Letting Go

T0355787

Letting Go

*Parenting Teens and Young Adults
in a Time of Uncertainty*

DEMIE KURZ

OXFORD
UNIVERSITY PRESS

OXFORD
UNIVERSITY PRESS

Oxford University Press is a department of the University of Oxford.
It furthers the University's objective of excellence in research, scholarship,
and education by publishing worldwide. Oxford is a registered trade mark of
Oxford University Press in the UK and in certain other countries.

Published in the United States of America by Oxford University Press
198 Madison Avenue, New York, NY 10016, United States of America.

CIP data is on file at the Library of Congress

ISBN 978–0–19–022245–1 (pbk.)
ISBN 978–0–19–022244–4 (hbk.)

DOI: 10.1093/9780190222482.001.0001

Paperback printed by Marquis Book Printing, Canada
Hardback printed by Bridgeport National Bindery, Inc., United States of America

MIX
Paper | Supporting
responsible forestry
FSC
www.fsc.org   FSC® C103567

Contents

Preface

Many years ago, I was the mother of two preschool-aged sons. My husband and I loved being parents. We were also very busy balancing our jobs and taking care of our children. We knew parenting would have its challenges. But what I didn't realize until we actually had children was how much uncertainty was built into the job! There was no shortage of advice in the popular press: "Don't use too much discipline or too little, monitor your children carefully, but don't be over protective." I was doing my best to raise children who would be safe and well-educated, and who would have an enjoyable childhood. But I wondered, Was I "helicopter parenting," hovering too much? Or maybe I was too laid-back? Was I failing to understand the latest trends in parenting?

I adored my sons, I was fascinated by all the new things they were doing, and they could be great fun to be with. At the same time, I found parenting very challenging; there were so many things to figure out and decisions to make. I often thought, "Why don't more people write about what it's really like to raise a child?" Bookstores are filled with books on parenting: "how-to" books, some by experts. But as one mother I interviewed for this book said, "Kids always want to do something new; every day I have to make decisions on the spot. How do I remember what some expert said about childrearing?" Deep down, I had the feeling that our sons would turn out to be fine adults, but the uncertainty never completely went away. As many mothers I spoke with said, "You never know what can happen, how your kids will turn out and what they could face in these tough times."

Our wonderful sons are now grown up. Like most children, they "got through" childhood, adolescence, and young adulthood, and have become very caring, responsible adults whom I am immensely grateful to have in my life. However, while at this time parenting for me is no longer the all-consuming activity it was when I had children at home, I have maintained a strong desire to understand more about the challenges of parenting and the larger forces that shape them. I have wanted to understand more because parenting is not only a fundamental aspect of the lives of mothers and fathers, raising the next generation is a critical societal task.

Unfortunately, despite the importance of parenting to the functioning of societies, the actual work of parenting—the endless tasks, the continual interactions with children and teens, and the constant decision-making in the face of uncertainty—still remains largely invisible in wider public discourse. The voices of parents, more often than not, go unheard. Parenting is typically assumed to be something mothers and fathers "just do," and mothers are widely believed to be "naturally" suited to raising children.

In this vacuum of information about what it actually takes to parent today, current popular narratives about parenting often blame parents, particularly mothers, for failures their children might experience. The dominant story we tell about parents in the United States portrays them—and, above all, mothers—as the ones who determine their children's success or failure; they are the ones who are ultimately responsible for whether their child finishes their education, stays out of trouble, and moves on to a productive life. These narratives have particularly blamed poorer mothers and mothers of color for failing to be good parents, often wholly discounting the challenges they face or the lack of accessible resources for their parenting. Because these narratives are so pervasive throughout our culture, when children face difficulties, parents can blame themselves, asking, "Is my parenting good enough? Should I be doing more? Will I be able to ensure that my children turn out alright?"

To gain more understanding of parenting, I interviewed mothers, who do the majority of the work of parenting. As I describe in the following chapter, I did also interview some fathers, who also play a very important role in parenting. I chose to focus on a particularly challenging time of parenting—adolescence—when children must gain more independence and autonomy as they move along the path to adulthood. Adolescence is often viewed as a time of teen rebellion, although as I demonstrate throughout this book, it is a much more complicated life stage for adolescents and for parents than the term "rebellion" suggests.

In this book I focus on how mothers manage the critical task of managing their children's transition from early adolescence to young adulthood. This is a task they refer to as "letting go," or "giving kids their freedom," allowing their children and teens to make more of their own decisions about their lives. Letting go is a challenging process. Mothers must shepherd their children safely from the dependency of childhood through to young adulthood. Parents are expected and expect themselves to be in control as they manage this process. They are held responsible for seeing that their children successfully complete secondary school, move on to college or some type of training, and become independent. At the same time, as adolescence progresses, parents must give over more control to their teens and young adults. To promote their autonomy, they must renegotiate control with their teens and young adults, allowing them to make more of their own decisions about their lives.

As the mothers I interviewed describe, letting go presents many challenges. On an ongoing basis, mothers must make important decisions as they try to ensure their teens' safety, for example—a key task of parenting. As teens venture farther away from home, mothers often find it difficult to get information and make decisions about the safety of their teens. How do they determine what activities are safe? When can teens be out on their own? How much trust should mothers put in their teens? What about cell phones? What amount of cell phone use is too much?

In this book, I demonstrate how parents engage in letting go in multiple arenas of the lives of their teens and young adults: in keeping their teenage children safe; in seeing that they successfully complete their secondary education; and in supporting them through college or some type of postsecondary training. As they balance the tasks of maintaining control and letting go in these arenas, parents must continually make difficult decisions. Often, they have to make these decisions without much information; communication with teens becomes more challenging as they make more decisions on their own. As the period of young adulthood has extended, mothers face new questions about when to give young adults financial and other assistance and when to push their young adults to take more responsibility for their lives.

Mothers' accounts of letting go also provide valuable insights into the parenting process. They demonstrate the ways in which parents do not simply guide their children in a "top-down" fashion. Children, teens, and young adults are an integral part of decision-making about their lives. Mothers describe their parenting as a negotiated activity, one in which teens and young adults are heavily involved in decisions about their lives. Parents must renegotiate issues of control with their teens and young adults. They face questions such as when should parents get "the last word?" When is it time to give over more control to teens? Parents face uncertainty in this process, as their teenage children grow and change and they must continually adapt.

Mothers' accounts of their experiences also show how vitally important resources are to the process of parenting. Parents cannot rely solely on their individual actions to ensure that their teens progress successfully on to adulthood. They require good neighborhoods, safe schools, and funds for extracurricular activities. As the mothers I interviewed make clear, parents are continually searching for resources that will improve their children's chances of success.

A fuller understanding of letting go is valuable for parents, researchers, and social policymakers. Seeing the complexities involved in this key task of parenting can help parents better understand that the challenges they face are not simply a product of their own individual actions but are shaped and influenced by wider social and economic forces. The accounts of mothers presented here also show the need for more research that incorporates the views of children and teens. In their descriptions of parenting, researchers often present parenting as a one-way process. However, mothers' descriptions demonstrate the negotiated character of parenting and the integral role children play in the process. Without a consideration of this crucial element of parenting, we risk overestimating the degree of control parents have in their ability to promote the success of their children. In this book, I argue for new models that incorporate the interactive, negotiated character of parenting, models that are sensitive to the myriad ways mothers must renegotiate control with their children and teens.

Finally, a better understanding of parenting demonstrates the need for more social policies that will support the work of mothers and fathers. In the US, parenting is viewed as a private endeavor that is the responsibility of individual mothers and fathers. Parents are held responsible for raising children, often without having access to the financial and other support necessary to ensure their success. Current narratives of parenting often fail to recognize and appreciate the value that raising children provides to the wider society, which depends on new generations to take over the societal work done by their elders. Raising successful children, teens, and young adults who remain safe, receive a good education, and go on to become responsible citizens is an essential public good and requires public support, including more funding for safe neighborhoods and good schools, which are critical to raising successful children. Policies that provide resources for lower-income families who live in underresourced neighborhoods with underresourced schools are particularly important for reducing the stark inequality of opportunity that currently divides lower-income from higher-income families.

The stakes are high for both parents and their children. While most teens make it through adolescence safely, finish secondary school, and move on to college or some type of postsecondary training, in our current era of rapid social and cultural change, they face a great deal of pressure. Adolescence and young adulthood are critical stages of life when teens and young adults need to gain the credentials necessary to succeed in an era of intense competition, when more and more education is required to attain lives of security and stability. This is also a time when teens and young adults can face risks. As I describe, a minority of teens and young adults get into more minor trouble, and a small group face serious trouble from drug or alcohol abuse or mental health challenges. It is essential that we provide the resources parents need to help them promote the success of their children, teens, and young adults.

In writing this book, I have been very grateful for colleagues who have provided encouragement and who read and gave feedback as I developed my ideas, including Marjorie DeVault early on, and, for the duration of this project, Annette Lareau. Their belief in what I wanted to write as well as their feedback on earlier versions of the manuscript were invaluable. I also thank the anonymous reviewers chosen by Oxford University Press, for their insightful suggestions about how to improve the manuscript. Additionally, I deeply appreciate the valuable feedback of others, including the late Robin Leidner, who read an earlier version of the manuscript. Others read different parts of the book, including Sarah Fenstermaker and Michelle Fine. Their insights and constructive feedback pushed my thinking forward. Of course, none of these people bear responsibility for any errors or limitations of the book. I have also benefited from feedback on various chapters that I received when giving papers at meetings of the American Sociological Society, the Eastern Sociological Society, and the meetings of the Carework Network.

I am also very grateful to Frank Furstenberg, currently the Zellerbach Family Professor of Sociology and emeritus research associate at Penn. He enabled me to interview some mothers who had participated in his Family Study project, and their accounts of raising teens and young adults deepened my understanding of parenting. Discussions with colleagues in the Department of Sociology at Penn and support from the Gender, Sexuality and Women's Studies Program provided further encouragement and resources for which I am grateful. And my most heartfelt thanks to my editor at Oxford University Press, James Cook, for his support and patience over the years, which have made this book possible.

Finally, I thank the mothers who agreed to be interviewed for this book. As their accounts indicate, parenting is one of the most central and deep-seated commitments of their lives, and a key part of their identities. Most mothers spoke of very enjoyable times with their teens or times when they were proud of their teens for their accomplishments in academics, sports, or the arts. After that, however, they would turn back to the subject of how challenging the task of parenting teenagers is, working to ensure their teens' safety, their successful performance in school, and their future well-being. This was what they wanted to discuss, and the mothers I interviewed seemed to find it valuable to have an opportunity to reflect on their experiences of parenting at this challenging time in the lives of their children. I would have loved to include the experiences of fathers, and teens and young adults as well. As I indicate in the appendix, I did interview a small group of each and learned important things from them, but it was not possible to report on these interviews and give full justice to their experiences.

In my own family, I am immensely grateful for the loving support of my spouse, Bruce, and our sons, our daughter-in-law, and our grandsons. Bruce is a valued intellectual companion, an excellent chef, and a great director of activities who helped get me out of the library! He is also a most wonderful father and grandfather. My adult "children" and my grandchildren are also very great treasures in my life—caring, talented, and fun!

Finally, I want to thank the friends who rooted for me over the years, encouraging me on. Please know that I have greatly appreciated your support!

1

Letting Go

An Introduction

Americans repeatedly ask how parents are doing. Media commentators regularly raise questions such as "Are mothers 'helicopter parenting,' micromanaging the lives of their children who then don't learn to make their own decisions? Are they failing to spend enough time with their children? Are they too lenient, too strict?" Questions such as these reflect the dominant narrative of parenting in the United States, a narrative of parental determinism that portrays parents, and above all mothers, as the ones who determine the success or failure of their children—whether their children complete their education, stay out of trouble, and move on to productive lives. This narrative has also blamed poorer mothers, and mothers of color in particular, for failing to be good parents, without taking into account the challenges these mothers face or the resources they can (or cannot) access.[1]

Of course, parents' beliefs, their love and care, and their endless work on behalf of their children have a profound impact on their children's lives and their chances of becoming productive members of society. However, this popular narrative of parental determinism is based on top-down models of parenting that are misleading. These models reflect an individualized view in which parents are portrayed as issuing directives to their children. In this framework, parents provide instruction, guidance, emotional support, and discipline to their children, who then learn appropriate ways of behaving. Mothers are expected to be in control of their parenting at all times. Based on these models, current narratives of parenting assume that if parents—and again, typically mothers—have sufficient motivation and commitment, they can raise successful children. If children have problems, it is because their mothers have failed to discipline them properly or spend sufficient time with them. Alternatively, other common narratives portray mothers as people

---

[1] S. Elliott and S. Bowen, "Defending Motherhood: Morality, Responsibility and Double Binds in Feeding Children," *Journal of Marriage and Family* 80 (2018): 499–520.

Letting Go. Demie Kurz, Oxford University Press. © Oxford University Press 2024.
DOI: 10.1093/9780190222482.003.0001

who are engaged in "overparenting," hovering, meddling, and intervening excessively in their teens' lives.[2]

Top-down models such as these do not accurately reflect the realities of mothers' lives. Mothers are not simply "in control" of parenting. Many things shape and constrain the process of raising children beyond parents' individual actions. The models that underlie these popular narratives of parenting also fail to portray the integral role children and teens play in the parenting process. They are not passive recipients of their parents' directives but instead continually respond to their parents' requests and initiate their own. Children are more powerful in family dynamics than prior research has suggested; they demand things of their parents in a way social scientists have not sufficiently acknowledged, and they can thwart their parents' best intentions. Furthermore, top-down parenting models often fail to convey the changing nature of parenting and the way junior high and high school years can bring about new and unexpected challenges for parents as well as adolescents.

It is critical that we understand more about the realities of parenting and develop models that are sensitive to those realities, including the multiple challenges and constraints mothers and fathers face. Raising the next generation is one of the most important tasks of any society. We have learned much from social scientists about parenting including parenting practices and their impact on children and teens, and the impact of race, class, and gender dynamics on parenting.[3] However, we have heard little from parents themselves about the ongoing challenges they face from children, and particularly teens, who develop strong opinions of their own and who are often in environments parents may not be familiar with, including social environments that are viewed as risky.

---

[2] K. L. Fletcher, E. E. Pierson, K. L. Speirs Neumeister, and W. H. Finch, "Overparenting and Perfectionistic Concerns Predict Academic Entitlement in Young Adults," *Journal of Child and Family Studies* 29 (2020): 348–357.

[3] Putting together an exhaustive list of all the social scientists who have researched in these areas would be impossible. To mention a very few, Lareau's work in sociology on parenting logics has been highly influential in shaping research on parenting. For decades psychologists Judith Smetana and Laurence Steinberg have provided valuable research on adolescence and parenting as well. Carework researchers have brought attention to the critical work of caregivers, including parents. Throughout this book I cite the work of many important researchers of parenting. A. Lareau, *Unequal Childhoods: Class, Race, and Family Life Second Edition With an Update a Decade Later* (Berkeley: University of California Press, 2011); L. Steinberg, *Adolescence* (New York: McGraw-Hill Education, 2020); N. Folbre, *For Love and Money: Care Provision in the U.S.* (New York: Russell Sage Foundation, 2012); J. Smetana and M. Rote, "Adolescent–Parent Relationships: Progress, Processes, and Prospects," *Annual Review of Developmental Psychology* (1) (2019): 41–68.

To develop a fuller understanding of parenting and a model of parenting that better reflects mothers' actual experiences, drawing from random samples I interviewed a diverse group of 118 mothers of teens and older teens entering young adulthood (ranging in age from 18 to 25). This group included mothers who are married, single, heterosexual, lesbian and gay, white, African American, and who are from different socioeconomic backgrounds. I chose to focus on mothers because—although many fathers are involved in parenting, and indeed a small number of fathers take primary responsibility for raising their children—in most families, mothers still perform more of the daily activities of parenting.[4] While I don't write about fathers or teens at any length in this book, I did interview small samples of each to gain some idea about their experiences, which helped inform my understanding of the parenting process more generally (see the appendix for further details on the sample).

I chose to interview mothers of adolescents and young adults to learn more about the process of raising children at a stage of life that many people view as particularly challenging. While raising children is demanding at any age, parents find adolescence to be the most difficult stage.[5] It is a pivotal time. Younger children, who are highly dependent on their parents, grow and change, becoming preteens, teens, and young adults who are expected to take more responsibility for their lives and work toward the traditional markers of adulthood—completing their education, moving out of their parents' homes, and gaining financial independence. As I will describe, throughout this period, teens begin to develop their own views and opinions, they challenge their parents more, and they go off on their own, away from adult supervision into environments parents may not know about. At ages 18–25, they enter a period known as young adulthood or "emerging adulthood." During this time, which has relatively recently come to be seen as a distinct stage of development, mothers and fathers face new challenges. Due to recent economic and social changes, finding work and becoming an adult takes much longer in the contemporary era, and young adults often continue to need parental support, particularly financial help, for extended periods.[6]

[4] In egalitarian and breadwinner wife marriages where fathers are the most involved, wives spend roughly two hours more per week on caregiving than husbands do and about 2.5 hours more on housework. R. Fry, C. Aragão, K. Hurst, and K. Parker, "In a Growing Share of U.S. Marriages, Husbands and Wives Earn About the Same" (Washington, DC: Pew Research Center, April 13, 2023).

[5] A. Meier, K. Musick, J. Fischer, and S. Flood, "Mothers' and Fathers' Well-Being in Parenting Across the Arch of Child Development," *Journal of Marriage and Family* 80(4) (2016): 992–1004.

[6] Jeffrey Arnett helped initiate the study of emerging adulthood. Many researchers have since pursued this field of study. A number of them are cited throughout this book. J. J. Arnett, *Emerging*

Mothers' accounts of parenting their teens and young adults provide valuable insights into the challenges and dilemmas parents face. In this book, I focus on what mothers described as one of the most challenging, unrecognized aspects of parenting: promoting the autonomy of their children, teens, and young adults—or what mothers call "letting go." As they described this process, mothers talked about "giving kids their freedom," allowing their teens to do more things and make more of their own decisions so they can become more independent and start taking more responsibility for their own lives. They portrayed this process as one that involves renegotiating authority and control with their children, teens, and young adults. This is a key task of parenting, and although it occurs at all stages in a child's development, it is particularly challenging during adolescence, when teens transition from the dependency of childhood, spend more time away from their family, and do more things without consulting their parents.

Psychologists believe that developing autonomy is a primary task of adolescence and young adulthood.[7] Many of them focus on the need for teens to develop psychosocial autonomy. Adolescents must "differentiate" and "individuate" from their parents and develop more emotional autonomy. They must forge their own identities. They must take more responsibility for their personal lives and become more independent from their parents.[8] However, while there is extensive research on how teens individuate, there is less understanding of the critical role parents play in promoting teens' autonomy. As teens grow and develop, parents must manage and guide this process to ensure that their teens develop autonomy in safe and productive ways, a process they identify as letting go.

Adulthood: The Winding Road from the Late Teens Through the Twenties (New York: Oxford University Press, 2015).

[7] M. Zimmer-Gembeck et al., "Autonomy, Development of," *Encyclopedia of Adolescence*, ed. B. Brown and M. Prinstein (New York: Academic Press, 2011), 1: 66–67; L. Steinberg, "Autonomy," *Adolescence* (New York: McGraw Hill, 2020), 246–271.
[8] For individuation, see B. Soenens et al., eds., *Autonomy in Adolescence: Towards Conceptual Clarity* (New York: Routledge, 2018).
The need for children to develop autonomy is an innate human need, but beliefs about what constitutes autonomy vary by cultures and subcultures. In the United States, autonomy is often equated with independence. The United States is a highly individualist culture with a stronger belief in individual independence than is found in more collectivist cultures. However the idea that people are truly independent or autonomous does not correspond to the reality that people's lives are embedded in relationships with others and that they are dependent on others for their social and often economic well-being. See K. N. Marbell-Pierre, W. Grolnick, A. L. Stewart, and J. N. Raftery-Helmer, "Parental Autonomy Support in Two Cultures: The Moderating Effects of Adolescents' Self-Construals," *Child Development* 90(3) (2019): 825–845.

When the mothers I interviewed spoke of letting go and providing teens with more autonomy and freedom, they described an extended social process, which I describe in this book. Mothers must see that their teens begin to take more responsibility for different aspects of their lives. Teens have to accomplish many tasks in order to move successfully through adolescence and on to young adulthood. They must complete the requirements of secondary school, which are more difficult than elementary school, and prepare for college or post–high school training. They must develop the ability to establish goals and stay motivated to accomplish them. They also need to safely navigate new social worlds outside home, which adults often view as risky. Mothers are tasked with enormous responsibilities for seeing that teens accomplish these tasks. They are expected to manage and control their children's whereabouts, their performance at school, and their ability to plan for the future. At the same time, they must promote their teens' autonomy and learn to let go.

Understanding the Process of Letting Go

In this book I explore the process of letting go as it has been portrayed by a diverse group of mothers. Their accounts not only provide important insights about parenting during adolescence, but about parenting more generally, and they point the way to a model of parenting that more accurately reflects the day-to-day realities of mothers' experiences. I argue that an understanding of letting go demonstrates the need for a negotiated model of parenting. The mothers I interviewed described the process of guiding their teens through adolescence while promoting their autonomy and letting go as a series of ongoing negotiations concerning important issues that affect teens' well-being and ability to succeed. At all stages of childhood and into young adulthood, parents and children negotiate. Parents negotiate with teens over how they can remain safe as they go out into new environments, how much time they should spend on schoolwork in an era when securing educational credentials is more important than ever, and how much planning they should do for their futures. Children and teens may agree and comply with their parents' requests, they may disagree and negotiate with their parents for more freedoms, or they may ignore their parents' wishes altogether.

As they engage in letting go, mothers face challenging decisions. They spoke of a continual balancing act between letting go and maintaining control, between creating rules and enforcing restrictions and allowing teens to do more on their own. Mothers create rules about where their children can and cannot go and establish curfews to ensure they come home at a time that is considered safe. They monitor their teens' compliance with rules and apply sanctions for failure to abide by them. They observe their teens' behavior to assess their emotional well-being, and they get to know their children's friends to ascertain whether they are engaging in activities they feel are appropriate. They work to assess whether their teens are staying on track with their schoolwork. At the same time, they must engage in letting go.

As they spoke about letting go, mothers described negotiating with their teens to manage their safety and see that they successfully completed their secondary education. They also described a continual process of renegotiating control. Mothers must turn over increasing control and responsibility to their teens, letting them do new things and allowing them to go new places without adult supervision. During childhood, parents maintain control over many aspects of their children's lives. During adolescence, however, teens gain the ability to negotiate for more control over their actions, and they increasingly simply take control of major decisions in their lives as they move into young adulthood.

The process of renegotiating authority and control, of course, occurs at all ages, but it is particularly challenging during adolescence, when teenage children make more forceful demands and begin to engage in more activities without adult supervision. These challenges to a family's usual way of doing things can feel threatening. Family members are expected to keep their place in the family order. When one member breaks informal rules and challenges habitual practices, it can disrupt the family hierarchy, one of the fundamental elements on which the family unit is based. This is what happens during adolescence as teens work to gain more autonomy.

At every point in their negotiations with teens, mothers face common challenges. Teens may communicate less with their parents, and they may be more resistant to their mothers' suggestions than they were as younger children. Mothers can't always trust what their teens tell them, and their children may not reveal everything mothers would like to know. As mothers described, there is "no manual" and there are few guidelines mothers can rely on as their teens grow and change. As their children venture out, it can be difficult to monitor all their activities, which are often in environments mothers aren't familiar with. This dynamic regularly makes mothers anxious for their children's safety.

Sarah, a white middle-class mother of three children (ages 16, 13, and 9), detailed the basic challenges mothers face in letting go, including deciding when to intervene in their teens' lives and when to let go and allow them make more of their own decisions: "I love being a parent," she said, "seeing the kids become individuals, seeing their interests, their relationships, my son can be really funny, sometimes he makes me laugh." She then continued:

> But it's especially tough now, it's easier when they are younger. When they are older and become teens you have to let go more, you don't always know what to do, it's harder—do you let them make more of their own decisions, do you let them make a mistake? Of course you can't let them make a really serious mistake. But do you do something or nothing? And you argue with them about these things.

As mothers engage in the process of letting go, they also work to gain resources for their teens. Resources are essential in raising children and teens who are able to succeed in school and move on safely to young adulthood—money for activities, school fees, counseling, sports, and for those who can, the ability to move to safe, resource-rich neighborhoods with good schools. Additionally, given the challenges of letting go and maintaining control, mothers rely on resources to manage the uncertainties of parenting. With teens having more freedom to be out on their own in new places that are potentially risky, parents need to be able to rely on safe environments. At a time when schoolwork in junior high and high school has become more difficult, mothers rely on schools to help their teens stay motivated in their studies and on track to graduate.

In this book, I focus on mothers' accounts of three critical tasks they face as they engage in letting go: keeping teens safe; seeing that they successfully complete secondary school; and launching them into young adulthood. I present what mothers described as the tasks of letting go in each arena, focusing on their interpersonal work with their teens and their work to gain resources. I describe the common challenges mothers face in letting go and highlight the ways that mothers with fewer resources face more challenges in guiding teens safely through adolescence and young adulthood. Parenting and letting go are embedded in unequal relations of social class, race, and gender, which enable some parents to provide valuable resources for their teens while others struggle to obtain the resources necessary to promote their children's well-being. While mothers face many common challenges, the conditions for promoting the success of children and teens are highly unequal.

Throughout this book, I focus primarily on the challenges of parenting adolescents and young adults, but I also note the times when parents enjoy their relationships with their teens and young adults. The mothers I interviewed love their children deeply, and they take pleasure in watching their growing mental and social capabilities. They find new interests in common, enjoy watching movies and TV together, attend their teens' school events and athletic games. Parenting can bring tremendous rewards to mothers and fathers. When teens and young adults are doing well, mothers described feeling pride in their children, and they can feel a sense of accomplishment at helping their children succeed. As a white working-class mother said:

> Parenting can be so rewarding, it's the ultimate reward when you see them independent and doing the right thing. Parenting is hard, there can be some tough going along the way, but it's wonderful to see these children you raise growing and learning and becoming more mature. It makes you really happy.

Speaking of her older daughter who has just graduated from college, another mother, who is white and middle-class, said, "We are very proud of our daughter. I could explode sometimes because she's just a really neat kid, she's a really neat kid. She's always excelled at things. And now she's graduating from college. She did so well, I know she will succeed in the future."

At the same time, while mothers expressed positive feelings when I asked them about the joys they experienced in parenting their teens and young adults, they quickly returned to the challenges they faced, reflecting the demanding new situations they encounter in the process of guiding their children through adolescence and letting go. They worry about their teens' safety and about their school performance in a society that requires more and more education to achieve an adequate standard of living. Some described the uncertainties of parenting and the difficulty of feeling effective. As Janelle, a middle-class African American mother, said:

It's hard when you don't feel effective, like when the kids are not doing chores or their homework and you don't want to just keep nagging. That's the hardest thing. I try things, like I try restricting them or I cook up a plan for positive reinforcement. And then it doesn't work.

Mothers also said they thought a lot about how their children's lives would look in the future. Will they be happy? Will they find a good partner? Will they be safe? Or will they experience substance abuse, health issues, or run-ins with the law?

The Importance of Understanding Letting Go and the Work of Mothers

An understanding of letting go and the challenges of parenting can make important contributions to public narratives of parenting, to research, and to social policy. Prevailing societal narratives about parenting typically ignore the tremendous amount of work involved, its challenges, and the multiple influences that can affect parents' ability to shepherd their teens safely through adolescence. Parenting is often viewed as something "natural" that mothers "just do" as part of their biological makeup. In the absence of more accurate models and a better understanding of parenting and its challenges, top-down individualist views of parenting have prevailed, reinforcing narratives that hold mothers responsible for what happens to their children and that blame them if their children have problems, no matter how much work and effort they may have undertaken on behalf of their children and teens. This can be painful for parents but particularly for mothers, for whom parenting is one of the most important parts of their identity, an identity in which they have invested enormous time and physical and emotional labor. These individualist perspectives also contribute to the view that parenting is primarily a private matter and that the wider society, including the government, bears little responsibility for supporting parents and families.

Moving beyond top-down, individualistic views and developing an understanding of the negotiated nature of parenting can contribute to the creation of new public narratives that benefit parents and promote new possibilities for research and more informed social policy. More accurate narratives and models can provide mothers and fathers with a greater understanding of the uncertainty of parenting, of how parents are not simply in control of their parenting, of how children and teens have an active role in the parenting process. More accurate narratives can also be valuable for mothers and fathers in seeing parenting within a wider context, as a process that is enabled and constrained by the resources parents can access—resources that are not available to all parents.

Mothers' accounts of parenting teens and young adults also demonstrate the need for more social policies to support families. Because they are responsible for raising the next generation, parents, and mothers in particular, have irreplaceable value. As one mother put it: "It's the most important job there is. The way I look at it, if you have a job, even a big job, and you drop dead, people would regret that, but almost immediately, they would get someone in there who picks up the pieces and goes right on." She added:

> If you're the mother and you drop dead, who picks up the pieces? It has a huge impact on a family, and in some ways, they never get over it. You're also forming lives, you're molding them. And then they'll grow up and influence other people and contribute to their families and communities. And you've had a hand in that. What we do is so important, even though we don't get recognized for it.

Despite how essential it is to social life, top-down models often portray parenting as a mostly private affair for which there is little wider social responsibility. As a result, while parents need resources to enable their children to move successfully through adolescence and into young adulthood, current social policies in the United States do not provide adequate resources to support the critical work that parents do. There needs to be increased government funding to provide equal opportunities for neighborhood safety and enrichment and for good schools that serve all communities. Without adequate funding, lower-income families and families of color will continue to struggle to achieve the outcomes that are required for their children to succeed in the United States today.

Finally, an understanding of the negotiated nature of parenting can contribute to research on the family. Both sociologists and psychologists have done extensive research on parenting, including some work on the parenting of adolescents and, more recently, on the period known as young adulthood.[9]

[9] Research on parenting during adolescence includes the work of Furstenberg and others, who provide valuable qualitative and quantitative data on management strategies used by parents to promote the well-being of their teens. F. Furstenberg, J. Eccles, Glen H. Elder Jr., and Arnold Sameroff,

In recent years, sociologists, following the work of Lareau and others, have examined parenting styles and their relationship to outcomes for children and teens.[10] Psychologists have also studied parenting styles and their relationship to cohesion and conflict in parent-teen relationships.[11] However, there is still too little research on the actual work of parenting and its ongoing challenges.

To gain a deeper understanding of the work involved in parenting teens, I have adopted a sociological perspective, one that focuses on the lives of individuals and groups and how they are shaped and influenced by wider social, economic, and cultural forces. Using qualitative interview data, for this book I focus on the interactions between mothers and their teens and young adults as well as mothers' work to gain opportunities and resources for them. The mothers I interviewed provide numerous insights into the interactive work that is an essential component of parenting, work that is often not visible in top-down models. Understanding these interactions enables us to see much more clearly the day-to day work of parenting and its challenges. Parents and teens continually negotiate over many things—what is safe for teens to do, how hard teens should work in school, and how teens should

Managing to Make It: Urban Families and Adolescent Success (Chicago: University of Chicago Press, 1999); S. Elliott, *Not My Kid: What Parents Believe About the Sex Lives of Their Teenagers* (New York: New York University Press, 2012); M. K. Nelson, *Parenting Out of Control: Anxious Parents in Uncertain Times* (New York: New York University Press, 2010); A. T. Schalet, *Not Under My Roof: Parents, Teens, and the Culture of Sex* (Chicago: University of Chicago Press, 2011). There is a growing field of research on emerging adolescence and the transition to adulthood. See M. C. Waters et al., eds., *Coming of Age in America : The Transition to Adulthood in the Twenty-First Century* (Berkeley: University of California Press, 2011); J. J. Arnett, *Emerging Adulthood: The Winding Road from the Late Teens Through the Twenties* (New York: Oxford University Press, 2015); F. F. Furstenberg, "Becoming Adults: Challenges in the Transition to Adult Roles," *American Journal of Orthopsychiatry* 85 (2015): S14–S21. This includes work demonstrating the impact of parents' social class position on their ability to provide support for young adults, support that increases their chances of obtaining good educational opportunities and good jobs in their future. In review of this research see E. G. van Stee, "Parenting Young Adults Across Social Class: A Review and Synthesis," *Sociology Compass* e13021 (2022): 1–16.

[10] Lareau describes "concerted cultivation" as a parenting style characterized by parents' actions to foster their child's talents by incorporating organized activities into their lives, and developing their child's ability to speak with adults and interact with social institutions. This approach provides valuable tools for helping children succeed in contemporary America. In contrast, working-class parents promote "the accomplishment of natural growth," an approach that gives children both clear guidelines and objectives and more autonomy in their leisure time to engage in their own activities but fewer skills for navigating institutional settings.

[11] Developmental and family psychologists have done extensive research on variations in parenting styles and parent–child relationship qualities. X. Bi et al., "Parenting Styles and Parent–Adolescent Relationships: The Mediating Roles of Behavioral Autonomy and Parental Authority," *Frontiers in Psychology* 9 (2018): 2187, https://doi.org/10.3389/fpsyg.2018.02187.

plan for their futures. Sometimes parents are able to persuade their teens of what they think is the best course of action; sometimes they are not.

Understanding these negotiations enables us to gain more knowledge of how parents exercise control in their parenting as they work to promote the success of their young adults and teens and about letting go of control. A focus on the negotiations that are at the heart of parenting, where children and teens sometimes dictate interactions and outcomes, provides a clearer view of the uncertainty in the parenting process, of what parents are and are not able to control. It also helps us see more clearly the critical role of resources in promoting teens' ability to move safely through adolescence to young adulthood.

The Mothers I Interviewed

As I explain in the appendix, my analysis of parenting teens and letting go is based on an interview study of a diverse group of 118 mothers of teenagers and young adults (ages 13 to 25). The majority of interviewees were drawn from random samples, and they include white and African American mothers, and married and single mothers. Some live in a place I call Northeastern City, and some live in the suburbs of that city. I asked mothers both specific and open-ended questions about the work they do on behalf of their teens and young adults and about the challenges and rewards of parenting more broadly.

In order to understand the variety of mothers' experiences, I interviewed an equal number of mothers from three social-class groups based on their education and occupation—upper-middle-class, middle-class, and working-class. Social class is a concept that is widely used to understand people's experiences, beliefs, and opportunities and to locate people's place in a society's broader social and economic hierarchy. The concept of social class is also frequently used to refer to people's access to social and cultural capital, including connections to people who have information about opportunities and resources and how to access them. From the samples I drew, I designated three different social class groups—upper-middle-class, middle-class, and working-class—based on commonly used indicators, including mothers' education, their occupation, and the median household income in their neighborhood. I also considered the impact of mothers' race on their experiences of parenting and the intersections of mothers' social class and racial background. I considered the impact of gender on their parenting and their views and varied treatment of their sons and daughters as well. For further details about the sample, see the appendix.

To provide background on the mothers I interviewed, I briefly describe characteristics of the mothers in my sample who are in different social classes and racial groups. In recent decades, income inequality has risen dramatically in the United States, making it increasingly difficult for many parents to ensure that their children will have a better life than they did growing up. Mothers have differing amounts of "family capital," financial capital, and social and cultural capital. This latter category is made up of family, friends, colleagues, and helping professionals who can provide information about how to promote the success of their children and teens—for example, by offering information about schools. Through their networks, upper-middle-class and middle-class parents can more easily learn about good schools and summer programs and get advice about applying to colleges. They can also afford good schools. Although my sample does not include mothers in the poorest neighborhoods, working-class parents, by contrast, tend to have much more limited access to good schooling for their children, as do African American parents who live in segregated neighborhoods. The institutional racism that is firmly entrenched in the social fabric of the US produces racially segregated communities where schools struggle to obtain adequate resources.[12]

Upper-Middle-Class Mothers

The upper-middle-class mothers in my sample have graduate degrees, and both they and their spouses work in professions that include medicine, law, architecture, psychology, social work, and upper-level educational administration. They send their children to private schools or to public schools that are supported by high property taxes, hoping to give them an advantage in

[12] T. T. Swartz, "Family Capital and the Invisible Transfer of Privilege: Intergenerational Support and Social Class in Early Adulthood," *New Directions for Child and Adolescent Development* 119 (2008): 11–24; K. Michelmore and P. Rich, "Contextual Origins of Black-White Educational Disparities in the 21st Century: Evaluating Long-Term Disadvantage Across Three Domains," *Social Forces* 101 (2022): 1–30.

Funding for education varies widely across and within states. The poorest districts, often those with more African American students, receive the least funding. B. Baker et al., "Is School Funding Fair? A National Report Card".

applying to high-ranked colleges. Many of them are anxious for their children to enter professional positions that come with high status and high pay. They travel in social circles where it is relatively easy to access current medical, therapeutic, and educational knowledge.

While these mothers live in mostly safe neighborhoods and have more economic security than other groups, they still experience certain anxieties about their teens' safety. They worry about drugs and alcohol, which they fear their teenagers will have access to in their communities and schools, and they fear their children could be hurt in car accidents in which they or their friends are driving. Like all mothers, they worry about information their teenage children can access through the internet and cell phones, which could lead their teens to engage in risky behavior.

Middle-Class Mothers

The majority of the middle-class mothers I interviewed have four-year college degrees; those who did not have at least an associate's degree. They work in the field of education as schoolteachers and counselors, nurses, and service providers in social service agencies. A few have started their own businesses. Half of these mothers live in a middle-class suburb and half live in middle-class neighborhoods in the city. The suburban middle-class parents live in three- and four-bedroom homes in housing developments that are considered safe. Most of their teens attend public schools that their parents believe are adequate or, as some said, "good enough." Like their upper-middle-class counterparts, middle-class mothers worry about drug and alcohol problems and car accidents.

The urban middle-class mothers I interviewed live in single-family and row houses that are usually in safe neighborhoods, although as their children become teenagers and circulate more widely throughout the city, these parents may worry more about their teens' risk of experiencing crime and violence. Their teens have choices of schools through a citywide system of public magnet schools that many are able to access. Some families send their teens to private Catholic schools. While the middle-class mothers I interviewed expect their teens to attend college, they worry about how they will be able to pay for college and talked about "watching our money."

Working-Class Mothers

The working-class mothers I interviewed have high school diplomas and work as administrative assistants, salesclerks, day care workers, medical technicians, home health aides, and nurse's aides. Except for a few who live in the suburbs, most of these families live in the city in working-class neighborhoods. Many of the working-class mothers have grown up in or near the same neighborhood they currently live in. Many live near family members who help each other with childcare and take care of family members who are older or disabled.

Like all the mothers in the sample, the working-class mothers I spoke with were very concerned that their teens attend good schools. Some of their teens go to public schools, and a few of them go to a magnet school. If they can afford it, some working-class families try to get their children into Catholic or other private religious schools, which they think will offer a better education for their teens than the typically understaffed and underresourced public schools they have access to. Working-class mothers are also very concerned about safety. Some live in stable neighborhoods. Some live in changing neighborhoods that have seen an increased prevalence of drugs, which they fear will bring crime and violence.

Gender

In recent decades, there have been major changes in the way the broader society views women and girls although stereotypes and discourses of traditional gender roles—breadwinner fathers and mothers as the primary caregivers of children—remain prevalent. Today, girls are often told they can achieve high-level positions and have successful careers. Following trends in the wider culture, the mothers I spoke to stressed the need for girls to develop qualities of strength and independence. They espoused an "empowerment" model of girlhood, something long promoted by African American mothers who have socialized their daughters to be strong and independent in the face of oppressive conditions.[13]

---

[13] For raising African American girls, see P. H. Collins, *Black Feminist Thought 30th Anniversary Edition: Knowledge, Consciousness, and the Politics of Empowerment* (New York: Routledge, 2022).

However, even as they work to empower their daughters and promote their independence, these mothers' messages can be undercut by fears for their daughters' safety. Mothers are surrounded by popular discourses that assert the dangers that are presented by girls' perceived sexual vulnerability. Mothers in the United States regularly hear media reports about the dangers of unprotected sex, sexual assault, and rape (including date rape). Some of these reports are sensationalized, but at the same time, parents face the reality that girls can be at risk of harm due to sexual violence.[14] Almost all the mothers I interviewed spoke of being more protective of their daughters than their sons. As one white middle-class mother with two teens in high school said:

> I worry about my son too, but it's harder with my daughter. I protect her more, she's more vulnerable, more could happen to her. And she has to consider her reputation. Women really have to put up their guard more. They have more restrictions, they have their reputation. My daughter wasn't happy when I told her these things.

As I will describe in Chapter 3, girls can also use drugs and alcohol, suffer from online bullying, experience depressive symptoms, and attempt suicide.

Up through their children's high school years, many mothers who are anxious about their daughters' safety can and do create more restrictions on their social lives. Once their daughters go away to college or move out of the house to work, however, mothers' ability to protect daughters becomes more difficult. If their daughters live at home while they attend college or work, mothers must loosen restrictions on their activities. By age 18, most girls simply start doing more things on their own, away from adult supervision.

Mothers also worry about their sons, their school performance, and the possibility that they will get into trouble. In terms of education, boys perform less well in school than girls. Girls account for two-thirds of high schoolers in the top 10 percent of their grade, ranked by GPA. They receive more college degrees than boys.[15] The lower rates of education make mothers worry about

[14] In 2021, 8 percent of high school students had ever been physically forced to have sexual intercourse when they did not want to. Centers for Disease Control and Prevention, "Youth Risk Behavior Survey 2011–2021: Data Summary and Trends Report" (Atlanta: Centers for Disease Control and Prevention, 2023).

[15] S. Reardon, E. M. Fahle, and R. C. Zarate, "Gender Achievement Gaps in the U.S. School Districts." *American Educational Research Journal* 56(6) (2019): 2474–2508; R. V. Reeves, *Of Boys and Men: Why the Modern Male is Struggling, Why It Matters, and What To Do About It* (Washington, DC: Brookings Institution Press, 2022), 6; National Center for Education Statistics, "Degrees

how their sons will succeed in the highly competitive challenges of today's labor market, where a college degree is necessary for getting an adequately paying job (or even any job).[16] Mothers also worry about their sons getting into trouble. In 2020, young adults ages 18 to 24 accounted for 19 percent of all arrests and 21 percent of arrests for violent crimes.[17]

Race

In my sample, there are a small number of African American mothers who are upper-middle and middle-class. The remainder are working-class and hold lower-paying service-sector jobs in healthcare and home health service, day care, and education. In recent decades, more African Americans have joined the middle and upper middle class, but due to racially based practices in housing, education, and employment that systematically discriminate against African Americans, their income and wealth are significantly lower than that of whites. Many working-class African American mothers live in communities where public funding for engaging, constructive activities has been dramatically reduced and where children attend schools with larger class sizes, fewer class materials, and little guidance counseling.[18]

In their roles as parents, African American mothers face serious challenges protecting their teens from racism. Given the widespread prevalence of racial profiling, African American mothers continually worry about the safety of their teens and young adults. While they also worry about their daughters, they experience an immediate fear for the safety of their sons, who are at greater risk of experiencing violence at the hands of police.[19] These mothers also worry about the racism their children could encounter in the workplace.

Conferred by Postsecondary Institutions, by Level of Degree and Sex of Student: Selected Years, 1869–70 through 2029–30," Digest of Education Statistics Table 318.10 (Washington, DC: US Department of Education Institute of Education Sciences, 2020).

[16] A. P. Carnevale et al., "Three Educational Pathways to Good Jobs: High School, Middle Skills, and Bachelor's Degree" (Georgetown University Center on Education and the Workforce, 2018).

[17] In 2020, young male adults ages 18 to 24 accounted for 19 percent of all arrests and 21 percent of arrests for violent crimes, four times higher than for girls. C. Puzzanchera, "Trends in Youth Arrests for Violent Crimes" (Washington, DC: National Institute of Justice, 2022).

[18] B. Baker et al., "Is School Funding Fair? A National Report Card" (Rutgers, NJ: Education Law Center, Graduate School of Education, Rutgers University, 2016); R. V. Reeves, Dream Hoarders: How the American Upper Middle Class is Leaving Everyone Else in the Dust, Why That is a Problem, and What To Do About It (Washington, DC: Brookings Institution Press, 2017).

[19] N. A. Cazenave, Killing Black Americans: Police and Vigilante Violence as a Racial Control Mechanism (New York: Routledge, 2018).

Their parenting experiences echo those reported in other research showing the challenges African American mothers face in raising children in a society where racial discrimination exists in many aspects of social life.[20] African American parents also have lower incomes than white parents and less access to resources for parenting.[21]

Overview of this Book

In each chapter of this book, I explore one of the key arenas of parenting where letting go takes place and describe the challenges mothers face in promoting their teens' autonomy while letting go. I demonstrate how mothers manage the process of letting go through their interpersonal work and their work to obtain resources. I highlight both the similarities and differences in what mothers face based on their social class and racial backgrounds.

In Chapter 2, I provide background on the changes mothers face when their teens enter adolescence and the challenges these changes pose for the process of letting go. Mothers of all backgrounds described their teens as "pulling away" during this time. Their teens begin to see things differently from their parents, they want to make more of their own decisions, and they challenge their parents' authority. In their interpersonal work, mothers experience new difficulties in communicating with teens. Increasingly they must negotiate over their teens' rights and privileges as teens demand to make more of their own decisions.

Like a lot of mothers, Allison, a white working-class mother of two children—a 17-year-old son, James, and a 14-year-old daughter, Cindy—finds a lot of uncertainty in the process of letting go. She reported that communication with her teens has become more difficult. She said, "James doesn't talk to me as much, which makes things harder. He's at that age, you know, and sometimes he gives me these looks like he's saying, 'You just don't get it.'" Allison wonders if James is really listening to her. She also reported

---

[20] D. M. Dow, "The Deadly Challenges of Raising African American Boys: Navigating the Controlling Image of the 'Thug'," *Gender & Society* 30(2) (2016): 161–188.

[21] On the one hand, African Americans are graduating from high school at the same rate as whites. The Black middle class has been growing, with half of African Americans holding white-collar jobs. At the same time, in 2020, median household income was $75,000 for white households, but only $46,000 for Black households and $55,500 for Hispanic households, figures which have changed only slightly since 1970. J. Bowdler and B. Harris, "Racial Inequality in the United States" (Washington, DC: US Department of the Treasury, 2022), https://home.treasury.gov/news/featured-stories/racial-inequality-in-the-united-states.

that he argues with her more than he did when he was younger. Allison said James is a "good kid"—he keeps up with his schoolwork and "doesn't get into trouble"—but she wished it were easier to get information from him.

Chapter 3 then examines the new challenges adolescent mothers face in keeping teens safe while letting go and allowing their teens more freedoms. Teens want to be out more and doing new things, they have increased access to information and activities which adults may consider risky. Andrea, a white upper-middle-class mother, said she feels less control over her teens' lives now that they are out of the house more. "It's more difficult as they get older," she said, "there are bigger problems. You worry. When they are young, you have them with you or they're with someone you trust, you know what's happening." But then, she said:

> You have to give them more freedom. It starts when they are teens, you are with them less and they can access so many things on their phones, on computers. You can't really know what your teens are doing. Out of the house you just have to give them the benefit of the doubt, you know, that they aren't getting into some kind of trouble.

Mothers negotiate with their teens about where they can go, and they monitor their teens' whereabouts as they go out on their own. However, all the mothers in my sample debate with themselves about how not to be too controlling, or, as one mother stated, how not to be "policing my teens all the time."

African American mothers face additional challenges. Ella, an African American working-class mother, fears for her sons' safety. Like other mothers, she particularly worries about the possibility of police harassment and violence toward young African American men. She said she frequently sees African American teens being stopped by the police. "I look out the window on the weekend," she noted. "Kids get stopped, then they can get arrested if they make a wrong move, especially the boys." She reported that her teens want to wear expensive sneakers, but she said that's a bad idea. "I tell them, 'You don't need those. Why do you need those, you can use just a regular pair.'" This is not because the shoes are more expensive, but because, as Ella said, "The police think they've stolen their shoes." Ella also said, "Girls can be targeted too, but they are not seen as such a big threat as the boys." When white mothers with resources worry about their teens' safety in their neighborhood, some are able to move to safer neighborhoods.

In recent years, parents have faced new challenges as rates of anxiety and depression among teens and young adults have reached disturbing levels. In 2021, 42 percent of high school students experienced persistent feelings of sadness or hopelessness during the last year and 22 percent considered attempting suicide, with girls experiencing more problems than boys. These problems are believed to have worsened during the COVID-19 pandemic, although the mental health problems of teens predate the coronavirus pandemic.[22]

Chapter 4 explores the challenges mothers face in letting go as they support their children's education. Parents' support of their children and their schoolwork is believed to be critical to teens' success in school in a world that requires more and more education to achieve an adequate standard of living. Mothers feel a tremendous responsibility to help their children be successful in school. They talk with their teens about assignments and deadlines, help them with problems, attend parent-teacher meetings, and meet with teachers to learn of their teens' progress.

At the same time, mothers pull back and urge their teens to take responsibility for doing their schoolwork. However, it can be challenging for mothers to let go of their involvement in teens' schoolwork given that the stakes for successfully completing secondary school are high. Mothers feel they cannot let their teens fall behind at a time when the successful completion of high school and college are essential for achieving an adequate standard of living. Some mothers describe their teens as liking school and doing well. Others describe teenagers who are not motivated and find schoolwork difficult. Still others report that their teens experience a lot of stress in school.

Elizabeth, a white middle-class mother, said she experiences a lot of frustration about her son Dan, a high school junior who scores high on standardized tests but whose grades are average and sometimes below average. In her view, Dan is not interested in working hard. She noted:

Dan is very into sports and watches a lot of sports on TV and on his computer. He is on his computer a lot but whatever he is doing, it still doesn't bring his grades up. My husband and I talk to Dan about how important grades are, especially now in his junior year. He says he wants to go to

[22] Centers for Disease Control and Prevention, "Youth Risk Behavior Survey 2011–2021: Data Summary and Trends Report" (Atlanta: Centers for Disease Control and Prevention, 2023).

college, and he certainly has the brains to do well in college. But he'll have to get good grades to get the financial aid he'll need to go.

Elizabeth concluded by saying, "We don't know what to do, we keep talking to Dan about this." Elizabeth said Dan's problems with motivation made it especially difficult for him to focus on his studies during the COVID-19 pandemic; he said he didn't like "going to school on a screen." Elizabeth thinks he only did the minimum amount of work to pass his courses.

Other mothers face teens who may be motivated but who experience stress over their school performance or the college admissions process. School work is harder in junior high and high school, and there is more pressure to do well in order to be accepted to college. Encouraging motivation and helping teens with stress is difficult work for all mothers. Those with resources, however, have advantages. They can access better schools that are likely to have more teachers and counselors who can address these issues.

In Chapter 5, I describe the process of letting go as it takes shape in later adolescence and emerging adulthood. In the current era, when a child turns 18, it means they have reached an age where they become legally responsible for their actions. However, that milestone is no longer the marker of achieving independence it once was. It now signals an entry into a new stage of life, young adulthood, which has become a critical time for gaining educational credentials that are essential for securing a place in a competitive economy. Young adults remain dependent on their parents during this time as they attend college, enroll in training programs, or look for work. Many parents provide financial support as they are able, however, at the same time, they ask themselves how long it is appropriate to support their young adults financially and in other ways and at what point their children have to take more responsibility for their own lives. As one mother described this challenge, she said it is not always clear where to draw the line and when to tell their children who have entered into young adulthood that they can no longer rely on their parents for financial support.

After their young adults turn 21, mothers engage in new kinds of interpersonal work to promote their children's independence. Increasingly, letting go involves pushing teens to take responsibility for their own lives. Some young adults are uncertain about how to plan for their future. Some are able to get jobs and begin to support themselves. Still others benefit substantially from financial support from parents and grandparents on into their twenties, which enables them to go on to postgraduate training and gain qualifications for higher-paying jobs. Other young adults, however, particularly those who have not received more education or training after high school, may have difficulty finding a job that will enable them to live on their own. Mothers worry about whether their children will be able to establish financial security in an increasingly uncertain economy.

As older teens move further into emerging adulthood, mothers reflect on the process of letting go and the changes they see in their children. Some are pleased about the path toward the future their young adult children are following, which they expect will lead to a good job or career and some type of financial security. Some described developing a more equal relationship with their young adults. They are happy they can be more like friends with their young adult children. However, when things are not going well for their young adults, or when they are not taking steps to prepare for their futures, mothers worry. They ask themselves how their children's lives might look in the future. Will they be happy and find a good life partner? Will they be safe, or will they experience issues with substance abuse, health issues, or trouble with the law? Will they have financial difficulties?

In the book's concluding chapter, I summarize key elements of the work of letting go. All mothers face difficult questions of how many restrictions they should place on their teens, how much to police their behavior, how hard to push them to succeed in school, and when to engage in letting go and trust that their teens will make good decisions. Mothers are expected, and expect themselves, to guide their teens safely through adolescence, to maintain control in the process of letting go. This is challenging. All mothers face a lot of uncertainty as they work with teens and young adults to promote their success. At the same time, those with resources have many advantages in ensuring their teens' successful passage through to young adulthood at a time when it is increasingly difficult to succeed in a highly competitive labor market where good jobs are not guaranteed.

It is essential to seriously consider the experiences of mothers, which provide us with the opportunity to develop much-needed revisions to our prevailing narratives and models of parenting. New models of parenting can expand our understanding of the range of forces that impact the work parents do. They can provide important insights for research, for social policy, and for mothers as well. As I demonstrate, the ability to raise successful teens is affected by many factors, not just individual mothers and fathers. Individualist narratives that circulate widely in public discourse contribute to the view that parenting is a private matter and that the broader society has little responsibility for supporting families. Far from being a private matter, however, parenting and raising the next generation are central tasks of any society. In closing, I offer recommendations for social policies that can provide the kinds of support families need to promote the ability of teens and young adults to move on to productive lives.

2
Becoming Adolescents and Pulling Away

As teens enter adolescence, mothers describe them as pulling away. They want more autonomy, or, as mothers say, they want more freedom. They want to do new things, they develop their own views of what they are entitled to do, and they spend more time away from home. Teens enter environments—both physical environments and online environments—over which parents have less control. These developments create significant changes in relationships between parents and their teen children. Mothers face new issues in their interpersonal work—in their communications with their teens, in managing negotiations and conflict, and in renegotiating issues of authority and control. As teens push for more freedoms, mothers "let go" of certain types of control.

As they described how their teens change and pull away, some mothers spoke about their teens "rebelling." For example, Beth, a working-class white mother with an 18-year-old daughter, Yvonne, who is a senior in high school, and a 16-year-old son, Tim, reported that Tim is "pulling away" from the family now:

> Through the end of ninth grade, Tim was very easygoing, easy to talk to. Then he became a typical teenager. Now he's like, "I have my own life," and his peers come before his parents. He likes to spend time alone or with friends. And I guess he also feels freer now to reject what his parents say. My daughter, she did all these things earlier. She's more confrontational, she pulled away at an earlier age.

Beth concluded by saying, "It's the rebellion thing." Beth's comments reflect widely held views of adolescence. In the popular view, pulling away is often referred to as rebellion. In my sample mothers sometimes said things like, "He's getting to be a teenager, he is going to start rebelling." Teens are seen as prone to defying their parents' wishes and engaging in activities parents and the wider society may not approve of.

Letting Go. Demie Kurz, Oxford University Press. © Oxford University Press 2024.
DOI: 10.1093/9780190222482.003.0002

When mothers spoke of rebellion, one of the things they were describing is a shift in their relationships with their teens. They feel their authority being challenged and they can have more difficulty monitoring their teens' activities and whereabouts. Elaine, an African American middle-class mother of three children (age 19, 16, and 8), described a major change in parenting as her children have become teens:

> They argue with you more. It's hard because before they are teenagers, you're the boss. You're the one that tells them what to do. But now they start telling you what to do and they rebel.

As Elaine described, it is more difficult to talk to her teenage son who feels free to challenge her authority. Teens increasingly claim the right to decide more things on their own, including where they go and with whom they spend time. It can be harder for parents to know what they are doing on social media or where their teens are. In concluding, Elaine said, "When they are out with their friends, you can worry, where could your teens be, what are they doing?"

At the same time, as noted in the previous chapter, parents and teens continue to have good times together. They can come to share new interests. Some parents become engaged with teens' sports teams and other extracurricular activities, they help teens prepare for school events, and they host their children's friends. Families can also enjoy vacations together. One mother said, "My son James is 16. He got a big part in the school play, he's very excited. We are helping him learn his lines. My husband and I and our daughter playact different parts, it's a lot of fun." Another mother said, "We are excited for my daughter. It turns out she is good at learning how to code, computer stuff. She and my husband are programming things together. I don't understand it a bit, but they love doing that."

However, while parents and teens continue to enjoy each other, as adolescence unfolds, the interests and experiences of parents and teens begin to diverge as teenagers spend more time in different social, emotional, and physical spaces at friends' houses or on social media. Teens can create psychological distance from their parents as they proceed with the tasks of adolescence, becoming less emotionally dependent on their parents and forging a new identity and sense of self as they seek more autonomy in their lives.

Divergence in the lives of parents and adolescents is propelled by the multiple changes teens undergo during adolescence, beginning with physical

changes. Teens experience growth in height and secondary sex characteristics, including breasts for girls and facial hair and a voice change for
boys. Due to improvements in nutrition and healthcare, puberty has begun
earlier—as early as age 8 to 13 for girls, and age 9 to 14 for boys.[1] In recent
years, more research has focused on how teens' brains change during adolescence. Neuroscientists have found that by mid-adolescence, teens develop
basic abilities in attention, memory, and logical reasoning that are at the
same level as those of adults. They can exhibit a certain degree of maturity
in a cognitive sense. However, brain functions that promote self-regulation
do not fully mature until late adolescence or even early adulthood. For some
teens, this leads to higher levels of what many adults view as risky behavior.
Other researchers note these changes but argue that it is important to consider not just the "maladaptive" but also the "adaptive" kinds of risks teens
take that can foster development and promote growth. Some teens take risks
in more positive arenas—auditioning for a school play, running for a student government office, trying out for a sports team—activities that can help
them develop goals and a sense of purpose.[2]

As their physical growth and brain development proceed, teens develop
more powers of reasoning and begin to think in more complicated, multi-
dimensional ways. They develop more sophisticated abilities to understand
that there are different ways of looking at a situation and imagining other possibilities for action. As a result of these changes, teens gain new perspectives
about their own mothers and fathers. They shed the idealized images of their
parents they may have previously held and begin to see them more critically,
including their weaknesses and flaws. They are more willing and able to
challenge and argue with their parents, and there can be increased conflict.
Teens' increased abstract reasoning skills also enable them to better understand the complexities of life, including its more fearful aspects. With these
more sophisticated powers of reasoning, teenagers find it easier to imagine

---

[1] L. Breehl and O. Caban O. (2023). "Physiology, Puberty." 2023 Mar 27. In: StatPearls [Internet].
Treasure Island (FL): StatPearls Publishing; 2024 Jan–. PMID: 30521248.
[2] According to brain and behavior research, at 15 years of age an average teen can perform at the
same level as an average adult in terms of basic abilities, including memory, attention, and logical
reasoning. More sophisticated cognitive abilities—including impulse control, the ability to evaluate
risks, and the ability to understand the consequences of actions—develop over time and on into a
young adult's twenties. L. L. Steinberg, *Adolescence* (New York: McGraw-Hill Education, 2020), 61.

what others are thinking of them, which can mean their sense of the negative side of things can become magnified.[3]

In the wake of these changes, teens experience increased emotional vulnerability and undergo a weakening of their identities and childhood selves. Before adolescence, children closely identify with their parents and are able to rely on them for a sense of a core, stable emotional self, but during adolescence, teens become more emotionally independent. They confront the task of developing new identities, a process that can be complicated and stressful. They face many choices, often beginning at school, where they typically find groups to identify with—the intellectual crowd, the popular crowd, the athletes, the arts crowd. Teens must develop gender, racial/ethnic, and sexual identities during this time. They "try on" identities by adopting new fashion choices, hairstyles, and musical tastes; they create online profiles; they choose new friends and begin romantic and sexual relationships; and they imagine how they want to be in the future.[4]

Divergence in the lives of parents and teens also takes place as peers come to play an increasingly central role in teens' social and emotional lives. In the US, not including the time they spend in school, teens spend twice as much time per week with peers as with their parents or other adults.[5] Peers can provide ways of being and feedback for teens that they do not get from adults. Peer cultures take many forms based on teens' racial/ethnic and sexual identities, their "popularity" rankings, and their interests in sports, music, popular culture, and other arts. Some teens are prone to risk-taking behaviors, and some take part in "delinquent" peer cultures, including those that promote drug and alcohol use. In the context of the peer group, teens can try on different roles, personalities, and identities.

Peers also play a role in teens' emotional development, helping them acquire new emotional centers and identities as well as new interpersonal and decision-making skills. As teens strive to expand their horizons beyond the advice and demands of their parents, it is peers who help them establish new emotional centers and cognitive frameworks that will enable them to forge and grow into their own identities.[6] Teens get a lot of emotional support from

---

[3] K. L. Mills, F. Lalonde, L. S. Clasen, J. N. Giedd, and S-J. Blakemore, "Developmental Changes in the Structure of the Social Brain in Late Childhood and Adolescence," *Social Cognitive Affective Neuroscience* 9(1) (2014): 123–131.

[4] J. E. Côté and C. Levine, *Identity Formation, Youth, and Development: A Simplified Approach.* (New York: Psychology Press, 2016).

[5] Steinberg, *Adolescence,* 126.

[6] B. Little, "The Role of Peers in Personality Development," in *Encyclopedia of Personality and Individual Differences,* ed. V. Zeigler-Hill and T. K. Shackelford (Cham: Springer, 2020), 4499–4504.

peers, who understand and share their condition of "frameworklessness," "a period of living in a 'no man's land,' of being on unfamiliar, unsteady ground, having left childhood yet remaining far from adulthood."[7] Teens' moods are at their most positive when they are with their friends, away from the adults who monitor their behavior. At the same time, while peers play a central role in teens' lives, peer culture can be stressful. As is well known, teens can engage in intense competition for popularity, they can judge each other harshly, and they can reject others to get ahead. Thus, while spending time with peers can help teens develop more autonomy, it can also be stressful. Some students report being bullied online.[8]

Cultural and technological changes can also impact parent-teen relationships and create further divergence. Kingsley Davis argues that due to rapid changes in contemporary societies, youth and parents find themselves in different social and historical contexts and develop more divergent views on a range of issues than do youth and parents in traditional societies. Parents may not be able to "catch up" with a teen's point of view or skills. According to Davis, this can result in a loss of "mutual identification" between parents and teens.[9] In the current era, as the use of the internet and social media have become central to social life, teens and young adults typically understand these technologies and become more proficient in their use than their parents and older relatives. When parents don't understand these new technologies and need help operating their computers or other devices, they often call on teens and are grateful for their help. As I will describe in the following chapter, it is certainly also the case that parents have many concerns about how teens are using these new media.

The Impact of Pulling Away on Mothers

In response to these changes and the distancing that typically occurs in their relationships with their teens, mothers continue to reach out to their

---

[7] V. C. Seltzer, *Psychosocial Worlds of the Adolescent: Public and Private* (New York: Wiley, 1989); Steinberg, *Adolescence*.

[8] J. W. Cohen and R. A. Brooks, *Confronting School Bullying: Kids, Culture, and the Making of a Social Problem* (Boulder, CO: Lynne Rienner, 2014). In one survey, half of teens reported being cyberbullied, including being called an offensive name, having false rumors spread about them, or having explicit images they didn't ask for sent to them. K. Schaeffer, "9 Facts About Bullying in the U.S." (Washington, DC: Pew Research Center, 2023).

[9] K. Davis, "The Sociology of Parent-Youth Conflict," *American Sociological Review* 5(4) (1940): 523–535.

children as they enter adolescence. They cook their teens' favorite food, order pizza, watch movies and television shows with them, organize special birthday celebrations, and include their friends at gatherings. If their teens are on athletic teams or in a theater group, parents attend their games and performances. They transport teens to events, extracurricular activities, and friends' houses, and they plan family trips they think their teens would enjoy. During these activities, mothers reported times of love and connection between themselves and their teenage children.

However, mothers in my sample also reported that the pulling away and distancing they experience with their teens during adolescence can affect the amount of time they spend together, the communication that takes place between them, and their ability to exercise authority and control. As Reed Larson and Maryse Richards describe, up until adolescence, parents can readily "sense strong internal centripetal forces that pulled the child back to the family each night." Younger children rely a great deal on their parents, typically communicate more openly with them, and ultimately must accede to their parents' authority. However, as teens spend more time apart from their family, they retreat to their bedrooms to be alone and spend time on their phones, texting and communicating with friends.[10]

Some mothers I interviewed find the changes in their relationships with their teens to be a major emotional adjustment. Cathy, a nurse who is a white middle-class mother of two teens, a daughter who is 14 and a son who is 16, said that she finds her teens don't want to spend as much time with the family as they used to. Cathy left her full-time job to work part-time so she could spend more time with her teenagers and make sure they were involved in safe, constructive activities. Her teens' pulling away weighs on her. She reported that things are different now at the dinner hour, which used to be an important time for the family to be together:

> My kids want to talk more to their friends, more than to us. They talk and text on the phone a lot. And then there is going to their room, like after dinner. Instead of sitting around at the dinner table talking like we used to, they want to go to their rooms.

[10] R. Larson and M. H. Richards, *Divergent Realities: The Emotional Lives of Mothers, Fathers, and Adolescents* (New York: Basic Books, 1994).

Cathy said that her father, who lives nearby, spends a lot of time at their house. She reported, "The kids used to want to sit around after dinner and be with my father and talk and play, it was really nice. Then they became teens and it changed, they want to finish dinner and go connect with their friends on their phones or on social media." Cathy went on to explain that these changes in her children also affect how they view holiday gatherings, which can make it harder to organize these occasions:

Having the family eat together, spending time together over meals and at the holidays, is very important to me. But it's different now. We do our holiday things, our traditions, and then the kids want to go be with their friends. It's a big change, it kind of upsets the apple cart about what to do on holidays.

Cathy finds these changes in family routines and traditions unsettling and is working to adjust to the new situation she finds herself in. She sounded alternately clear and uncertain about how to do this. As she tried to reassure herself that her teens would become close to the family again in the future, she noted, "I tell myself to be flexible and it will all come around again. It can be upsetting, but it's their thing. They want to be with their friends, I have to step back, they aren't as dependent on me anymore. I have to let them be more independent, but I'm not really sure how you do this."

Several mothers described their teens as becoming more like "strangers." Their teens begin to dress differently, play different kinds of music, and respond to their parents differently. One mother said it felt like her teens were "joining a tribe." If their teens stop responding to them in friendly ways, some mothers can experience anxious thoughts like, "What if we are never close again?" One mother imagined what she felt could be one of the worst things that could happen when she said: "You don't want to lose your kids, like if they get really defiant, kids can run away." While mothers used to feel more unconditional love from their children at an earlier stage of development, they reported that during their children's teenage years, they could not count on expressions of love from their teens. They experience fewer of the positive times they enjoyed when their children were younger.

Joleen, an upper-middle-class African American mother, is an educational consultant and a mother of two teen girls (ages 13 and 16). She described how she was trying to adjust to the fact that she couldn't show physical affection toward her daughter. She said, "I can't kiss or hug her anymore. And talking is hard. But of course she can show physical affection towards me. Last weekend we watched a really beautiful movie. And at one point, my daughter puts her head on my shoulder. There's her head, on my shoulder! But I didn't even think of reaching back to her, I just sat there like a mummy! But," she said, laughing, "I'll take that." Joleen said these changes are difficult to adjust to:

> I found her pulling away very hurtful. It broke my heart, I felt like I'd been stabbed in the heart. One minute it's "I don't want to be anywhere near you," and another minute she comes and sits on my lap.

However, Joleen reassured herself by saying, "I've read a lot, I know this is what she is supposed to do." Joleen has also found a way to communicate with her daughter when talking doesn't work. "Sometimes I write notes to her. I write when I get frustrated, when I feel she is not listening. I try to be more positive—to get rid of the judgmental, negative stuff. And she writes notes to me." Joleen concluded, laughing, "Her notes are kind of offensive though."

Carla, a white upper-middle-class mother of 15-year-old twin boys, made a revealing statement about how things have changed since her children became teenagers: "You can't control as many things, you are not the be-all and end-all," she said. "It's a humbling thing to be a parent. Teens can be obnoxious. It changes you." She explained further:

> You become vulnerable in a new way that gives you depth. It can make you a better person. I guess if you were already fairly healthy, it can make you healthier. And I guess if you were already having trouble, it could really put you over the edge! [Laughing]

Carla's comments summarize what many mothers feel about their teens during adolescence, including the emotional changes and evolving sense of self that can occur in the life of mothers, as well as changes in what they can control.

It is important to note that a small number of mothers did not feel much distancing from their teens. Some teens and some parents have times where they feel a lot of connection with each other. A white upper-middle-class mother I interviewed said, "When people talk about how difficult teenagers are, I don't relate to it. My daughters are wonderful, they are just a pleasure to be with. We can talk things over and make our decisions." Similarly, a middle-class African American mother said she, her husband, and their 16-year-old son and 18-year-old daughter are a close family and get along well. "We can always talk about anything," she said. Some mothers experienced distancing with one teen but not another. Some mothers said they were more bothered when they felt this distancing with a first child, but by the time their younger children became teens, they were more used to the idea that teens distance themselves from their parents.

Letting Go and New Challenges in Parenting

As their teens pull away, the mothers I interviewed reported new challenges in communicating with them, in managing negotiations and conflict, and in renegotiating issues of authority and control. All of these challenges underlie the work of managing teens' passage through adolescence and letting go. During this stage in teens' lives, mothers and teens must renegotiate rules and practices in relation to teens' social activities, their schoolwork, and family relations. As they face these new challenges, mothers can experience uncertainty about how to adjust their parenting strategies. Mothers referred to the fact that there are no widely accepted guidelines for parenting teens, there is "no manual." As one mother put it, "There's no universal codebook for parenting, there's no manual, a big fat thing in a vault in London that gives you a standard. Everyone just has to find their way through this, it's a big challenge." Mothers often referred to "parenting as you go" or "learning as you go."

Communication

Mothers I interviewed said they work to keep lines of communication with their teens open through talk. Talk is work; it is a key medium of parenting and an essential part of caregiving.[11] It is critical for staying connected to children and teens and understanding what they are thinking, and for exercising control—instructing teens, getting them to do certain things, and

[11] M. L. DeVault, *Feeding the Family: The Social Organization of Caring as Gendered Work* (Chicago: University of Chicago Press, 1991).

forbidding them from doing other things. The mothers I interviewed reported new challenges in communicating with their teens. As one said:

> Starting around when they are 13 or even earlier, they start pulling away. You don't know if they are really listening to you or how much they are telling you. They also get sneaky, it's harder to keep track of them when they don't tell you things. And then you worry. Where are they? What could they be doing?

Research shows that adolescents, and college students as well, report frequently concealing things from parents or lying to them.[12] Teens do this in order to avoid parental disapproval, protect their parents' feelings, and assert control over decisions they believe it is their right to make.[13] Challenges in communication can arise because teens want to create more buffers or distance between themselves and their parents and develop a more private self. Researchers have argued that the failure to disclose things is a normal part of developing autonomy and that the ability to have a private self is part of growing into adulthood.[14] Withholding information can also be a way for teens to exercise "strategic interaction," a process Erving Goffman describes as the way each party in an encounter, knowing what the other party thinks and wants, takes actions that will most likely secure the outcome they desire. Knowing what their parents will disapprove of, teens find that the strategy of failing to disclose things can further their goals.[15] Some researchers find that parents are not always aware of this and that they overestimate the degree to which their teens are disclosing things.[16]

When they discussed communication with their teens, some mothers said they had good communication with their children. As one mother noted: "I have a close relationship with my daughter and she talks to me about everything, absolutely everything." However, many noted that they find it more

[12] J. Smetana, M. Villalobos, M.Tasopoulos-Chan, D.C. Gettman, and N. Campione-Barr, "Early and Middle Adolescents' Disclosure to Parents About Activities in Different Domains," *Journal of Adolescence* 32 (2009): 693–713.

[13] M. Gingo, A. D. Roded, and E. Turiel, "Authority, Autonomy, and Deception: Evaluating the Legitimacy of Parental Authority and Adolescent Deceit," *Journal of Research on Adolescence* 27 (2017): 862–877.

[14] H.-Y. Chan, B. B. Brown, and H. von Bank, "Adolescent Disclosure of Information About Peers: The Mediating Role of Perceptions of Parents' Right to Know," *Journal of Youth and Adolescence* 44 (2015): 1048–1065.

[15] E. Goffman, *Strategic Interaction* (Philadelphia: University of Pennsylvania Press, 1969).

[16] J. G. Smetana, *Adolescents, Families, and Social Development: How Teens Construct Their Worlds* (New York: Wiley Blackwell, 2011).

difficult to communicate with teens. This creates challenges for parents. The mothers I interviewed reported that there are times at the dinner table when they can't get their teens to say much of anything, or when their teens respond to whatever their mothers say with an answer like "Okay" or "Fine." Some teens may find it's too hard to explain all the new things in their lives that parents don't share. Some may not want to talk as much because they feel talked down to.

Elizabeth, a social worker, is a white middle-class mother with a 15-year-old son, Tom, and a daughter in college. She described a time when Tom went on a camping trip with friends. After previous trips, Elizabeth said Tom always shared his experiences with her and her husband. But this time, when Tom came home, he said, "Hi, Mom," and immediately called a friend to relate the details of the camping trip. Elizabeth never heard much about the trip. She said, "Tom talks on the phone with friends now. Supposedly it's about schoolwork." Elizabeth continued, "He just doesn't tell me things, he used to tell me all kinds of things. I told my daughter, 'When you come home from college, you need to know that your brother has become a teenager.' I just thought she should know." Elizabeth spoke with some sadness and missed the connection she had with her son, but like other mothers, she also did emotion work to reassure herself. "I'm glad I understand that this is supposed to happen," she said. "I took psychology courses in college, I learned about how teens do this in my courses in child development. That makes it easier, and most of the time, I don't take it personally. And I know things will change, it will get easier."

Joan, a white upper-middle-class single mother, reported that communication is something she particularly worries about because, on a day-to-day basis, it is only she and her daughter in the family. Her daughter's father lives in another city and only sees their daughter every few months. Joan's account highlights the critical role communication plays in carrying out the tasks of parenting:

> What I worry about isn't drugs or anorexia, I worry about her stopping talking, about silences. My daughter and I are in a dyad, that's the least stable unit. When there's no talking with two, it's loud. With two of us, we have no buffers. It's hard if we don't talk with each other, we're in the same space, it's so obvious we are not communicating, but we have to get things done.

Joan said her daughter has a bigger tolerance for unresolved conflict than she does: "But she does get it that it's just the two of us and she has to communicate too." Joan also voiced an another concern about communications with her daughter:

> Sometimes I wonder, will she shut me off? I have friends whose sons did. Then in college they changed and got more communicative. [Laughing] Then they said, "Our parents changed." Joan's that her daughter could "shut her off" illustrates the important role that communication plays in mothers' ability to carry out the tasks of parenting.

While mothers can have similar problems with girls, some mothers noted that talking becomes a particular issue with their sons, who they report are less willing to engage in conversation than their daughters. Farah, a middle-class African American mother who has a 14-year-old son and a 16-year-old daughter, finds herself in what sounds like a power struggle with her son, Malcolm, over his lack of communication with her. She said:

> It's a little harder to get through to a boy than it is a girl. I have a real hard time getting through to Malcolm. Where, you know, I'll sit down and talk to my daughter and it seems to sink in. With him it doesn't, it's a couple of times you go around before it finally sinks in, what you're telling him.

Farah continued, "You know, he's just real hard to talk to. You'll talk about one thing and he'll come out with something else completely different." She said she tries to figure out why Malcolm won't communicate more, noting, "A lot of times, I kind of think he's just doing that to try to avoid things, it's just that he doesn't seem to under . . . I don't know if it's he doesn't understand or he doesn't want to understand what you're trying to say." Farah said, "Sometimes Malcolm drives you crazy when you try to talk to him." Other mothers similarly reported that it is more difficult to communicate with their sons, who can see details of their personal lives as more private than their daughters do, a pattern which has been reported in various studies.[17]

As mothers adapt to their teens' changing status and the fact that their children can withhold information, they engage in strategic interactions to exercise control and get teens to do the things they want them to do. They work to frame issues to get their children to listen and not "tune them out," and they

[17] J. G. Smetana, *Adolescents, Families, and Social Development.*

determine when and where to raise issues with their children. The mothers I interviewed also reported that they work to develop strategies of communication that don't make them sound as if they are telling their children what to do, which they feel could backfire and decrease their ability to get their teens to do what they want them to do. Louise, a white upper-middle-class mother who teaches at a community college, said, "You have to be careful how you talk when you want them to do something. I can't sound too much like I'm making them do things, you really have to restrain yourself, you have to hold back from saying things and bite your tongue." Louise said that as a teacher, she has learned about the importance of framing her talk as a strategy to get teens to agree with her point of view:

> The thing is, I guide students all the time, I know what works. You have to say things in a certain way, like you can't just be telling them what to do anymore, you have to get them to accept things you're saying for themselves.

Geraldine, a working-class African American mother of two daughters (ages 14 and 16), described a strategy she calls "waiting." She said, "There are some rewarding times because we are close and they will come to me, you know, eventually." Geraldine said you have to choose the right words: "I say, 'Lord let me be able to say the right thing, please give me the right thing to say when they finally come to me.'" But most of all, she said, "You just have to wait." She noted that this was a hard thing to do:

> Sometimes you're waiting and you're looking at them. You want to talk about something, you try to talk. It seems like something is going on and you want them to talk to you.
> But you just have to wait. Or then pretend that you don't realize they are upset, you know? And then maybe finally they'll tell you something, like what's wrong or what they are upset about.

Geraldine hopes that her strategy of "pretending" will get her daughter to reveal what's on her mind, but she seemed uncertain about this.

Nadine is a white middle-class mother. She works as an accountant in a local business and has a 12-year-old daughter and a 14-year-old son, Jeff. Like Geraldine, she spoke about "waiting" and also about "backing off" in her communications with her son:

We have always had very open communication. We can share, Jeff's comfortable talking about how he's feeling with me. He's been close to my husband also. They've done things together, especially as Jeff is getting older, not so much when he was younger.

However, Nadine also stated that she experiences challenges in communicating with Jeff. She said, "Of course, sometimes he hasn't been close to either of us. You know how teens are, they keep things to themselves. It's always a struggle to communicate, but I'm involved as much as they will let me be." As she decides how to respond in this situation, she spoke about "backing off":

Now that they are getting older, I have to back off more. It's hard. The kids don't want to tell you as much, and you can't look like you are prying. You have to back off, you have to wait for the opportunity to talk with them, you just have to wait. They want to talk more to their friends, more than to their parents.

Nadine and Geraldine both hope that backing off and not appearing to pry can create more opportunities to talk with their teens. However, as Nadine said, it can be a "struggle" to communicate. Nadine also believes there are gender differences in how she and her husband communicate with their teens. She stated that while her husband is now more involved with their teens than he was when they were younger children, "I've always drawn Jeff out more where he can talk about emotional feelings."

To get information from her teens, Margaret, a white middle-class mother, talked about planning the location as well as the timing of her talks. She said:

I'll tell you the perfect time to get my kids is in the car. I say, "We're going to have a talk." They are like, "Oh!" I turn the radio off and with their being in the back seat, they can't get away. It is the perfect time to say whatever you want to them. Another mother, however, reported that the strategy of planning a talk in the car with her son did not work for her: "He just gave me short answers."

An additional strategy mothers use involves enlisting the help of other family members—fathers, siblings, cousins—in communicating with their teens, hoping that another person who carries some authority or is close to their teenage child can help reinforce their arguments. Yolanda, an African

American middle-class mother who works as an administrator at a local school, enlisted the help of her husband in talking to her son Paul. She reported that she did this to avoid sounding like she was "lecturing," which she felt was not helpful in promoting conversation with her son. As she put it, teens can see mothers as "Always wanting something, always trying to get them to do something. So," she said, "If I see a situation coming, I tell my husband, 'Honey, when you get a chance, could you talk to Paul about such and such a thing?' He can engage Paul in a conversation more than a lecture." Yolanda said that her husband and Paul have always been close, that her husband has been a very involved parent, and that now that Paul is an adolescent, he and his father share even more, particularly around their interest in sports.

Yolanda may also want her husband to speak to Paul because she, like many mothers, believes that fathers and sons can have a special bond. As she noted: "I think with the male child, the father, you know, they can form up a bond with that male child. From even just day-to-day activities that guys do." Yolanda said she believes that "Fathers can have special times with daughters too, but I think there are certain things that mothers and daughters share and certain things that fathers and sons share that are going to be different, although I have a special relationship with Paul too." Perhaps consciously or unconsciously, Yolanda also thinks that Paul views his father's authority as a male as more legitimate than hers.

Some mothers believe it can be important to try and talk with their teens on a more equal level. In contrast to Yolanda, Joyce, a white middle-class mother of a 10-year-old son and a 15-year-old daughter, felt that her husband does not understand how to craft his style of communication to be sensitive to their daughter's need to be talked to on a more equal basis. Joyce said that while her husband can be helpful in certain aspects of parenting, this was not the case in terms of talking with their daughter. Because of this, she thinks about when to include him in conversations:

> In some ways, my husband helps a lot with raising our daughter, driving her places and things, but in some ways, he does not help, like talking to my daughter. She tells me, "You understand and Dad doesn't." When he talks to her, he sort of reverts to being Dad—kind of the dominant one. My daughter rejects that.

Joyce said she thinks, "Fathers aren't warm and fuzzy. They just say, 'This is the rule,' then there's no discussion. It's a different style, I engage in a conversation."

Some of the mothers I interviewed said that fathers have more distant relationships with their teens, particularly their daughters, that they are not typically involved in day-to-day talk with their teens. Fathers often become involved with teens through sports, leisure activities, and sometimes through homework and school projects. However, they can be less connected personally and emotionally to their teens, and they may not talk or empathize with their teens as well as mothers do, creating what has been called a "closeness gap." Consequently, fathers may also experience less of the defiance, arguing, and complaining that can be part of interacting with teens.[18]

Negotiations between Parents and Teens and Increasing Conflict

As teens venture out to new places and participate in new activities, mothers engage in negotiations with them about curfews, coed parties, tattoos, piercings, girlfriends, boyfriends, time spent texting or on social media, video games, homework, and going to friends' houses. Sometimes negotiations between parents and teens go fairly smoothly. However, the mothers I interviewed also reported that they have experienced more conflicts with their children during adolescence. One middle-class African American mother reported that she was having more arguments with her teens and that, "Sometimes, it's like they've taken psychology classes and they come back and play mind games with you and they say, 'If you do this, I'll do that for you!'" Another mother said: "Kids argue back all the time. You think it's settled, you've argued about it three times, and then they come back again and start arguing. They could have 15 go-arounds!" These conflicts can take an emotional toll on mothers. It is an adjustment to be challenged by one's teen after an earlier period of childhood in which children certainly challenge their parents' views but also show more deference to parental authority, as well as more love and affection.

As I described earlier, changes in teens and the resulting divergence in parent-teen relationships are often described as teen "rebellion." The widespread belief that teenagers rebel and actively reject their parents' beliefs

[18] Larson and Richards, *Divergent Realities.*

arose earlier in the twentieth century.[19] The idea of adolescent rebellion is not universal, however. Amy Schalet, for example, argues that in the Netherlands, Dutch people have a less adversarial view of adolescence and don't see teens as rebelling. They see teens' passage through adolescence as taking place without a break or separation between parents and teens and without much discord. According to Schalet, the Dutch believe that teens and parents can work out new agreements for teens' increasing autonomy within the family. She argues that the American belief in intergenerational conflict can be traced to widely held views of individualism, which stipulate that developing a self that is independent of the family requires "breaking away."[20]

While the term "rebellion" is widely used in the United States to describe teen behavior that is challenging to adults, as I noted above, it does not capture the actual complexities of how parents and teens negotiate over teens' increasing autonomy. Adolescents assert their own views and disagree with parents, sometimes arguing strongly against them. This happens particularly at the beginning of adolescence.[21] At the same time, the majority of teens do not repudiate adult values or engage in a wholesale rejection of their authority; rather, most adolescents share their parents' values and respect their parents' rules, although they wish their parents were less strict. In multiple studies of families from different ethnic and racial backgrounds, Judith Smetana found that only a small number of families could be characterized as angry and highly conflictual. The majority of families—at least half—reported frequent conflicts that involve bickering and squabbling but that are relatively low in intensity and not excessively angry or hostile. The remainder of families are "easygoing" and don't experience many conflicts.[22] Some argue that at least in the American context, rebellion should more accurately be considered "individuation," or the work of teens to develop a self that is separate from their parents.[23]

[19] G. Palladino, *Teenagers: An American History* (New York: Basic Books, 1996).

[20] A. T. Schalet, *Not Under My Roof: Parents, Teens, and the Culture of Sex* (Chicago: University of Chicago Press, 2011).

[21] Steinberg, *Adolescence*, 104.

[22] N. Campione-Barr and J. G. Smetana, "Families with Adolescents," in *APA Handbook of Contemporary Family Psychology: Foundations, Methods, and Changing Forms* Vol. 1, ed. B. H. Fiese, M. Celano, K. Deater-Deckard, E. N. Jouriles, and M. A. Whisman (Washington, DC: American Psychological Association, 2018), 593–609.

[23] J. Jager, C. X. Yuen, D. L. Putnick, C. Hendricks, and M. H. Bornstein, "Adolescent-Peer Relationships, Separation and Detachment from Parents, and Internalizing and Externalizing Behaviors: Linkages and Interactions," *Journal of Early Adolescence* 35 (2015): 511–537.

When mothers spoke about rebellion in interviews, they typically described times when their teens challenge their authority. They stated that in their children's elementary school years, they had arguments, but as parents, they usually got the last word—that is, "Because I told you so" still worked. As one mother said, "Ages 7 to 11 are great. But teens are more independent, not like little kids, they're cooperative." Other mothers said things like: "Teens think they know everything"; "They are standoffish"; "They can be like, 'What do you know?'" Another mother said, "He's starting to mouth back, I can see he's getting a tongue."

As teens begin to question their parents' authority and develop their own views of what they should and shouldn't be allowed to do, mothers and teens must negotiate over their differences. Sometimes parents hold fast to their positions and expect their teens to concede. Sometimes teens return to an argument or a difference with their parents with more information, and parents decide they will give their teen permission to do something. In other cases, mothers and teens can have a serious disagreement which might involve yelling. As one of the mothers I interviewed said, "Things can become emotional very quickly." Conflicts can lead to good discussions and promote more understanding. But they can also take a toll, break down trust between parents and teens, and, at least temporarily, poison the atmosphere. A few mothers mentioned not talking with their teens for a short period after a fight. After a conflict, mothers also noted that they can sometimes question themselves. As one mother reported, "My daughter would keep saying to me, 'You're too hard on me, you're not giving me enough space.' I really thought about that, I had to think, 'Is this my fault?' And then after a while I realized [with feeling] it's not my fault. I am doing the best that I can. It's her too."

When conflicts or heated negotiations occur, they can become emotional because each party feels their basic rights are being challenged. For mothers, this includes their parental authority and their knowledge of what they believe is safe and in their teens' best interests. For teens, it includes the rights they believe are now theirs, including decisions about who their friends are, what their curfew times should be, and how they should dress. Many conflicts between parents and teens develop over relatively small issues that do not involve a rejection of parental values but arise over teens' belief that they now have the right to control certain aspects of their personal lives. What can make these conflicts over small things contentious is that parents and teenagers are not only negotiating over the substance of a particular issue but over who has the right to decide issues concerning teens' lives.

For the most part, teens agree with their parents and accept their authority when the issue is a moral one (for example, cheating on a school test or stealing) or one involving clearly identifiable issues of safety (for example, drinking and driving). They also agree on basic values such as the importance of hard work, education, health, and safety. However, parents and teens tend to disagree over who has authority over issues such as curfews, leisure time activities, the use of cell phones and social media, clothing and hairstyle choices, the cleanliness of their rooms, hours devoted to sleep, and dating. Teens typically view these decisions as personal matters which they have the right to control. Part of developing agency and identity as a person involves the ability to make decisions about personal issues, something teens begin to claim is their right.[24]

Deirdra, a working-class African American mother, was experiencing conflicts with her 15-year-old daughter, Latoya, about the clothes Latoya wanted to wear and the money she wanted to spend on her hair. Deirdra doesn't believe in spending a lot of money on material things. As she said:

> The big thing with Latoya is she's complaining because with the hairstyles and the clothes she wants, you know, I wasn't willing to put out whatever kind of money she wanted to buy the clothes and pay for what she said she needed to keep up her hair.

According to Deirdra, Latoya argued hard for her views: "She said she didn't want to go to school because other kids would make fun of her or whatever. But I have a hard time putting so much emphasis on material things." Deirdra then spoke more generally about the tension in their relationship, tension that can arise over the question of who has the right to make particular decisions:

> Latoya's got that teenage thing. Everything's gotta be done her way now. She thinks everything should go her way. And like I say to her, "It can't go your way all the time." It's arguing, it's the constant arguing. I think every parent goes through it. About when she wants to come in and go out. About her chores because she doesn't wanna do the work she's supposed to do.

---

[24] Smetana, Adolescents, Families, and Social Development.

Deirdra reported that she and Latoya do have some good times. "We can get along pretty well," she noted at one point. But then she said, "I guess every four months we get into it." In concluding, Deirdra said, "I'm hoping this is a phase that she'll hurry up and jump out of."

Another example illustrates how negotiations between mothers and teens over a fairly minor issue—in this case, how many ear piercings a daughter can have—can become contentious and emotional when each party feels they have the right to control a particular behavior. Anne is a middle-class stay-at-home mother of two daughters (ages 14 and 12) and a son (age 10). She described a time when her older daughter, Shannon, at age 14, disobeyed her. Shannon had two piercings in each ear but decided she wanted more. Anne thought this was a bad idea. Anne said that a few days before our interview Shannon had gone to the mall with a friend. Shannon said she wanted to get another ear piercing in each ear. Anne said she is against this and that she thought Shannon could regret getting so many piercings. "Shannon already has two ear piercings on each ear, that's enough," she said. "I told her I would not give her permission to get another one, that she could regret this when she applies for jobs. But Shannon went against that." Anne continued, "Even after what I said, when Shannon came back from the mall with her friend and her friend showed me that she had gotten more piercings, I asked Shannon what she had done at the mall. Shannon didn't say anything, but she kind of pushed her hair back and I could see she got another piercing in each ear."

Anne was angry about what Shannon had done, and she believed she had the right to discipline her over this incident because she had broken what Anne said was their agreement about an acceptable number of piercings:

> I said to Shannon, "You disobeyed me." She quibbled with words and said, "I thought you just said you wouldn't want me to, not that I couldn't." I said, "I made it perfectly clear, I was very, very clear—not another earring."

As a punishment, Anne grounded Shannon for a week, a common punishment used by parents that requires their teens to stay home and not attend social events for a certain period of time. Anne acknowledges that Shannon saw things differently. She noted, "Shannon thinks I'm heartless and cruel. She thinks, 'It's my body, I can do what I want.'" But Anne believed she had the right to make a decision about ear piercings because they could negatively impact how Shannon would be perceived by the adult world—for example, if she was trying to get a job. And she believed that Shannon deserved a punishment "because Shannon defied me, she's testing me."

Anne said she is tired of the conflicts between herself and Shannon. She believes these conflicts are about "nothing unusual," but she is tired of the tension:

Shannon has a chip on her shoulder. Everything is a major battle; it seems like overnight I became stupid. Nothing unusual, no green hair, no belly button piercings. I never thought I would find myself saying this but now I think, "It will be fine when you go away to college. I'll miss you but things will be a lot easier."

Anne's comment that "It seems like overnight I became stupid" would resonate with other mothers. Anne said these conflicts have negatively affected their family life. She said that Shannon doesn't show any "blatant disrespect"; she wouldn't allow that. However, she said, "It's not easy to take, it gets old. Sometimes I just want to have a normal conversation because the attitude affects everything, like conversations at dinner." In another comment that would undoubtedly resonate with many mothers, Anne concluded, "And then you go out with your husband for dinner and argue about how to handle it."

The incident between Anne and Shannon reflects how conflicts can arise because parents see teens as defying conventional norms. The mothers I interviewed sometimes saw issues in terms of what is considered socially appropriate, conventional behavior, or "how things are done." As mothers and fathers try to ensure that their teens develop the personal qualities necessary for success in their lives, they typically believe that teens should conform to certain social conventions: appropriate dress, polite behavior, regular sleep patterns. They believe that conforming to these norms will help their teen children acquire the social and psychological competencies they need for their future life and work. As adolescence progresses, however, teens, who often view these same things as a matter of personal choice, can become more resistant to their parents' requests that they conform to dominant norms of polite behavior, appropriate dress, and proper demeanor.

Mothers also reported negotiating over what they will and will not do for their teens. To avoid conflicts between herself and her 15-year-old son, one mother, Elaine, tried to be clearer about when she was willing to change her plans and drive her son somewhere. As parents do with many issues, she was trying to set boundaries with her son concerning what she was willing to do for him:

> And then my son and I have conflicts about driving her places. He always tells us at the last minute. The problem is his school is in another neighbor-hood and most of the kids in his class live in that neighborhood. So I feel I should drive him.

Elaine continued, "Recently, my son's friends have been calling him on Saturday morning and saying, 'We're all going to—wherever—so come over and we'll make a plan.'" Elaine said at first she thought, "Okay, I guess I should drive him there." But now she said, sounding confused, "I'm thinking, no, I really need more planning on this. I mean I have my plans, too. I need to talk to my son about this, he's got to let me know these things sooner."

As noted earlier, conflicts between mothers and teens are more frequent at the onset of adolescence.[25] One white working-class mother, Maureen, re-ported that as her daughter became an adolescent, she and her daughter had more conflicts and her daughter also became harder to talk to. Then at 15, her daughter changed and became easier to be with. Maureen is not sure why this happened. She said she and her daughter used to "go at it" a lot. She said:

> She wasn't real bad, I mean she's not a bad kid, she's a real good kid. She just, she's mouthy like any girl, you know. And that's basically what it was like, she could make a face at you if she didn't like what you said and you know, nothing real major just, we clashed a lot.

Maureen said that as time went on, the communication between her, her daughter, and her husband has become easier:

> After she turned 15, things got better. Right before it was like you had to pry things from her. And then after she turned 15, it was like she just started coming to me. I mean, she even goes to my husband now too, she even talks to him now. Him and her get a long a lot better.

---

[25] I. H. A. De Goede, S. Branje, and W. H. J. Meeus, "Developmental Changes in Adolescents' Perceptions of Relationships with Their Parents," *Journal of Youth and Adolescence* 38(1) (2009): 75–88.

Maureen continued, "It was like after she got out of eighth grade, it was like this magic thing happened. [Laughing] I don't know what happened, but that's when I noticed the change, after she got out of eighth grade."

While the majority of conflicts between parents and teens are over relatively minor issues that become contentious in the short term, there can also be conflicts that involve more serious, deep-rooted differences and painful, even long-lasting feelings. These kinds of conflicts may not resolve as teens progress through adolescence and can persist into the future.[26] Elsa, a white upper-middle-class woman, had serious conflicts with her 13-year-old daughter at the time of her divorce. Elsa said things are better between her and her daughter now, but for the two years after the divorce, things were difficult, and she blamed herself for their conflicts:

> At the time of the divorce, my daughter would just get really angry at me—call me names, blame me for everything. I tried not to get angry back. I went to see a therapist, and she really helped me with that, she helped me to see why my daughter was doing that. I also made sure my daughter had a good therapist.

Elsa noted, "One really important moment was when I went to a therapy session with my daughter. The therapist said to my daughter, 'It's easier to be angry with the one you know is going to be there for you, isn't it?' And my daughter acknowledged that was true, that her dad was not going to provide as much support for her as I was." Elsa said, "That was very important to me, it helped me see that it wasn't just me doing something wrong. There is still some tension between us, but things are better, and I am hopeful that in the long run, we'll be on good terms."

At times, however, conflicts between teenagers and their parents are resolved not by listening or through compromise but by one party giving in or walking away in anger. For example, a white middle-class mother named Jean reported that her husband Jack and her 16-year-old daughter, April, got involved in a serious conflict in which they were both very angry. April challenged her father about his right to ask a lot of questions about where she had been and what she had been doing. Jean said April told her father she was angry that he didn't trust her and that he talked down to her. Jean said she

---

[26] K. Agillias, *Family Estrangement: A Matter of Perspective* (New York: Routledge, 2017).

wasn't there, but she was sure April "had an attitude" when she spoke to her father. And then, she said:

> Jack hit her in the mouth, not too hard but she has braces, and they cut the inside of her lip. So of course she was real upset, and I was upset with him for like two weeks for hitting her. I even slept with April in her room I was so upset. Since then, my husband and I have settled our differences about what happened.

Jean said April and Jack don't get along at all: "They argue and argue. I keep telling her that it's because they're just the same but I mean to the point that she does not, just does not get along with her father at all." She continued, "They are both to blame, although now Jack is trying to make things better, but April won't." Jean said her husband has a significantly different relationship with their other daughter "who lets everything roll off her back," whereas "April's the opposite, she's more sensitive and takes everything personally":

> April and my husband both have to give a little. It's been going on for over a year now that they're at each other's throat, and I tell her, "You sound exactly like your father when you talk that way." But then words come out of his mouth that make her more upset.

Jean indicated the conflicts between her husband and daughter have taken an emotional toll on her. "I'm just tired of being the middleman you know? It gets very tiring, and it's painful," she said. However, recently Jean noted that she had become a little more hopeful about the situation: "Actually we all ate out at a restaurant recently, and the two of them were so civil, I thought I was at somebody else's table. So it's, it's possible."

Exercising Control

In early adolescence teens begin claiming the right to more freedoms, and trying to get their parents to grant their wishes and demands.[27] Using information they gather from peers and social and mass media, they develop

---

[27] Steinberg, *Adolescence*, 104.

ideas about new types of freedoms they would like. Parents then have to decide how to respond to these requests. Do they grant them, negotiate over
them, or deny them and potentially face a conflict with their teens? Mothers,
particularly if they are worried about their teen's safety, wonder when they
should exercise their authority and when they should let go, relinquish control, and allow their teen to make their own decisions.

During their children's adolescent years, mothers use a number of
strategies—persuasion, reasoning, directives, making rules about what is and
is not permissible—to maintain control. Mothers can withhold resources,
including money teens need to buy things they want or go out with friends.
They can bargain with their teens, permitting them to do certain things
in exchange for their willingness to abide by rules, and they can withhold
privileges, such as staying out later at night or going places alone without
adult supervision. They can "ground" their teens for a certain period of time.

Many mothers I interviewed struggle with finding a balance between restrictiveness and permissiveness. Some of them framed this issue in terms of
how "strict" they should be; others debated whether or not they should be
a "friend" to their child. Some mothers from all backgrounds believed that
being more of a friend to your teen is a good thing, even for maintaining control, while others did not. Esther, an upper-middle-class African American
mother, said she does not believe in being a friend to your child:

> I would say that in being a parent, you should have soft but firm discipline.
> And that you should always be a loving adult but an adult, not a friend. And
> you have to listen to your child and support your children.

Rosa, a white middle-class mother, said she is trying to be both a friend
and parent and finding it difficult:

> Being a parent is hard, I have to say I don't always enjoy it. I want to be their
> friend, but I also want to be their parent. Right now, I don't think my hus-
> band and I are either very good parents or very good friends.

Rosa said she sometimes questions the parenting strategies she and her husband have used in the past. She noted, "Maybe we should be harder on them
and discipline them more. The way we were raised, was that better? Our
parents were stricter, are we too laid-back?"

Arlene, a white working-class mother with two daughters (ages 16 and 17) voiced a different view. She stated that her daughters are her friends and that this has real benefits. She said, "My kids are my friends. You have to be their friend or they're not going to talk to you." She then continued, "They're not going tell you their problems if you're just a mom. If you're just a mom, they're not going to say, 'Mom, I'm having a problem with my boyfriend.' They're going to talk to their girlfriend. I want to be my kids' friend." Arlene concluded, "Even my son has no problem talking to me about anything."

Germaine, a white middle-class mother who has one son, Miles, a junior in high school, said she, Miles, and her husband, Jimmy, have a close relationship, doing things together regularly. Jimmy and Miles are particularly close, she said: "They are best friends. Jimmy is a great Dad. Starting when Miles was younger, even though he had friends, Jimmy was his best friend; they were buddies, they would watch sports on television together, go to ball games together." Germaine's comments reflect how a teen's personality can affect their relationship with their parents, as well as how a parent chooses to exercise their authority. According to Germaine, "Miles has never been that kind of a child that I've had to be real strict with." Germaine suggested that the reason for this is that "Miles has never been too demanding, he doesn't ask for too much, that's just the way he is."

Chareen, a working-class African American mother, described the conflicts she has had with her husband, Aldon, over issues of permissiveness and restrictiveness. Chareen said that Aldon has much stricter, more traditional ideas about childrearing and control than she does and that they disagree about how to handle Kaylee, Chareen's 17-year-old daughter by a previous marriage. Chareen said, "I've read some books on teens and families, and my husband, Aldon, kind of scoffs at them." Chareen said she has learned that Kaylee will listen to her, that she can reason with her. Aldon, however, believes Chareen should be stricter with Kaylee. As she noted:

> He feels that I try to use too much psychology and what I really need to do is smack Kaylee's hand. That's kind of his approach. "You don't do what I say, then I beat obedience into you." And I can't say that I haven't tried to smack my daughter when I've gotten desperate.

Chareen said that Aldon feels that she's afraid of her daughter. However, based on what she has learned from experience, her observations of Kaylee's behavior, and what she has read, Chareen believes that Aldon's stricter approach and use of physical punishment is ineffective. Over time, Chareen has worked to develop strategies of talking and reasoning that she feels are more effective in getting Kaylee to comply with her wishes. As she noted:

> I realized early on that beating—whereas maybe with some personalities that might help at a point, you know, but not with Kaylee. My daughter is a strong-willed child. I am stubborn, but I mean, she's got me beat by miles. It just will not help, if anything, it'll cause more resentment and to try to reason with her is sometimes better. There are times where she will dig her heels in and she just, you know, will not, she will refuse to see your point. And at those times, I let her alone.

Chareen also stated, "If it's an issue where she's threatening my authority I will put my foot down. But I know from experience and just knowing her, that, like, you can reason with her." Lareau argues that reasoning is primarily a middle-class parenting strategy. Chareen is a working-class mother, but based on her experience, she has come to view reasoning as an effective strategy to use in resolving differences with her daughter.[28]

Anthea, an African American working-class mother of a 16-year-old son, a 15-year-old daughter, and two younger children (ages 9 and 3), struggles with balancing restrictiveness and permissiveness in her parenting. She is separated from her husband, who rarely sees the children. Anthea said she is stricter with her teens since becoming a single parent:

> Now I have to make all the decisions. It used to be that they would come to me for things and say, "Come on, Mom, let's do this or that," and maybe I would say, "Yes" and their Dad would say, "No." I was softer, now I'm stronger.

Anthea's comments reflect tensions in letting go. She said, "I'm strict now because I have to be as a single mother, but I'm not too strict. If you're too strict, it just backfires. Like with my daughter, if I told her she couldn't go out, she would anyway. I have more control if I talk to her and try to convince her of what I think is best. Then she listens more."

[28] A. Lareau, *Unequal Childhoods: Class, Race, and Family Life Second Edition With an Update a Decade Later* (Berkeley: University of California Press, 2011).

Anthea's comment that being too strict can backfire now that her daughter is a teenager illustrates changing patterns of power and control. Her daughter can now do more of what she wants regardless of what Anthea says, and Anthea believes she will have more control if she trusts her daughter. Presumably, she means that if her daughter feels trusted, she will be more inclined to at least listen to her mother as well as share more information.

The challenges contemporary parents face in exercising appropriate control reflect wider debates in the United States about approaches to child-rearing. These conversations and arguments can be confusing. According to Ann Hulbert, throughout the twentieth century, experts' advice on issues of discipline and control alternated between advocating for strict rules and punishments for children on the one hand and "listening to the child" on the other, or between "hard" and "soft" approaches.[29]

In my sample, mothers across all social classes and racial groups talked about whether or not to be a "friend" to their teens, but for some time, researchers have found differences in the ways parents from different social classes exercise power and control. For example, Margaret Nelson, along with Annette Lareau, argues that middle-class parents reason with their children, negotiate with them, and give them choices.[30] By contrast, working-class parents tend to be more restrictive in their child-rearing practices, demanding compliance with their authority and expecting their children to obey their directives. Researchers have not found these more restrictive practices to be negative or dysfunctional, but rather argue that working-class parents use them because they live in neighborhoods that are less safe, which leads them to put a high priority on ensuring that their teenage children obey family rules as a way to protect them.[31] African American parents have also been found to use more strict discipline and demand more obedience from their children than white parents, an approach that is similarly believed to reflect a desire to protect their children, who may face environments that are unsupportive and sometimes hostile to racial minorities. At the same time, researchers find that African American parents are also warm and nonpunitive, an approach that produces positive outcomes for children.[32]

---

[29] For further discussion of "hard" and "soft" approaches to parenting, see A. Hulbert, Raising America: Experts, Parents, and a Century of Advice About Children (New York: Vintage Books, 2004).

[30] M. K. Nelson, Parenting Out of Control: Anxious Parents in Uncertain Times (New York: New York University Press, 2010); Lareau, Unequal Childhoods.

[31] F. F. Furstenberg et al., Managing to Make It: Urban Families and Adolescent Success (Chicago: University of Chicago Press, 1999). For African American parenting, see also Smetana, Adolescents, Families, and Social Development.

[32] Smetana, Adolescents, Families, and Social Development.

While these findings are robust and have held up over time, regardless of how strict their child-rearing practices are, African Americans, like all the parents in my sample, must also let go and renegotiate issues of authority and give up some of their control over their teenage children. Furthermore, as teens demand more autonomy and spend less time under adult supervision, mothers can't control them in the same way they did when they were younger children. One working-class African American mother, Alberta, described how she went to see a counselor when she realized she couldn't just tell her teenage son what to do anymore. She said:

> I was having trouble with one of my sons when he became a teenager so I went to a place that does counseling—my sister told me about this place. I believe you have to be very firm with kids, and with teenagers especially—they can get in so much trouble, especially Black boys. But my son wasn't listening, nothing was working.

Alberta said that after she went to some counseling sessions, "I changed." She ended a power struggle by "listening," which she says is more effective than "hollering":

> I realized the way I was strict and the way I hollered wasn't effective anymore. My son was getting older, I couldn't just tell him what to do. So I stopped laying down the law all the time.
>
> One day it just came to me. I realized it was more effective not to holler and be so rigid. So I changed my approach, and I started talking calmly and asking my son how he felt about things.

Miriam is a white middle-class divorced mother who has a female partner and shares custody of her sons (ages 12 and 16) with her ex-husband in an amicable arrangement although her sons live with Miriam and her partner more than with their father. She reported having worked through a power struggle by listening. She said, "My younger son is in a pretty mellow place, although he's just starting, you know, to be rude, to talk back, to be challenging sometimes. It's the older one, Ryan, who I had the conflicts with starting when he was about 14 or so." Miriam said the conflicts were over household chores that Ryan no longer wanted to do, a common type of conflict between parents and teens during adolescence. Miriam said that her conflicts with Ryan lasted for over a year. She felt they were stuck in a pattern. She would ask Ryan to do chores, then he would resist. "It was over the little everyday things like taking out the garbage, washing dishes—he was resisting doing his chores," she said. "We had serious conflicts, they were power struggles but not over anything big like using drugs or some big terrible thing." Miriam found these conflicts "painful." She said she felt that as the adult, she had to do something to improve the situation. She said:

> We were both locked in the struggle. I think we were both very unhappy about it but we couldn't do anything. It was upsetting me a lot and I felt I was the parent, the one who was older and I was more experienced in the world, so I felt it was up to me to be the one to give more, although I definitely expected him to give some too. [Emphatically] I was clear, I wasn't going to be the one who was going to do this alone.

As parents and teens negotiate over who has the right to make certain decisions, the conflicts that arise between parents and teens are often over, as Miriam said, "everyday things."[33] After thinking hard about how to improve her relationship with Ryan, Miriam shifted her strategy and tried to signal to him with her tone of voice and overall demeanor, as well as her words, that she wanted to talk seriously with him about making things better in their relationship:

> I tried to show by how I presented myself that I was really sincere about wanting to make things better between us and I acknowledged that I had contributed to our miscommunication too.
>
> Ryan responded right away, telling me that he wanted to change things too. So it's been more than six months now and we haven't gotten into power struggles. So I think we're through it—I hope so anyway. We're both trying to talk things through without getting so irritated.

According to Miriam, she was successful in ending her power struggle with Ryan by taking the initiative and stepping out of the traditional parent role, putting herself on a more equal footing with her son and telling him she believed she had played a part in their miscommunication. This has led to

---

[33] J. G. Smetana, "Goals, Goal Pursuit, and Adolescent-Parent Relationships," in *Self Regulation in Adolescence*, ed. P. Gollwitzer and G. Oettingen (New York: Cambridge University Press, 2015), 243–265.

their ability to "talk things through," she said, and, at least for the time being, reduced the conflicts between them.

As teens grow and change, mothers continue to wield influence and control. They can provide or threaten to withhold things their teens want, such as money, permission to attend social gatherings, and transportation to events. They create rules and threaten to impose punishments. They can also use guilt to pressure their teens. As one mother said, "When Jerome refuses to do his chores, I really land on him. I say, 'I'm taking care of this family—your dad's out of work, Grandmom's sick, and you aren't helping at all. All you think about is yourself.'"

At the same time, mothers reported that their ability to control their teens' actions is decreasing over time. Ella, a working-class African American mother, has a 16-year-old daughter, Kiara, and two sons (ages 15 and 10). Ella said that now, she and her daughter have more "power struggles." Kiara demands a justification for doing the things that Ella asks her to do, and according to Ella, she feels more entitled to say "no":

> You tell teens to do something and they start saying, "Why?" If I say, "Please watch the little one," or "Please go to the corner store and get some bread," my daughter says "Why?" My younger son, when I ask him to go to the store, he will. My daughter will always say "Why?"

Ella said, "Sometimes she just won't go. If I'm busy and tired, I just give up and do it myself later. When that happens, it feels like I lose." Ella isn't happy about "losing" or having her daughter refuse to do something Ella wants her to do. "It makes me mad," she said.

Margery, a white upper-middle-class mother of a 15-year-old daughter, said she feels she has less power. "You do still have power at this stage in your relationship with your teen," she noted. "And of course you have the power of the purse, and general power. But they are getting more power as they get older, and so our power is waning. You know when they're younger it's, 'You do it because I said so,' although I know that may not be the best. They are little people. But they get taller and more like adult-like, and then your power is waning."

As adolescence progresses, teens gain the ability to do more of the things they want to do. If they choose, they can ignore mothers' advice, tell half-truths, conceal things, and refuse to do things when they are asked. While parents can enjoy many things about their teens as they watch them grow and learn new things and become more sophisticated in their thinking, teens can become unpleasant and they can "leave" emotionally, which can be painful for parents. Teens can also literally leave, disappearing and going to friends' houses and other places, not telling parents where they are.

The new powers teens gain as adolescence progresses often force mothers to make changes such as compromising on rules, allowing teens to go out more on their own, and becoming less restrictive. Mothers also find that it can be harder to punish their teenage children. Several of the mothers I interviewed who were finding their teens particularly difficult to manage talked about "running out of punishments." Willa, a middle-class African American mother of a 15-year-old son, for example, stated that it's more difficult to punish teenagers:

> It can be hard to punish teens. There have been times when my son was asserting his power a lot—doing exactly what I didn't want him to do. So I would give him a punishment—no TV, or being grounded.

However, Willa said, "If you ground them, you have to stay around. If he's grounded, I don't want him to watch TV. But if I go over to my sister's across the street, he would watch TV. So I got a lock for the door of the room with the TV. I'm not crazy about grounding, but there's not much else for a punishment except taking away cell phones. I took away my son's cell phone once for a few days, that seemed to make a big impression."

Finally, it is important to note that in certain types of families, authority relations between parents and teens take different forms. Parents can suffer from physical and mental illnesses, which may prevent them from parenting and exercising as much authority as they would like. Teens may take on additional responsibilities to help the family cope. In some families with fewer resources, there are teens who have part-time jobs and who routinely provide essential financial help or help caring for dependent family members.[34]

---

[34] For teens providing resources and help to their families, see J. Roksa, "Intergenerational Exchange of Support in Low-Income Families: Understanding Resource Dilution and Increased Contribution," *Journal of Marriage and Family* 81 (2019): 601–615.

Coming Together

While parents and teens experience divergence in their relationships, as noted earlier, they also enjoy family events together. Parents organize outings with their teens to activities that they like. They encourage their teens to invite friends over. They attend events where their teens participate—sporting events, plays, art exhibits, and academic competitions.

And while parents can feel upset with their teens and worry about them, they can also feel proud of them. As one mother said, "I feel good because I like my children, I try to enjoy their being teens, their growing up, their coming to maturity. People at my job have met my [16-year-old] son and they tell me, 'Your son is wonderful, we like talking to him, he's maturing so nicely.' That makes me feel good." Parents are proud when their teens experience success, such as when they win a sports competition, secure a major part in a school play, or get a good grade on a school project they worked hard on. Parents admire their teens when they overcome difficulties as well—a rough patch in a relationship with a friend or a bad grade in school. Parents feel happy when teens show kindness toward a family member—a grandparent, a sibling, a friend. When the son of one of the mothers I interviewed left for college in another part of the state, she said, "I miss him, and I miss his friends. I loved it when his friends came over—they were so lively. It was more fun when they were here."

Conclusion

As teens change physically, emotionally, and socially throughout adolescence, the process brings significant changes to their relationships with their parents. During this time, mothers experience their teens as "pulling away." A distance can grow between mothers and teens, who begin to develop their own views, share less of what is happening in their lives, and become more assertive with their demands. Mothers and teens continue to have positive times. Mothers appreciate their children's new talents, and they still do fun things together. However, mothers also experience new challenges. It can become more challenging to communicate with their teen, to get information from them and check up on what they are doing and where they are. Mothers must negotiate new agreements about going out, spending time on social media, and completing schoolwork on time. Sometimes their interactions with their teens go smoothly, but the possibility of conflict increases, particularly in the early stages of adolescence as teens are developing their own view of what decisions about their lives they should be allowed to make. In these moments, mothers can experience "power struggles" with their teen children.

These major changes in the relationships between mothers and teens shape both the challenges mothers face and the strategies available to them in carrying out the work I describe in the following chapters: how to promote their teens' autonomy while also working to keep them safe; how to ensure that their children complete their secondary education; and how to see that they successfully move into young adulthood and gain the preparation they need for adult life. On an ongoing basis, mothers and fathers face questions of how restrictive or permissive to be, of when to be a "friend" to your child and when to "let go." As mothers engage in the process of letting go, they find that being too strict can "backfire," and that meting out punishment is often less effective than it was when their children were younger. They still have leverage in their negotiations with teens—they have money that their teenage children need, they provide transportation, and they can punish their teens by grounding them or taking away their cell phones—but slowly, the balance of power begins to shift.

3

Keeping Teens Safe at a Time of Risk

Keeping children safe is one of the most critical tasks of parenting. Above all else, parents are expected, and expect themselves, to see that their children, teens, and young adults remain safe. It is a task that becomes particularly challenging during adolescence when teens go out with friends to new places, make more of their own decisions, and spend more time on social media. It is essential for teens to gain greater freedoms as they progress through adolescence. As they participate in new activities, they make new friends, learn new skills, and grow into new identities.

Parents, of course, understand this, but at the same time, they worry about their teens' safety. As one mother said, "These are scary times. There is so much freedom. It seems like there's a lot more drinking and drugs now. A girl can get a wrong boyfriend." Mothers' worries can become exaggerated in the current atmosphere of what has been called a "culture of fear," an atmosphere in which politicians and the media gain attention by making dire warnings about the risks children and youth face.[1]

Mothers' fears have some basis in fact. Although the majority of teens remain safe, many adolescents of all races and class backgrounds engage in behaviors that parents worry could harm them, including the use of alcohol and drugs.[2] Some teenagers get into more minor trouble; they are caught drinking in parks or at social gatherings, or they receive citations for

---

[1] B. Glassner, *The Culture of Fear: Why Americans Are Afraid of the Wrong Things* (New York: Basic Books, 2018). Advice provided to parents about teens' internet use likewise focuses on the need to protect children and teens from harmful information, rather than the benefits informaton on the internet can provide. L. E. Harris and J. A. Jacobs, "Emerging Ideas. Digital Parenting Advice: Online Guidance Regarding Children's Use of the Internet and Social Media," *Family Relations* 72 (5) (2023): 2551–2568.

[2] In 2021, 23 percent of high school students drank alcohol, 16 percent used marijuana, 18 percent used an electronic vapor product, and 13 percent used certain illicit drugs (cocaine, heroin, methamphetamines, hallucinogens, or ecstasy). Centers for Disease Control and Prevention, "Youth Risk Behavior Survey 2011–2021: Data Summary and Trends Report" (Atlanta: Centers for Disease Control and Prevention, 2023). In 2022, 52 percent of high school seniors used alcohol in the last 12 months, 31 percent used marijuana, and 27 percent vaped nicotine. R. A. Miech et al., "Monitoring the Future National Survey Results on Drug Use, 1975–2022: Secondary School Students" (Ann Arbor: Institute for Social Research, University of Michigan, 2023).

Letting Go. Demie Kurz, Oxford University Press. © Oxford University Press 2024.
DOI: 10.1093/9780190222482.003.0003

breaking city or town curfews. A smaller number experience serious harm due to car accidents, homicide, suicide, or sexual assault.[3] Teens who live in underresourced neighborhoods face the most immediate danger and the greatest risk from violence, drugs, and gangs. African American mothers fear that their children will become victims of gun violence as well as racial profiling and harassment by the police.[4] Parents also worry about the rising rates of teen mental health problems. In 2021, 42 percent of high school students experienced persistent feelings of sadness or hopelessness.[5] In my sample, a small number of mothers reported that their teens have gotten into serious trouble, including two teens who had been arrested for drug use, one teen who had been assaulted in a failed robbery attempt, one young woman who experienced a serious eating disorder, and two teens who had tragically died from drug overdoses.[6]

[3] Car accidents: car crashes are the second-leading cause of death for teens in the United States. In 2020, roughly 2,800 teens in the United States ages 13–19, or almost eight teens every day, were killed in motor vehicle crashes and about 227,000 were injured in motor vehicle crashes. Centers for Disease Control and Prevention, "Teen Drivers and Passengers: Get the Facts" (Atlanta: Centers for Disease Control and Prevention, Nov. 21, 2022). Suicide: in 2021, 22 percent of high school students seriously considered attempting suicide during the past year, with female students more likely than male students to consider attempting suicide. Centers for Disease Control and Prevention, "Youth Risk Behavior Survey 2011–2021." Sexual assault/violence: in 2021, 8 percent of high school students had ever been physically forced to have sexual intercourse when they did not want to (14 percent of female students, 4 percent of male students). Centers for Disease Control and Prevention, "Youth Risk Behavior Survey 2011–2021." Deaths by homicide: homicide is the third leading cause of death for young people ages 10–24 and the leading cause of death for non-Hispanic Black or African American youth. Each day, Emergency Departments treat over 800 young people for physical assault–related injuries. Centers for Disease Control and Prevention, "Preventing Youth Violence" (October 25, 2023). In 2020, more than five thousand youths under 17 suffered gunshot wounds. A quarter (1,250) died, the highest number of deaths ever recorded up to that point. Gun Violence Archive (Washington, DC: Gun Violence Archive, 2021).

[4] F. Baumgartner, D. Epp, and K. Shoub *Suspect Citizens: What 20 Million Traffic Stops Tell Us about Policing and Race* (New York: Cambridge University Press, 2018); N. A. Cazenave, *Killing Black Americans: Police and Vigilante Violence as a Racial Control Mechanism* (New York: Routledge, 2018). African American children and teens are disproportionately affected by gun violence. In 2019, Black children and teens made up 14 percent of the child and teen population but 43 percent of all child and teen gun deaths. Children's Defense Fund, "The State of America's Children 2021: Gun Violence" (Washington, DC: Children's Defense Fund, 2022).

[5] Centers for Disease Control and Prevention, "Youth Risk Behavior Survey 2011–2021."

[6] Reports of more serious trouble from my sample: upper-middle-class mothers (all white): arrest for leaving the scene of a car accident the teen was involved in; arrest for drugs found in the search of a car; suspension from school for being caught using marijuana; expulsion from school for repeated alcohol violations; arrest and probation for drawing graffiti on public property; hospitalization due to anorexia. Middle-class mothers (one African American, the remainder white): a girl suffering from depression; a girl given a short suspension from school for drinking at a party where the police were called and her school was informed; a boy arrested for shoplifting; a girl who abused drugs for close to two years; a boy arrested in a park for the possession and selling of drugs. Working-class mothers (two white, the remainder African American): a girl who was held up at knifepoint on the street and robbed (she was not injured); a girl arrested for shoplifting; a boy convicted of robbery and sent to prison; a boy and girl in the same family who died of drug overdoses; a boy sent to prison for drug dealing; and the nephew of an African American mother who died from a gunshot wound.

Determining what is safe, and letting go and giving teens permission to do more things on their own, presents numerous challenges for parents. The mothers in my sample feel an ongoing need to monitor their teens' actions to ensure their safety. At the same time, they support their teens' needs for autonomy—their ability to be with friends and go out more without adult supervision. Ruthana is a white working-class mother who has three children (ages 6, 11, and 13). Her 13-year-old son, Tom, entered junior high school last fall. Ruthana lives on a residential city street with small two- and three-story brick row houses and says her immediate neighborhood is "stable." She knows her neighbors, many of whom have children, and they feel the street is safe. But Ruthana worries. She said, "When teens get older and go out you can really worry, we're never that much in control of all the things that could happen to them. Outside forces are there." Ruthana said it was easier to supervise her children when they were young, but she said, "That's a lot harder now, teens have to go out, they have to go places on their own, I know that, but you worry a lot, you never know what these kids are thinking." As she spoke about her worry and about what she felt was her decreasing ability to ensure her teens' safety, it was not clear what "outside forces" Ruthana was referring to, but she said she worries more since there have been reports of drug dealers coming into nearby neighborhoods.

As mothers balance their desire to create rules and restrictions to keep their teens safe with their need to give them more freedoms, they described a key challenge—how to engage in letting go while not "policing" their teens all the time. Caroline, a white upper-middle-class mother of two daughters (ages 11 and 15), lives in an affluent area of the city that is considered safe. She says she has a privileged life, her children go to private school, and she and her husband, a business executive, do not have financial worries. However, reflecting mothers' fears about the risks teens face in contemporary life, she noted, "It doesn't get easier when they become teens, it gets more difficult

N.B.: These figures cannot be considered representative of all teens and young adults in the sample. It cannot be determined from the mothers' accounts whether they reported all instances of trouble their teens and young adults had encountered. One mother reported that her daughter had to be hospitalized for anorexia, a potentially life-threatening mental health disorder that primarily affects girls. Nine percent of the US population will have an eating disorder in their lifetime. Two to three times as many females as males contract this disorder. This very serious mental illness puts people at higher risk of suicide. Twenty-five percent of people with an eating disorder attempt suicide. Deloitte Access Economics, *The Social and Economic Cost of Eating Disorders in the United States of America: A Report for the Strategic Training Initiative for the Prevention of Eating Disorders and the Academy for Eating Disorders*, Harvard T. H. Tan School of Public Health, Harvard University, June 2020, https://www.hsph.harvard.edu/striped/report-economic-costs-of-eating-disorders/.

because your kids are away from you more and you don't necessarily know where they are, but you don't want to be policing them all the time." Caroline said she uses the cell phone to "stay connected": "When my kids are away from home, I use the cell phone and text with them a lot, they have to tell me where they are. They are pretty good at answering my calls." However, as she spoke about the benefits of cell phones, Caroline said she faces questions about how often to use the cell phone to monitor her teens:

> I don't know how much to call them—am I calling or texting too much, too little? They have to learn to manage in the world and keep themselves safe, and sometimes I have to let go.

Given the dangers mothers believe their teens could face, how do they manage the process of letting go while keeping their children safe—removing restrictions on their ability to go out, to be with friends, to spend time on social media—without "policing them all the time"? As they face this challenge, the mothers I interviewed said they work to develop trust in their teens. When they trust that their adolescent children will abide by rules they have created and act safely, they feel they can allow them to make more of their own decisions, do new things, and go new places. However, as mothers described it, developing trust is not a straightforward process, it is ongoing, and can be challenging.

I begin this chapter with mothers' accounts of the key challenges they face in their work to promote their teens' safety, including how to trust their teens to use good judgment and stay out of trouble. Mothers face new issues of control when it comes to monitoring their teens and knowing their whereabouts and whether they are accessing social media safely. While parents are urged to educate their teens about safety and know their whereabouts, teens often hold different views about safety. In the second part of the chapter, I present mothers' accounts of the process of letting go, of ceding more control to their teens while their teens increasingly take control of their own social lives. As I describe, mothers also work to obtain more resources to promote teens' safety, including constructive activities in safe neighborhoods. Providing safe environments for their teens is a high priority for all mothers. However, while their accounts show many similarities in their approaches to keeping their teens safe, based on their social class and race, mothers face different challenges in mobilizing resources that can increase their teens' safety.

Challenges in Maintaining Control and
Keeping Teens Safe

Mothers describe a variety of challenges as they work to monitor their teens to ensure their safety while at the same time engage in letting go, or as mothers often say, "giving kids their freedoms."

Maintaining Control and Developing Trust

As the mothers I interviewed work to develop trust in their teens, to assure themselves that their children are developing good judgment and will make the right decisions about safety, they face uncertainty. Joellen, a white middle-class mother with four children—two college students (ages 19 and 20) and two teenagers (ages 14 and 16)—stated that she has trust in her children and that her teens "have always been able to do a lot of things." She said, "I'm not Attila the Hun, although I guess you would have to ask my kids. But I don't need to control them that much because I trust them," although she added, "With the condition that they have to tell me what they're doing, where they are, and who they're with. I always have to know." So far, Joellen said:

> I trust them because they have never broken our trust. I don't know what we would do if we lost that trust with any of the kids, like if we found them smoking marijuana in their room or something.

Of course, Joellen can't be sure what her teen children are doing at all times. As noted in the previous chapter, teens sometimes lie or fail to disclose things when they believe their parents would not understand them or would disapprove of their behavior, or when they believe certain decisions—such as who their friends are, what hours they keep, and what events they attend—are theirs to make.

Jan, a white upper-middle-class mother of two teens (ages 16 and 17), reported that she is not sure she can trust her teens. She noted:

> I trust my kids but, ah, I don't trust them. I'm sure they are doing things I don't know about—drinking, and not drugs I hope. I trust them, but you never know. And then there are their friends, you don't know what they will do.

Like many mothers, Jan draws on her own past in thinking about safety. "I think of myself and what I did, you know, drinking and smoking pot," she said. She concluded with a statement attempting to reassure herself but one that also reflects the limitations of her ability to know what her teens are doing: "I guess what I don't know won't hurt me."

Paulette, a middle-class African American mother, has twin 13-year-old daughters and a 16-year-old son. She similarly reflected on her difficulties in knowing what her teens are doing when they are away from adult supervision. She said, "I don't think they're doing anything like drinking or drugs, but how do you really know? They don't tell me everything." In a telling phrase, Paulette said, "You'd like to be a fly on the wall and hear what they are talking about." She further commented, "You never know what they might be doing, if they might be hiding things or lying, and you never know when you might get a call from the police or from a hospital about something bad that happened, that would be so terrible." Then, like Jan, Paulette reflected on herself and her own behavior as a teenager: "We all know we did those things when we were young. Now," she said, "it's scarier, they are older and out more and you wonder what are they doing":

> I tell you, I never say, "My kids would never do like drugs or something." You absolutely never know. I know some really good parents whose kids have gotten into bad trouble.

Paulette concluded, "I worry, but now that my kids are teens, I know there are some things I have to let go."

In the face of these uncertainties, mothers develop a variety of strategies to keep their teens safe. As their children go off more on their own, mothers lecture their teens about safety and create rules and policies about what is permissible. They negotiate with their children about where they can go, they modify rules over time, and they let go of restrictions. However, as they are developing trust in their teens' decisions, they face ongoing challenges.

Getting Teens to Listen

Mothers continually offer advice to their teens, warning them about trouble and urging them to take safety precautions. However, like many mothers Janice, a white working-class mother, doesn't feel confident that her 14-year-old daughter, Amber, listens. She said, "Amber's a good kid, but I worry, I talk to her all the time about keeping safe." Janice believes that Amber "tunes her out" when she tries to warn her about issues of safety. She said there is no immediate danger on their block of city row houses. It is safe, and the street is narrow, so neighbors run into each other and share news and concerns. However, Janice said, "Two blocks away, the neighborhood's going down." She said there are some houses in disrepair and that recently there were several robberies there.

Janice said the fact that she doesn't think Amber listens to her "scares" her, that, "A lot of times, Amber doesn't believe that anything can happen to her in this neighborhood. She feels it's the safest neighborhood anywhere." Janice has persisted in trying to convince Amber that there are dangers to worry about in the neighborhood. She said, "I tell her 'Amber, no, it's everywhere, you heard about it, the drugs, it's in this neighborhood too. You might not hear about it, but it's here.' But Amber doesn't seem to think anything can happen here."

Aisha, a working-class African American mother of two sons (ages 16 and 11), also fears she is not being heard, that her sons are not listening to her concerns about safety. She said she particularly worries about "peer pressure." As she noted:

> The peer pressure is terrible. You can tell them all you want in the house. You can talk all the time until you're blue in the face. But when they go out on the street, the group takes over. What you said isn't there.

Aisha fears that her older son, Kamal, could get into trouble by hanging out with teens who do "risky things." As she said, she believes that in these circumstances, "the group takes over."

Despite her concern about not being heard, Aisha also talked about a recent incident when she thought that Kamal did listen to her and take her advice, although initially, she wasn't sure. Aisha had recently given Kamal a suggestion about how he could avoid trouble, but she didn't know if he had listened. She said:

> I told Kamal, "If you're worried that your friends are going to do something bad, just tell them you're sick or you don't feel good. Because if you're with a group and you're not doing anything bad but they get in trouble, you might

get in trouble too." Kamal hasn't really gotten in trouble, but some kids he knows have.

Aisha now thinks that Kamal has actually used the strategy. When he came home recently, he was holding his stomach. Aisha said, "I asked him, 'What's the matter?' He said, 'I don't feel good,' and then he went and lay down on the sofa." Aisha then said:

A little while later, down on the corner we saw a police car with the lights blinking. I was very concerned, I said, "What's going on out there?" Kamal was quiet. I asked him, "Kamal, tell me, do you know what's going on?" I don't think Kamal really wanted to tell me, but he said, "Wayne and the other guys were going to try to take some stuff from the store on the corner, I guess they did."

Aisha said, "I was really angry about what those kids were doing, but I was happy because it seemed like Kamal had done what I suggested—tell the other kids he wasn't feeling well to get away from a situation that was not good where kids were going to steal something." She concluded by saying she would never remind Kamal that she had suggested he could tell friends he felt sick if he sensed trouble. She wants to make Kamal think this was his idea, which would hopefully increase the chances he would avoid trouble on his own in the future.

Mothers develop a variety of strategies to "get through" to their teens and get them to listen. Some reported continually talking with their teens, trying to drive home messages about risks and safety. Jill, a white upper-middle-class mother with a 14-year-old daughter named Harper, said she exaggerates as she tries to get Harper to listen to her. She said, "I'm concerned about things that could happen, like drugs and alcohol. With drugs, I talk about all the problems they can cause." To increase the chances that her daughter will listen to her, and to boost her credibility and not seem hypocritical, Jill has also acknowledged to Harper that she and Harper's father, her husband Ed, used marijuana in the past. Jill said, "Ed and I sat down with Harper and we told her, yes, we smoked marijuana. But our pitch was, 'Now it's different, it's more dangerous.'" She said that Harper has a friend who had a terrible reaction to drugs, and Jill thinks "that scared her a little."

Respecting Teens' Privacy

Another challenge mothers face in keeping teens safe is how to get information from them while also respecting their privacy and trusting that they are making good decisions about their safety. To develop more autonomy, teens need to cultivate a more private self. The account of Sue Ellen, a white middle-class mother of a 16-year-old daughter named Joy and a 13-year-old son, provides insight into some mothers' conflicting feelings about getting information while not seeming too intrusive. She noted, "You have to give kids privacy, including privacy they can have with their friends." She recently faced the question of how much privacy to give her daughter and whether she could trust her when she was at a sleepover at a friend's house. She said:

> I have a few conflicts with Joy. She is sometimes late for her curfews, and I always worry, where is she? Like, she was at a sleepover last night, but I had a little thought, is that really where she is? Did she and her friends sneak off somewhere? Can I really trust her the way I used to? I thought of calling or texting, making up some stupid question, but I didn't. Anyway, she would see right through it.

In deciding whether she could trust Joy, Sue Ellen decided not to check up on her, not to "make up some stupid question" as a pretext for being in touch with her because, as she said, "We don't have any real problems. I know her friends, I know their mothers, we compare notes. I want to respect her private time with her friends." Sue Ellen concluded by saying that based on the fact that Joy has mostly stayed out of trouble, she can trust her:

> It would be different if Joy and her friends had gotten in trouble, that happened only once. I got a call one time—she and her friends were at the police station. They'd been hanging out in a town park one Saturday evening—it's a safe place, but they didn't leave by 8:00 in the evening when the park closed. The police came, and they ran away, so they got picked up.

Sue Ellen said, "I think it was good they had to go to the police station once. If that's the worst thing that happens, I don't worry too much—no problem, nothing happened, no legal trouble." She explained, "I don't worry to death but that's because so far, they haven't gotten in any real trouble. I still keep a step ahead of Joy. She knows she has to answer her cell phone." However, even as Sue Ellen said that she still "keeps a step ahead" of her teens, she acknowledged that, at this point, there are things about her daughter's life she can't control. As she put it, "I can't just follow my daughter around all the time. I know that and she knows it."

When considering privacy, some mothers talked about situations in which they would look at their teens' personal things that they would otherwise consider private. One mother noted, "If I go into their room to bring some laundry or something, I wouldn't open their drawers or their school bags." However, she said, "It would be different if I suspected something serious— you know, drugs or something." Laverne, an African American working-class mother who said she has a close relationship with her 15-year-old daughter, stated that she trusts her daughter and only reads the texts on her phone every once in a while to get more of an idea of what her daughter is thinking. She had insisted that her daughter share her cell phone password when she bought the phone for her daughter, "But," she said, "I don't want my daughter to know that I do this because she would be hurt if she felt that I didn't trust her."

There are some mothers who believe they need to do whatever it takes to get information about what their teens are doing, which sometimes means they disregard issues of privacy. How a mother views this issue can be based on her social class as well as how much she trusts her teen. Some working-class mothers place less emphasis on their children's privacy in light of the fact that they believe their teens face more immediate danger.[7] Sondra, a working-class African American single mother of a 13-year-old girl and a 15-year-old boy, gave an account that fits this pattern. Sondra lives in a stable working-class African American neighborhood. She stated that when her children complain that they don't have any privacy, she agrees. She said she tells them, "There is no privacy for you in this house, I have to know what you are doing. I'll go in your room anytime, I'll read anything."

Sondra said, "There's all kinds of things going on out there that they could get into. I have to know, I'm a single mom, it's just me." She said the kind of

---

[7] Nelson argues that professional middle-class parents are more willing to trust their teens because they believe that their teens internalize parental values as children. These parents believe they can rely on their active presence and hovering in children's lives to exert more subtle control. Working- and middle-class parents, however, who tend to be more ambivalent about trusting their teens, want to set clear limits and engage in direct control. It is also the case that because working-class teens often face more immediate environments that are less safe, parents may be more hesitant to rely on trust in their work to keep their children safe. M. K. Nelson, *Parenting Out of Control: Anxious Parents in Uncertain Times* (New York: New York University Press, 2010).

close monitoring she does has contributed to her teens being "Good kids. They haven't gotten into trouble and they are doing well in school." Her son is in an accelerated academic program. Sondra concluded, "I always keep on them, I do, there's too much going on out there."

Alexis is a white upper-middle-class mother of a 16-year-old son, Aaron. She spoke about the fact that situations are always changing—an activity that appears to be safe and trustworthy at one time may not be at another time—and that assessing teens' trustworthiness is never a finished process. Some mothers said they regularly find themselves having to reassess whether their teens are trustworthy. Alexis spoke about how she has been monitoring Aaron's whereabouts for safety and has developed trust in his decisions. She and her husband have also been pleased that Aaron's best friend, Brandon, seems to be a trustworthy person. However, Alexis also noted, "Yesterday, one of our friends told me that Brandon is getting a reputation as a heavy drinker, that people sometimes see Brandon drinking heavily with friends. Our friend said she wouldn't trust Brandon to have good judgment." Alexis said she and her husband were going to bring this up with Aaron: "We've told him we want to have a serious talk. He knows we don't want him drinking a lot." She said they were particularly concerned about alcohol use because there is a history of alcoholism in their extended family, and she noted, "We wonder if we need to check up on Aaron more and not just assume he is staying out of trouble."

In dealing with the challenges involved in keeping their teenage children safe—getting them to listen, giving them more privacy, and assessing their trustworthiness—some mothers talked about how they have developed unobtrusive ways to monitor their teens' activities. They may try to obtain information by eavesdropping or listening in on their teens' conversations as they talk on the phone or visit with friends at home. Mothers who drive a group of teenagers to an activity may use the opportunity to listen to their conversations in the car, hoping to learn more about their teens' ideas and activities than they would from a one-on-one conversation. Some mothers try to get other people to talk to their teens, often family members, to learn more about whether their teens are keeping safe. Still others watch for signs of behavior they might not approve of.

Maryanne, a white working-class mother of three children (ages 17, 15, and 13), lives in a stable working-class neighborhood. She laughed as she talked about how, after her teenage children come back from being out at social events with friends, she tries to smell for alcohol on their breath without their knowing. She said:

I'm like a sergeant. When they come back after being out with friends I tease them, and I say, "Oh, you've been hitting the bottle" or something like that, and they say, "Oh no, mom." I'm not sure if they know that I'm also checking to see if I smell anything, if there is some sign they could have been drinking.

Maryanne also encourages her teens to "hang out" at their house with friends. "It's better they be with their friends at home than off somewhere else," she noted. "They can have their space in the family room or out in the backyard at the pool. Of course, I can hear a lot of what they are saying through the kitchen window if they are in the backyard." One mother said that when her children became teens, they remodeled the basement to be a place where their teens could "hang out with friends. We tell them it's their space, but we can also use it to check up on who our son is spending time with."

Cell phones have proven to be an extremely useful tool for parents to communicate with their teens and check on their whereabouts. The vast majority of teenagers in the United States have access to a cell phone.[8] For mothers, cell phones provide assurance that they can at least potentially always reach their teens and that their teen can call or text them if they need help. As one mother said, "I sometimes make up reasons to text my kids. I say there is something I need to tell them, but mostly I'm checking up on them. I usually get an answer, or a string of emojis, almost like they know what I'm doing, like 'Mom, I'm ok, don't worry.'"

At the same time, cell phones have limitations as tools for monitoring. Because they are not connected to a particular place, parents must rely on their teens to answer their phones or respond to their texts and tell them where they are. Teens don't always answer, however. There are apps for tracking other people's whereabouts based on their cell phone numbers. One mother said she had used such an app when her daughter started going out on her own with her friends in high school. She deleted the app when her

---

[8] Ninety-eight percent of teens ages 15 to 17 and 91 percent of teens ages 13 to 14 have access to a smartphone. Pew Research Center, "Teens, Social Media and Technology 2022," August 2022, https://www.pewresearch.org/wp-content/uploads/sites/20/2022/08/PI_2022.08.10_Teens-and-Tech_FINAL.pdf.

daughter went to college. A white upper-middle-class mother groaned and said her 16-year-old son checks his texts and phone messages from time to time, but when she calls, she thinks, "He looks at the phone and sees it's me and doesn't answer." Anita, a middle-class African American mother of a 14-year-old boy, said that even if her son is reliable in calling her, she can't be sure he is telling the truth when he says he is at friends' houses in the evening:

> I want to know where Antoine is. And how I deal with it is the cell phone. He has to call me or text me and let me know wherever he is, like if he is one place and then goes somewhere else. And if I can't answer, he has to leave messages and I listen to the messages.

However, as she said, "Of course he could be lying about where he is, but I can't follow him everywhere." Digital controls for cell phones and computers that enable parents to monitor children and teens' communications and locations are widely available; however, teens who are savvy about navigating technical aspects of the internet and social media can often figure out how to get around these controls by deleting an app, resetting their phones to the initial factory settings, or accessing a non-network hotspot.[9]

While cell phones can be a valuable tool for staying in touch with teens, and while the majority of teens report that social media can provide meaningful connections for them with friends, wider social networks, and support groups, the majority of parents are worried that their teens are spending too much time in front of "screens"—on social media, instant messaging, gaming, downloading music—and that there is too much inappropriate content on social media. Teens report spending many hours a day on phones and screens, including social media.[10] Mothers also worry about online

---

[9] To bypass internet filters, for example, teens can also use a family password to create their own, download a VPN, and use extensions to bypass filters their parents may have set up on their computers. T. Jones, "10 Easy Ways Kids Can Bypass Internet Filters | Parent Should Know," FamliSafe, 2022, https://famisafe.wondershare.com/internet-filter/get-around-internet-filters.html.

[10] In 2023 a third of teens reported that they used YouTube, TikTok, Snapchat, or Instagram constantly. YouTube is the most widely used platform, with 70 percent of teens saying they look at YouTube daily, and 16 percent of them reporting that they are on YouTube almost constantly. Fifty-eight percent of teens use TikTok daily, and 17 percent of teens describe using TikTok almost constantly. About half of teens use Snapchat and Instagram daily. Overall, a third of teens use at least one of these five sites almost constantly. Pew Research Center, "Teens, Social Media, and Technology." Boys use more screen media than girls (76 minutes a day more, on average, among tweens, and 74 more minutes among teens). Black and Hispanic/Latino children use more screen media than white children (a difference of about two hours a day between Black and white tweens, and two and a half hours a day between Hispanic/Latino and white tweens). Tweens (children 9–12) and teens in lower-income households use more screen media than those in higher-income households. V. Rideout

bullying, including name-calling, spreading false rumors, and physical threats, dynamics that are experienced by half of teens.[11] Some researchers find a link between teens' use of social media and higher rates of anxiety and depression, particularly among teens who spend more time on social media. The US Surgeon General has warned that teens who spend more than three hours a day on social media, which the majority of teens do, face mental health risks, including depression and anxiety.[12]

Many parents restrict how much time their teens can spend online or on their cell phones.[13] Mothers I interviewed said they develop rules for their teens' use of cell phones. They reported making rules about when it's appropriate for their teens to use their cell phones for talking and texting and when the devices must be turned off. Mothers who are paying for teens' phone plans can decide whether to get a prepaid plan that limits the number of calls and texts a teen can make. Mothers can also exert pressure on their teens to comply with their rules by telling them they will check their phone to see who they have been in contact with. Almost half of parents say they will look through teens' cell phones. If teens violate rules about cell phone use, mothers may restrict their phone usage or take the device away completely.[14]

The mothers in my sample vary in how strictly they monitor their teens' cell phone use. For example, Charmaine, a single working-class African American mother of two boys (ages 12 and 14), describes a stricter approach to cell phone use. She said she checks her teens' cell phone bills to see whom they have been calling:

et al., "The Common Sense Census: Media Use by Tweens and Teens, 2021" (San Francisco, CA, Common Sense Media, 2022).

[11] E. A. Vogels, "Teens and Cyberbullying 2022" (Washington, DC: Pew Research Center, 2022).
[12] Office of the Surgeon General, "Social Media and Youth Mental Health: The U.S. Surgeon General's Advisor" (Washington, DC: Office of the Surgeon General, 2023). Jonathan Haidt argues that as a result of the widespread use of cell phones, the "play-based childhood" of earlier decades has been replaced by a "phone-based childhood" or a "rewiring of childhood," which has led to the rise of attention problems, loneliness, and mental health problems among children and teens. J. Haidt, *The Anxious Generation: How the Great Rewiring of Childhood is Causing an Epidemic of Mental Illness.* (New York: Penguin Press, 2024).
[13] Sixty-two percent of parents of 13- to 14-year-olds say they limit how much time their teen can be on their phone, and 37 percent of parents with a 15- to 17-year-old limit their time. M. Anderson, M. Favario, and E. Park, "How Teens and Parents Approach Screen Time," Pew Research Center, March 24, 2024, https://www.pewresearch.org/internet/2024/03/11/how-teens-and-parents-approach-screen-time/.
[14] Sixty-four percent of parents of 13- to 14-year-olds say they look through their teen's smartphone, and 41 percent of parents of 15- to 17-year-olds. Anderson et al., "How Teens and Parents Approach Screen Time."

For their cell phones, I check the cell phone bill every month. If I don't recognize a number, I ask them "Who is this?" I tell them, "Your cell phone is for safety and getting in touch with me." Of course they think it's for talking to their friends.

Charmaine said, "If they are abusing how they use their cell phone, I ground them and say, 'Give me the cell phone.' And I can take away the TV and their video games too." Recently, after checking the messages of one of her son's cell phones to see how often and when he had been using his phone, Charmaine did take it from him. As she said:

The other day, I told my 14-year-old son to hand over his cell phone, and I checked his messages. I realized he had made a call on his phone at 12:30 at night. I said "No, that's no good. Hand over your phone, I'm keeping it for now. You have to know there are consequences. If you disobey, there will definitely be consequences."

In this case, Charmaine kept her son's phone for four days. She said, "That's the way life is. You can go down this path or go down that one, you have to know there are consequences."

As teens move through adolescence, parents' policies on cell phone use can change. One white middle-class mother I interviewed said she and her husband have given up monitoring their daughter's cell phone use. She is 17 and is entering her senior year in high school. This mother suspects that her daughter is using her cell phone late at night, something she and her husband have told her not to do. But she said, "We have three kids and we both work. Our schedules are packed, and we go to bed tired, earlier than our daughter. So this is something we're just letting go now." A white upper-middle-class mother says she and her husband have also pulled back in their attempts to monitor their teens' cell phone use. They created a rule that their teens (ages 13 and 15) must leave their cell phones downstairs when they go upstairs to bed. However, she said, "We know the kids can find ways around that."

Because it's difficult to monitor all aspects of cell phone and computer use, social media affects the power balance between parents and teens. An upper-middle-class African American mother said she was angry about the content of material on the internet that her teens were able to access:

I am so mad at those media people. The kids can get anything on their phones and see anything—awful things. The media people are taking control away from us. And they keep saying, "First Amendment, First Amendment." I don't think so, I don't think it's such a First Amendment issue.

Echoing her, a white middle-class mother said, "Parents just don't have much power. We've lost the war on what our teens are exposed to in the media. We don't have big advertising budgets and PR [public relations] people." Her comments reflect some of the challenges parents face in monitoring their teens' use of digital technologies and the information teens can access. These challenges are amplified by the fact that new digital technologies are continually appearing and changing.[15]

Letting Go: Maintaining Control and Granting New Freedoms

For parents, the process of letting go while monitoring their teens' safety changes as adolescence progresses. Mothers described different trajectories in this process. In some cases and for some issues, mothers maintain control over how this process unfolds. In other cases, mothers have less control.

Developing Trust

When mothers trust teens, letting go and allowing them to do more things on their own can be a straightforward proposition. Nicole, a white middle-class mother of a 16-year-old daughter, Elizabeth, said she trusts her daughter. Nicole said Elizabeth is a pleasure to be around, she's "a happy kid," and she has nice friends. As she put it, "We like her friends, we like to have them over." She continued:

---

[15] Harris argues that the world of children and teens has shifted increasingly to the digital realm, creating more complex and daunting challenges for parents. She claims that to oversee their children's and teens' activities in the digital world requires that parents develop "a meaningful degree of digital literacy" and knowledge of digital technologies. A. J. Harris, "Understanding the World of Digital Youth," in *Adolescent Sexual Behavior in the Digital Age*, ed. F. Saleh et al. (New York: Oxford University Press, 2016), 24–42.

My daughter is the kind of teen where you have confidence that she will make good decisions and do things right. And she has what every parent wants, good values and intelligence. So I don't worry about her doing new things, she's ready, I trust her to do the right things.

Nicole uses the evidence of her daughter's good behavior to arrive at the decision that her daughter is "ready" to do new things. She is allowing her to go to coed social gatherings at friends' houses because, as she says, she trusts that her daughter will "do the right things." Similarly, an upper-middle-class African American mother named Miriam gave her 15-year-old son, Malcolm, permission to go on a three-day camping trip with friends. An adult drove the group to the camping venue and stayed at another campsite nearby to give the teens privacy. Miriam said, "I don't know if some of the kids smuggled in some alcohol or smoked marijuana—they're not supposed to. But so far, Malcolm's been good—we've been able to trust him."

Madeleine, a white upper-middle-class mother, has two daughters, a 16-year-old named Olivia and a 14-year-old. Madeleine went to greater lengths than most mothers I interviewed to develop trust in her daughter's judgment. She felt she needed to investigate whether her daughter was correct when she said she was engaged in a safe, appropriate activity. Over the summer, Olivia, who is in the drama club at her high school, was invited to play a small part in several performances of a community theater group. Madeleine agreed that Olivia could participate, but she did not want her daughter to go to cast parties after performances. Madeleine didn't like the fact that there were people in their twenties and older drinking alcohol at the parties. According to Madeleine, "I said to Olivia, 'Look this isn't right, you can't go.' She said, 'Yes it is, you don't understand, it's fine.'" Madeleine felt she had no way to judge for herself if the parties were appropriate for someone Olivia's age, and she continued to forbid her to attend.

However, Madeleine said, "Olivia kept at me to let her go, she said she had the right to go. So I said to her, 'Okay, if you want to go to a party with this group, I need to go to one first.'" According to Madeleine, Olivia was upset about this. She said, "You can't do that, you're intruding on me these are my friends, I can't have my mother coming to the party." Madeleine said that Olivia told her, "You don't trust me," to which Madeleine replied, "Well, I'm coming.'" Madeleine said:

So I went to one of the plays. It was a terrible production, I had to put up with that. Then I went to the cast party. I could see it was a good group, the younger people and the older people had a lot in common, they really shared this interest in the theater.

As for underage drinking at these parties, Madeleine noted, "There was no question the younger people would not drink the wine and beer and whatever else was there. It was like at our house, when we have people over and the older people drink alcohol and it's just understood that the younger people don't." Madeleine stated that Olivia resents the fact that she insisted on coming to the party:

> I said to Olivia, "This is great." Olivia said, "Why didn't you trust me?" I said "Look, I could have done two different things that would have been a lot easier than going to a play I don't understand and a party where I don't know anyone."

Madeleine said she could have made two other choices: "I could have just said 'No,' or, 'Sure, just go'—that would have been easier. But this is the way I felt I had to do it." Madeleine attended a play she said was "terrible," but she learned what she needed to know. She was pleased with her effort because she got to see the situation for herself and confirm Olivia's belief that everything was safe.

For other mothers, trust is developed as their teens become older and they have had more time to observe their behavior. Danielle, an African American middle-class mother with two daughters (ages 16 and 13), said she recently trusted her older daughter to go to the beach with two friends—both of them boys and one of whom had had his driver's license for only a year. She said:

> My daughter told me on Friday that two boys had asked her to go to the beach for a day, and she asked me if she could go. They are friends, boys she knows well, and their mothers are friends of mine. They were driving to the beach to visit a teacher of theirs at his family's beach house. I said, "Sure, you can go."

The fact that the teens were going to visit with a teacher at his summer home undoubtedly made the event seem safe because Danielle knew the teacher. It is also the case that Danielle has developed more trust in her daughter as she has gotten older. She said, "I have seen her make good decisions like with the kids she hangs out with WHO are good." Reflecting the passage of time, Danielle said, "So things can change, I wouldn't have allowed this a few years ago. She's getting more mature, it's really nice to see."

Negotiating Agreements

Letting go also takes shape through the negotiation of new agreements that involve teens gaining more control over their own decisions. Sometimes these negotiations take place amicably. At other times, they become heated, often when teens become angry, either because they feel their mothers or fathers do not trust them to behave well or because they feel it is their right to make their own decisions about their participation in an activity.

As mothers negotiate with teens about issues of safety, they have various forms of leverage. They might deny their teens permission to participate in an activity. They may withhold monetary resources teens need to attend an event, they may set conditions for driving a teen to an event. If they find their teens have disobeyed their wishes or rules, mothers may take their teen's cell phone, withhold their allowance, take a television or computer out of a teen's room, or ground them. As adolescence progresses, however, the power balance between parents and teens shifts, and teens gain more control over the decisions affecting their social lives.

If mothers think teens' wishes are, in the words of one mother, "reasonable," parents and children can more easily negotiate and make decisions about teens' new rights and responsibilities. This is the case for Amelia, a white working-class mother of a 16-year-old daughter, Hannah. Amelia described negotiating and sometimes "haggling" with Hannah to arrive at decisions about activities her daughter wants to engage in. She said:

> Hannah still follows the rules. And maybe part of that is because I negotiate and I still really consider what she wants to do and where she wants to go. I'm still on her side. If I can give my permission, I will. Like changing my mind and saying she can go to an event. But then if I say no, it's really no. So out of a struggle we might be having, I remind her that if it's something reasonable, I will try to accommodate her wishes.

Amelia expects Hannah to come up with good reasons for why she should do a particular thing and said that in negotiating with her, she shows Hannah that she takes her needs seriously and will try to accommodate her wishes:

> She may come back and haggle some more, and it's possible I would change my mind. I figure that my daughter is entitled to two rounds of haggling, and if she comes up with good reasons for what she wants to do, I'll consider it.

While Amelia seems to have worked out a strategy for negotiating with Hannah—waiting until she hears a good enough reason for giving her daughter permission to do something—she said she can find the process difficult. As she noted, "It's hard to disappoint her when I don't give her permission to do what she wants." Another mother, a working-class African American woman with a 16-year-old son, described arriving at decisions in their negotiations in a similar way. She said, "If my son comes back a third time with a good argument, I'll probably let him do what he wants."

Mothers and teens also negotiate over rules, a process that can involve conflicts and more extended negotiations. Eleanor, a white middle-class mother who lives in the city and has an 18-year-old son, Bill, and a 14-year-old daughter, described a protracted struggle over a rule that she and her husband, Jim, established with Bill when he was 14. Eleanor said, "We were pretty strict with Bill in those early teen years, we had rules. Some of his friends didn't seem to have rules." Eleanor and Jim made a rule that Bill couldn't stop at a video arcade that was close to the route Bill took on his walk home from school. Eleanor said Bill was very unhappy about this. When she and Jim first made the rule, Eleanor said, "I had to battle with Bill for three days. I began to really doubt myself. It was hard." Several years later, however, after Bill had turned 18 and was a senior in high school, Eleanor said her son had come to appreciate this rule:

> One night at dinner Bill said, "That was a good rule you had about the video arcade." Jim and I said, "What do you mean?" He said that one time, despite the fact that he was not supposed to, he had gone to the arcade with a friend and was playing a game. All of a sudden, Bill told Eleanor, a guy grabbed him from behind and said, "Give me your money." Bill told Eleanor the man pinned him up against the wall but Bill yelled really loud so everyone in the arcade could hear him, and the man let him go and ran away.

While mothers like Eleanor sometimes "win" in their negotiations, slowly but surely, teens gain the upper hand in negotiating more decisions. Letitia, a working-class African American mother of three children (ages 17, 15, and 13), including two daughters, changed her views of what was appropriate for her 17-year-old daughter when her daughter convinced her that she was being too restrictive. Letitia says she worries more about her daughters:

> Now they are teenagers, now I know I have to let go. I thought I needed to protect my daughter more than my son. But my daughter started telling me it wasn't fair, she was being too restricted. I told her I understood, but it's because of society—girls can be hurt by bad guys taking advantage of them.

But Letitia changed her mind about what restrictions to impose on her daughter. She said that her daughter kept challenging her and telling her that she was too strict, that she had to let her do more things. As Letitia noted:

> Then I changed. I always felt that protecting my daughters was the most im-portant thing. But my daughter said, "You can't hold me back." She helped me. I thought I was helping her. The kids see things differently.

Letitia continued, "I know my daughter is strong and has a good head on her shoulders—she doesn't get into trouble, she tells us how she is doing—but I still worry more about her and my other daughter more than our son, al-though I know bad things can happen to boys too."

Janice, a white upper-middle-class mother, reported a difficult negotiation she and her husband had with their 17-year-old son, Jeff, shortly after Jeff got his driver's license; it was eventually resolved in Jeff's favor. Jeff had a strict curfew of midnight, but one night, he didn't come home until about 12:45 a.m. Janice said, "We couldn't get through to him on his cell and he forgot to call. We were really, really worried." Janice said that after Jeff got home, they had a "blowup," something that rarely happens in their household. "My hus-band got really angry at my son and yelled," she said:

> When it cooled down, we sat down at the table to talk and had a lot of back and forth. It turned out that Jeff had to drive his friends all over the place to take them home. He goes to a private school and his friends live all over so that's why he was late. He said that could happen again and that our curfew wasn't reasonable.

At the end of their conversation, all three agreed on a new curfew, 12:30 a.m., for Jeff. Janice said she thinks Jeff "won that one." Her use of that phrase seems to reflect the fact that she feels she "lost" in this encounter. She would like to have Jeff's earlier curfew remain in place but, as she put it, "Jeff was arguing so strongly, my husband and I gave in." Jeff seems to be gaining more control in his relationship with his parents, undoubtedly due to his age as well as his forcefulness in arguing his case.

As teens progress through adolescence, mothers' accounts reveal a changing power balance between themselves and their teens and a shift in the boundaries of parental authority. As teens gain more ability to make their own decisions and act on them, mothers engage in letting go, dropping certain rules and restrictions, giving their teens more privacy, and acceding to their children's demands for more control over their own decision-making. One mother of two teens (ages 15 and 17) described not only how the "power balance" has shifted as her teens have gotten older but also how her "power is waning":

> I feel like I still have a lot of control, but not in the same way as I used to. They get taller and more adult-like, they're with their peers so much, they can get all that information on TV, the internet, social media, the power balance has shifted. They are getting more power and our power is waning.

She concluded, "Fortunately, we feel like our son is on a good path forward. He wants to go to college."

The Role of Institutions

The process through which teens gain more autonomy also occurs as they participate in organizations outside the family or in paid work. Teens who participate in summer camps, school trips, sports activities, arts clubs, or work for pay at full- or part-time jobs, typically gain more responsibility and freedoms, sometimes more freedoms than their parents would necessarily allow them. Lynn, a white upper-middle-class mother, for example, referred to experiences her 18-year-old son, Sam, gained on a trip to Europe with a school soccer team when he was 16. Lynn said, "When I first heard about this trip, I told Sam, 'No, you're not old enough.' I felt the kids would have too much time on their hands in a strange city—actually, they were going to two cities." But Sam persisted, saying, "Why can't I go on the trip?" Lynn said that because Sam "kept at" her, she called mothers whose teens had been on the trip in earlier years and asked them if the coach was a responsible person who knew how to make sure the teens were safe. According to Lynn, "They said yes, the trip had worked out fine. There are good rules, the kids follow them," so Lynn decided it was all right for her son to go. Lynn feels Sam learned important things on the trip:

> It was great for Sam. The coaches showed them the public transportation system in each city and how to buy tickets and let them explore the cities with their teammates. Sam was responsible, he made it work. I'm sure he saw and did some things, tried some things that may not have been so good, but overall, it went very well.

Although Lynn said she was initially skeptical, she came to view the trip as a positive experience and a turning point for her son. "It was a kind of coming of age," she noted, "that's what I call it. If you had asked me this spring if I would have let my son go on a trip to Madrid and Rome and wander off with his friends, I would have said absolutely not, no way." Of course, Lynn and her husband were able to provide this opportunity for their son because of their privilege. It goes without saying that many families cannot afford to send their teens on such a trip, which Sam's school was not supporting financially.

As they get older, teens also gain more autonomy through rites of passage that are institutionalized in law. Obtaining a driver's license and being able to drive represents a significant turning point in adolescence. Depending on the state, teens can get driver's licenses at age 16 or 17. Being able to drive— and certainly, having access to a car—is a highly valued marker of autonomy for teenagers, of being able to go places on their own in a way that provides them much more freedom to go out on their own than they have previously enjoyed. Mothers also cited a positive aspect to their teens' driving. If they have contributed financially to the purchase or upkeep of a car, for example, parents can use this as leverage to demand that their teens use the car to help them.[16] They can come to rely on teen drivers to help with errands—picking up food at the store or picking up a younger child at school or a sports

---

[16] A. L. Best, "Freedom, Constraint, and Family Responsibility: Teens and Parents Collaboratively Negotiate Around the Car, Class, Gender, and Culture," *Journal of Family Issues* 27(1) (2006): 55–84.

practice. As one mother said, "It's great, Sarah is still at that stage where she loves to drive. She'll pick up the younger kids after soccer practice, she'll go to the store if we need things."

At the same time, as teens begin to drive, parents experience new worries. Rates of teen car accidents are high.[17] Some mothers and fathers prepare for this time by enrolling their teens in driving programs, lecturing them about safety, and placing conditions on their getting their driver's licenses. They draw up agreements about who will pay for insurance, gas, and repairs, and what will happen if teens get into an accident. Sheila, a white middle-class mother, said, "I know it's time for our daughter to start driving, but I feel like with the car I have a whole new set of worries." Sheila and her husband read an article about teen driving that made them particularly nervous: "They said that for a teen to turn into a really good driver, they should have many, many hours of supervised driving." After doing more research about teen drivers and their higher accident rates, Sheila and her husband made rules. As she noted:

> We made our daughter read the article, and then we sat down and made a plan. After she gets her license, one of us still has to be in the car with her until she gets more driving experience, and after that, for a while, she can't be driving other kids around in the car.

Mary Ellen, a white middle-class mother, described her anxiety when her son Jake began driving the day after he got a driver's license:

> Jake passed the driving test on a Friday afternoon. Of course, the next morning, Jake wanted to drive to his friend Jonathan's house. We had agreed that his first day of driving alone in our car, I would follow in our second car. Jake drove fine, but I was nervous—there are some places where you have to cross a big road and there are no traffic lights.

Mary Ellen's comments also reveal her belief that her son's ability to drive represents a major turning point in his life:

---

[17] See Centers for Disease Control and Prevention, "Teen Drivers and Passengers."

We got to Jonathan's house, and Jake and Jonathan just started talking and laughing the way they usually do. I went right to Jonathan's parents and I was, like, "Oh my god, this changes everything." And it does.

Mary Ellen's belief that "this changes everything" is another example of an arena in which parents' authority can be superseded by wider societal authority. Parents can still make rules about driving, and Mary Ellen said she and her husband are requiring that Jake pay for his insurance and gas for the car from his earnings from his summer job. But if a teen wants a driver's license and can pass the test, they are legally entitled to drive. Mary Ellen now trusts Jake to drive safely, though she said she still worries:

> We worry when he's out in the car. And he's just not around as much since he got his license. I know this is good and he is taking more responsibility, he has to pay for his insurance and his gas, but you worry.

Finally, some teens acquire more autonomy in their relationships with their parents earlier than others due to family circumstances such as physical or mental illness, or drug and alcohol addiction. Patricia, a divorced white working-class mother of a second-year college student named Sophie, reported that she suffered from severe depression during her daughter's last years of high school when the treatments her doctor gave her were not working. Sophie is now in her second year of college, and Patricia said she and Sophie are close. However, Patricia says she was not able to be as much help to her daughter during her high school years as she would have liked, which makes her feel sad. Patricia's ex-husband, Sophie's father, had moved to another state and only saw Sophie a few times a year. Fortunately, she said, "Sophie understood my situation and was very sympathetic, I feel so grateful. She got herself breakfast and made breakfast for me before she left for school. She became so responsible, helping me and all."

Patricia said she feels guilty about not really "being there" for her daughter in the way she wanted to. She wasn't able to go to many of Sophie's events at school or plan many outings for herself and Sophie. She says, "We checked in and talked every day before Sophie went to school and when she came home. She showed me her grades, she was doing well in school, I listened and tried to be helpful when she described her schoolwork, she didn't get into trouble as far as I know." Patricia says Sophie did get a lot of support from the family that was renting the other side of her row house. They had a daughter a little younger than Sophie, and they would invite Sophie over to their house to hang out with them when Sophie wanted. The two girls liked each other. Patricia said she also alerted a school counselor to the situation, and he stayed in touch with Sophie during this time. Although her depression was difficult to treat, Patricia says her doctor finally found medications that worked to diminish the symptoms. Sophie successfully finished high school and Patricia reports that Sophie is doing well in college now.

Teens Gain Control

Finally, as teens get older, there are more and more times when mothers no longer control the process of letting go. Teens just start to do things on their own, some of which mothers don't necessarily approve of. Sue Anne, a white working-class mother, for example, acknowledged that there are many things she and her husband can't prevent their 17-year-old daughter, Katie, from doing now. She said, "I picked Katie up recently from a friend's house, and I could tell she'd been smoking pot." She said she hadn't thought Katie would smoke marijuana, which she had been told not to do. "I said to Katie, 'You've been smoking pot, why did you do that?'" Katie said, "Yeah, I did, I know it's not great but I just had to try it." Sue Anne noted:

> What are you going to do? You can't control what they do all the time. But I told her [speaking firmly], "It just makes you stupid and you'll get in trouble, so it's not a good thing to do, don't do it!"

She continued, "If she were younger, I would have really yelled at her, but she's going to be 18 soon—that's going to change things, and I don't want her to stop talking to me." While Sue Anne wasn't pleased about this, she worked to reassure herself, noting, "But Katie talks to me, that's good. And then you listen and make your comments and suggestions and you hope that they will make good decisions."

One mother described how a recent incident revealed that she has lost control over the actions of her son. Sharon, a white middle-class mother, has two sons (ages 17 and 12). She is divorced, and her ex-husband lives in another part of the state and is rarely in touch with the family. Sharon said that her older son, John, is not listening to her and not doing what she asks. When he goes out, he is not answering his cell phone as he did in the past. She said:

It's much harder to be the parent of a teen, it can be scary. I want to know where John is. His curfew is midnight on weekends. In the beginning of high school, it was 10:30, then I kept making it a little later. I really want to know where John is and who he's with, but it's not working.

Sharon described a recent incident that was frightening for her. She said, "Last Friday, I didn't get home from my job until late." She groaned as she said, "It's a new job, and my boss decides to call a meeting at 4:45 on a Friday afternoon and it wasn't over until 6:15." She called her sons in the afternoon when she got this information. They were both home, her older son had picked up his brother at his after school program, and they had come home for dinner. Sharon told them she would be late, but she would get dinner ready quickly as soon as she got home. She said, "My sons said they would be at home when I got there. But when I got home, they weren't there, the house was empty." Sharon was scared. "I panicked, it was horrible, I couldn't get through to them on their phones." Sharon found her younger son fairly quickly. "He was nearby playing outside with a new friend down the street, he had left his phone inside at the friend's house," she said. "He was fine, but John was doing his usual, he wouldn't answer his phone. He didn't come home at midnight and I couldn't get ahold of him."

Sharon said that after John leaves his job at a local supermarket on Fridays at 10:00 p.m., John goes to a friend's house, where she says he usually hangs out. But when she called there, the parents didn't know where John and their son were. John and his friend had apparently gone to someone else's house, and John didn't let her know where he was or that he would be returning home later than usual. Sharon stayed awake worrying, waiting for John to come home or contact her. He didn't come back until 1:00 a.m. Sharon said, "When he finally came home, I told John I was very angry that he didn't call or answer his cell phone, that I was really worried, and that we would have to talk the next day."

The following day, Sharon said she sat her sons down and talked to them about the importance of staying in close touch with her. "I was very stern," she said. "I said to them, 'People who live in the same house need to know where each other are.' But [looking and sounding upset] it didn't work with John. He just got up and started walking away. It was like, 'Why are you interfering in my life?'" This incident certainly reveals the significant tension that exists between Sharon and John at this time. It also shows that John is not interested in communicating with his mother or following her rules, at least for the time being. Sharon obviously feels not only anger but a sense of powerlessness at this time that her older teen son is so willing to rebuff her efforts to keep in touch with him to know he is safe. Furthermore, she doesn't have a partner or her ex-husband, the children's father, to help reinforce her authority. Her comments about a late Friday afternoon meeting at work also illustrate how the structure of the workplace can impede mothers' ability to monitor their teens.

Yolanda, a working-class African American mother, found herself in a similar situation. She moved back to her parents' home two years ago, after she separated from her husband, who she said was using drugs. Yolanda has four children: three sons (ages 17, 15, and 9) and a daughter (age 3). She said that just a few days ago, for the first time, her older son Shawn didn't come home until long after he had told her he would:

> My son Shawn really got me angry on Sunday. I was out with the other kids during the day and when I came back, he was gone. And he didn't come back in the evening, and then not at 11:00 or 12:00 or 1:00. He didn't call, and I couldn't get through to him on his cell. I waited and waited. Do you know when he came back—1:30 a.m.!

Yolanda said Shawn started to tell her a story about what happened, which made her angry:

> He had this stupid look on his face, he knew he'd done wrong. He started to tell me about how he'd gotten on a bus and it went the wrong way. I just told him to leave the room and go to bed. I knew he was going to lie and that was going to make me angrier. I think he might have gone with his friends to that big music festival going on now in the city and then stayed out later than he should have.

Yolanda punished her son, but she said it didn't have the desired effect. She said, "I told him he had to stay at home next weekend, and I took his phone away for a few days. He acted like that didn't bother him. That got me really angry, like he was defying my authority. I was really upset, even more upset when he said the punishment didn't matter. I didn't yell at him, I just wanted him to go to his room." Echoing other mothers quoted earlier, she said, "Yelling doesn't do any good, it just gets me more upset." In talking about this incident, Yolanda also expressed fear. "I really worry, it's not safe out there," she said. "There was that jogger who was killed in that fancy neighborhood; she was out running at 6:30 in the morning. Who would have thought that wouldn't be safe?" Yolanda said she hopes that Shawn's punishment, not seeing his friend the following weekend as he usually does, will make him think twice about doing this again.

Both of these mothers, one white and middle-class and one African American and working-class, are single. Some researchers have found that overall children in two-parent families have better behavioral as well as cognitive outcomes than children raised in single-parent (typically single-mother) families, particularly boys.[18] It is beyond the scope of this book to evaluate the connection between family structure and teen outcomes but as I describe later in this chapter, it is certainly also the case that married couples sometimes lose control of their teens.

Resources: Activities and Neighborhoods

To promote their teens' safe progression through adolescence and provide them with enriching experiences, parents work to support their teens' interests and enroll their teens in activities.

Activities

Access to constructive activities and other resources promotes positive outcomes for teens. As mothers work to manage the uncertainties of keeping teens safe, and of maintaining control while letting go, they rely on resources—safe neighborhoods with public parks and swimming pools, private clubs, summer camps, libraries, and after-school and weekend activities. The mothers I interviewed spoke of using activities to keep teens "occupied," "out of trouble," "in with a good crowd," and "not having too much time on their hands." They work to get teens into activities during after-school hours and on weekends, including sports and church activities, arts programs, and neighborhood groups. Researchers have found that teen involvement in these kinds of activities is correlated with positive outcomes, including staying

[18] M. Wasserman, "The Disparate Effects of Family Structure," in *How Cultural Factors Shape Economic Outcomes* (Princeton, NJ, and Washington, DC: Woodrow Wilson School of Public and International Affairs and The Brookings Institution, 2020), 55–81.

out of trouble and becoming more engaged at school.[19] Adolescents raised in resource-deprived neighborhoods with little social cohesion and few social support systems are at increased risk of delinquency.[20] Some researchers find that there are class differences in the types of activities parents prefer for their children; middle-class parents tend to exercise concerted cultivation and seek to enroll their children in activities that will actively promote their particular talents.[21] And of course there are class differences in terms of access to activities. The gap between what higher-income families and others can spend on enriching activities for their children has grown dramatically in recent years.[22]

Some upper-middle-class mothers use their financial, social, and cultural capital to enroll teens in activities that will not only engage their interests and keep them occupied but will also further their chances of acceptance at competitive colleges. They are very aware that college-bound teens need to demonstrate both academic success and involvement in extracurricular activities. These families have many more resources to pay for activities that meet their teens' specific interests in the arts, sports, and technology. As Monica, a white upper-middle-class mother said, "When our daughter told us she was interested in painting, we got her a teacher who had a studio nearby. The same thing with music. She said she wanted to play the violin, so we got her a violin and found someone who could teach her. We try to respond to her interests." Monica continued, "She likes these activities, and we like them because then she's not on her phone. They get her away from all that social media stuff. And she has to think about her resumé for college." Monica made no mention of the cost of paying for these activities. A white upper-middle-class mother named Pamela described the priority the family puts on supporting their daughter's participation in sports. Her daughter plays varsity tennis at her school. Pamela and her husband pay for extra coaching for their daughter, and for travel to games in other towns. Their daughter's team is hoping to

---

[19] R. J. Sampson, *Great American City: Chicago and the Enduring Neighborhood Effect* (Chicago: University of Chicago Press, 2012).

[20] D. Wang, J. K. Choi, and J. Shin, "Long-Term Neighborhood Effects on Adolescent Outcomes: Mediated Through Adverse Childhood Experiences and Parenting Stress," *Journal of Youth and Adolescence* 49(10) (2020): 2160–2173.

[21] M. Nelson, *Parenting Out of Control*; A. Lareau, *Unequal Childhoods: Class, Race, and Family Life, 2nd Edition with an Update a Decade Later* (Berkeley: University of California Press, 2011).

[22] "Enrichment expenditures" for things like trips, books, and tutors are around 10 times higher for families in the top quintile for income than for those at the bottom. R. V. Reeves, *Dream Hoarders: How the American Upper Middle Class is Leaving Everyone Else in the Dust, Why That is a Problem, and What To Do About It* (Washington, DC: Brookings Institution Press, 2017).

make it to the state championships. If their daughter's team advances, they will qualify for national competitions. Pamela and her husband will provide the funds and transportation their daughter will need to participate in the tennis program.

Middle-class mothers I interviewed seek out activities that will promote good values through sports or church activities, keep their teens occupied and out of trouble, and will look good on their record for applying to college or getting jobs. Some middle-class mothers reported that in their community many teens participated in sports and that many fathers and a few mothers become volunteer coaches. A smaller number of these mothers reported getting their teens involved in religious activities. Trudy, a middle-class African American mother whose family are Jehovah's Witnesses, said their religion helps them fulfill two sets of goals—it ensures their teens follow in the family's faith tradition, and it keeps their teens safe. She says she is able to control many things about her teens' lives—their friends, their after-school activities, their interactions with the opposite sex—because her children's social activities all take place at church and with church friends. As she said, "One way I know they are safe is I get them all into church activities. We don't want them in with all those other bad influences." Fortunately, her children like these activities, although her oldest son was unhappy when she and her husband forbade him from joining the high school football team. "But," she said, "he mostly got over that, and he's involved in church clubs and social activities, and he has a girlfriend now, from our church." She concluded by saying, "He's become a fine young man."

Often there are fees associated with enrolling in extracurricular activities, and because of the cost, working-class mothers are at a disadvantage in selecting programs for their children. However, a number of working-class mothers in my sample do seek out activities that their teens will like, that are low-cost, and that will keep their teens safe and off the streets, including church and sports activities. One working-class African American woman whose husband had recently died got her son involved in a Big Brother program, an organization that provides mentors for young people. She said her son developed a good relationship with his big brother and they attended baseball games together. Her son went on to attend a local university. A white working-class mother found an after-school program in filmmaking that her son was interested in. A working-class African American mother spoke of her strenuous efforts the previous summer to get her daughter into a church summer camp even though she didn't want to go. She said:

Last summer I pushed her on that church bus every morning, I pushed her if I had to, I couldn't let her be here alone while I went to work. And I wanted her to learn some things too, not just do nothing all summer.

This mother said, "And I feel really good that my daughter never got into trouble and she got her high school diploma. She's in a good training program now." The efforts of these working-class mothers undoubtedly provided their teens with valuable opportunities, as well as keeping them safe.

Neighborhoods

As noted previously, one of the most important assets for promoting teens' safety and well-being is a well-resourced neighborhood. Mothers want to live in neighborhoods that maximize their family's well-being and their children's chances for success. If they feel their neighborhood is not safe, those who are able try to move to what they believe will be a better place to live and raise their teen children. Abigail, a white middle-class mother of two children (ages 8 and 13), described her family's direct experience of the differences between well-resourced and poorer neighborhoods. A few years ago, she, her husband, and their children left the city neighborhood where their children were born and where they lived close to other family members. Abigail reported that their city neighborhood of white middle- and working-class residents was "going down" and becoming less safe, so they moved to a suburb they felt was safer and would have more opportunities for their 13-year-old son, Paul.

Abigail said, "It was a "really good move for the family, we like the community here." She said there are a lot more activities for Paul, "and he's in with a good group of kids and parents who have the same kind of direction that we'd like, you know, to push him into." Abigail said their old neighborhood doesn't offer many activities for teens anymore:

Paul is in Scouts here, and as far as I know, there's not even a Scout troop in our old neighborhood anymore. [Speaking sarcastically] It's more fashionable just to hang out and, I don't know, be cool.

Abigail did express one regret, however. She said, "We miss being close to our family who are still in the old neighborhood, we go back there when we can."

An African American working-class mother, Cheryl, also told a story of finding a better neighborhood for her children, one with more challenges. Cheryl and her husband have a 16-year-old daughter and two older children (ages 29 and 23). When the older children were teenagers, they sent them away from the city neighborhood where they live to the South so that they could live with her parents. She felt her teens would be safer there. Cheryl's story reveals a number of things: the distressing lack of safety in her neighborhood; the significant amount of work it took to provide a safe environment for her teens; the support Cheryl had from her family; and the need for her to be separated from her children in order to ensure their safety.

Cheryl said conditions in their neighborhood had worsened as her older children were entering their teenage years, but she and her husband could not afford to move to a safer neighborhood. So they contacted her mother and father who lived in a southern state. As she noted:

> The gangs got worse here and they would fight in the streets. And a couple of times it was so many boys right there in that intersection [pointing out the window], it would terrify us. Trying to catch somebody to beat him up and kill him and stuff. When things got bad we called my mom and dad down in [southern state] and told them about the situation. My dad asked me did I want them to take the boys down there. I said, "Well, Dad, you all are getting up in age." He said, "We can handle them." My sons stayed there for three years.

Sending her children down South required Cheryl and her husband to engage in various kinds of logistical work. She said:

> The school down there wanted out-of-state fees and all kinds of stuff. Somebody at the school board told my dad, if your daughter gives you temporary custody of their sons, it won't be all that much trouble. So it would be just like they were your children and you wouldn't have fees.

Cheryl and her husband talked it over and then found a lawyer who was able to turn over temporary custody of their sons to her parents with the understanding that Cheryl and her husband would support them financially and regain custody when their children returned home. The two older children stayed with their grandparents through their high school graduation. She said they have come back home and are doing well now. One attends a local community college, and the other is working in his uncle's contracting business. Cheryl's 16-year-old daughter has been able to stay with Cheryl and her husband because their neighborhood has become safer. The drug dealers had been driven out by the police and a local community organization, so, as Cheryl said, "things changed."

Cheryl said she is grateful that she was able to send her children to live with her parents in the South. However, she spoke with sadness about the time she missed with them. She said, "We knew we had to do this even though we missed our sons, sometimes terribly, but we went down to see them as much as we could." Cheryl said she and her husband felt they had to do this "because in [town in a southern state] they didn't have a gang problem there." Unlike more well-off mothers, who can move to safe neighborhoods and customize environments for their teens, in the absence of social policies that would provide affordable housing in better neighborhoods, lower-income families have far less ability to move their families to safer environments.

It is also the case that moving does not always mean that parents will be able to achieve their goals of ensuring their children's safety. One white working-class mother reported that their family had moved to their current neighborhood in a suburb that they knew would be safer than their inner-city neighborhood, but that their son has never managed to feel comfortable in their new neighborhood. She noted, "He feels out of place in the suburban school here, where kids have more money. Every weekend he leaves to go back and hang out with friends in our old neighborhood in the city." This mother said: "Our son spends a lot of with his buddies, I hope they don't get into trouble, it's just like he didn't really move. We'd like to see him more."

Trouble

While the majority of mothers I interviewed reported that their teens remain safe during their adolescence, for some, managing their teens' passage through adolescence involves dealing with "trouble." As described earlier, mothers in all class groups in my sample recounted incidents of their teens engaging in what parents and the wider society view as "problem behavior"—including underage drinking, using drugs, and receiving police citations for violating town curfews. A smaller group of mothers reported that their teens got into more serious trouble—a mental health crisis, drug abuse, and arrests for using and selling drugs. Dealing with trouble requires a lot of time, thought, emotional work, and the mobilization of resources on the part of all parents. Some mothers with resources are able to reduce legal penalties for their teens by hiring lawyers and other professionals to secure better outcomes for them, including keeping legal charges and convictions off their teens' records.

Mental Health

As noted above, large numbers of high school students are facing mental health challenges. In 2021, 42 percent of high school students experienced persistent feelings of sadness or hopelessness, including 57 percent of female high school students and 70 percent of LGBQ+ students. Similar rates of African American (39 percent) and white students (41 percent) reported experiencing feelings of hopelessness. Forty-two percent of high school students also reported that for two weeks in a row they felt so sad or hopeless on a daily basis that they stopped doing their usual activities. Twenty-two percent of high school students considered attempting suicide and 18 percent made a suicide plan. Overall, girls experienced greater mental health challenges than boys.[23]

Several mothers in my sample reported that their teens were experiencing mental health challenges. A white middle-class mother named Nora said that she and her husband Dave worried when their 15-year-old daughter Chloe began withdrawing from the family when she came home from school. Chloe spent most of her time in her room, and it was harder to get her to talk to them. At first, they thought maybe she was "just being a teenager." However, as Chloe began looking more and more sad and depressed, Nora and Dave went to her room one evening and said they had to talk with her. Nora said, "We told her, 'We're not leaving your room until you tell us what's going on with you. We love you and we are worried about you.'" After a period of silence, Chloe agreed to talk with them and said she was experiencing a lot of stress at school. She said her friends were "turning on her," she wasn't being invited to do things with her friendship group anymore, and this was making her feel terrible. And she said she didn't like most of her teachers. Nora said she and Dave told Chloe how sorry they were that this was happening and thanked her for sharing with them. Nora noted:

---

[23] Centers for Disease Control and Prevention, "Youth Risk Behavior Survey 2011–2021."

It was very hard to see Chloe so sad, plus we weren't sure what to do. But we really wanted to do something, we know that depression can get bad, we have some relatives who have experienced that.

Nora says that "if Chloe doesn't start to feel better, we'll insist she go to a therapist, we'll help her do that." Nora said she would like to talk to a therapist herself, to get advice on what she and Dave can do to help Chloe. She is also going to talk to the school counselor because, she said, "maybe she can give us some advice." Nora concluded, "I'm trying to remain hopeful, there are things we can do, but of course I am worried."

Edith, a white upper-middle-class mother, described the challenging time she has had keeping her 16-year-old daughter, Amanda, who has been diagnosed with anorexia, healthy and safe. When Amanda started high school, she joined the track team. The coach said she was happy to have Amanda on the team but told her and her parents that she, like all members of the team, would be weighed on a regular basis to make sure her weight didn't drop below the required level. If Amanda started losing weight, she could be suspended from the team.

Edith said Amanda loves track, she likes the team, and she was performing well. "But," as she noted, "Amanda was always talking about how she weighed too much. She started worrying more, obsessing about her weight, weighing herself all the time. Then we started worrying more. She wasn't eating very much. She wouldn't tell us how much she weighed." Edith said, "Then the track coach contacted us and said she was going to be weighing Amanda more, that Amanda was getting close to a weight that would mean she would be suspended from the team until she could get her weight back up." Edith let Amanda's doctor know about this. Her doctor said she wanted Amanda to come to her office weekly to be weighed.

It was at this time that Edith said, "It all turned into a crisis." One week at the doctor's office, a nurse realized Amanda had been putting stones in her pocket while she was being weighed to make herself heavier. Edith said:

This really scared us. It meant we couldn't trust Amanda to be truthful about how she was handling her weight issue. We told the track coach and the coach said she would suspend Amanda from the team for the rest of the season, which was actually almost over.

Edith and her husband then contacted an out-patient treatment center for eating disorders and enrolled their daughter in an intensive program that met every day for three weeks. Amanda was able to begin attending the program a short while later when school ended. Edith said the treatment Amanda has received has helped and her weight has stabilized. She said, "We're happy about this, but of course Amanda will have to show real signs of improvement before they let her join the track team in the fall."

Amanda was fortunate that she was able to get treatment for her anorexia. Her parents had insurance that paid some of the cost, and they were able to cover the rest. There was also a well-respected treatment center near where she and her parents live. There is not only a rise in diagnoses of mental health disorders among adolescents; there is also a large shortage of treatment facilities. The number of residential treatment facilities declined by 30 percent between 2012 and 2020.[24] Adolescents experiencing a mental health crisis often end up in hospital emergency rooms and stay there overnight or for several days.[25]

Alcohol and Drugs

The mothers I interviewed believe there is a good chance their teens will drink alcohol and try or use marijuana, just as many of them did when they were young, and they know their teens may not be telling them about their use of these substances. They exhort their teens not to drink excessively or use drugs. Several mothers in my sample reported incidents with alcohol and marijuana that were upsetting and stressful to manage. A white upper-middle-class mother, Georgette, discovered that her 15-year-old son, Adam, had taken alcohol from their liquor cabinet and shared it with friends who had spent the night, breaking the rule that he was not allowed to drink with friends in the house. That night Georgette and her husband were with friends who lived down the block for a few hours that evening. When they came back home, there were no signs that Adam and his friends had been drinking. However, while Adam and his friends slept the next morning,

[24] Substance Abuse and Mental Health Services Administration, "National Mental Health Services Survey (N-MHSS): 2020 Data on Mental Health Treatment Facilities" (Rockville, MD: 2021).

[25] M. Richtel, "Hundreds of Suicidal Teens Sleep in Emergency Rooms. Every Night," *New York Times*, May 8, 2022, https://www.nytimes.com/2022/05/08/health/emergency-rooms-teen-mental-health.html.

Georgette went to get something in the basement and found empty liquor bottles hidden there. She said, "I was so angry at Adam, he absolutely knows this is against the rules. I spoke to him very sternly and told him he would be punished for this. I felt really embarrassed too. I immediately called the other parents and told them what happened." Georgette and her husband decided to ground Adam, making him stay home and not attend social events for three weekends. Georgette said, "I don't feel this will happen again, at least for now. Adam knows he would get a worse penalty."

June, a white, divorced working-class mother, received information from her older son that her younger son, 16-year-old Joey, was smoking marijuana regularly, something he was forbidden to do. She took a variety of actions to make him stop. She said:

> Last summer, one of my older sons told me that Joey was drinking and doing pot with another boy. I didn't like that boy, he was always getting into trouble. Well, that was it. The next day I took Joey to (a drug treatment center). I called ahead of time and told them the situation. Joey got a lecture. I didn't want to fool around, I took him right there. I took him a few times.

Besides taking Joey to the drug treatment center, June drew on other resources to "scare" him and show him how she would punish him if he continued to use marijuana:

> I took Joey to a Navy recruiting station where you sign up to be a sailor.
> I made like I wanted him to be a sailor, but I was really trying to scare him.
> And I had some of our family who are police talk to him.

June also tried to locate Joey's father, her ex-husband, who had not been staying in touch with Joey. She had heard he was back in the area, so she got in touch with him. June said, "Kids needed a father, that's what I told him, I said, 'Joey really needs you now.' So he got involved and talked to my son a lot. It's good, they are staying in touch now." June believes that Joey has stopped using drugs since this incident, but she is requiring him to check in with her regularly when he is out of the house and inform her of his whereabouts.

Fights

When teens have conflicts with each other, they sometimes occur in the form of verbal insults and put-downs, either in person or on social media. Sometimes, conflicts take the form of physical fights. While there is physical fighting between girls, the reports given by several working-class mothers in my interview sample were about physical fights between teenage boys. African American mothers said they worry in particular about their sons, whom they believe are under pressure to engage in physical conflict as part of the struggle to maintain respect for themselves and avoid being targeted for violence, which requires being willing to threaten violence themselves. This is part of the "code of the street," a display of aggression that may require engaging in physical fights to avoid being victimized.[26]

Harriet, a working-class African American mother with a son named Travis (age 14), gave an account that reveals the burdens African American mothers carry when they are trying to get their teens not to engage in fights. She said, "You have to worry so much about young Black males in our society. It's scary how fast they can get in trouble with the police, who think they are doing something bad, it's really scary. And they can get in fights with other teenagers and get hurt." She worries that "Black males want to prove themselves, they want to be a man." Harriet said, "I talk to Travis all the time about the streets. I say to him, 'Stay to yourself, stay away from the crowd.' I'm constantly telling him, 'If somebody insults you, don't respond back, walk away. You are your own person, you don't have to prove yourself.'" She continued, "Fights are bad because the police can get involved and young Black men can be arrested or even shot and killed—it's very scary. I tell Travis over and over, 'If the police stop you, you must stop everything, do not move, do not put your hands in your pocket, be very polite, do not challenge police!' I remind him of this all the time, I've got to get him to see that this is really serious."

In the case of one African American family, the work to manage their son's fights with peers extended over time and was emotionally draining. Audrey, a middle-class African American mother of two sons, one who is 12 and going into seventh grade and the other one who is 15 and going into tenth grade, spoke of a very upsetting time after her older son, Jamal, was engaged

---

[26] E. Anderson, *Code of the Street: Decency, Violence, and the Moral Life of the Inner City* (New York: Norton, 1999).

in a conflict with another teenage boy. Audrey, her husband Michael, who works at an engineering firm, and their sons live in a middle-class African American neighborhood that is considered fairly safe but is surrounded by neighborhoods that are considered less so. Audrey spoke of her and Michael's work to manage Jamal's feelings and actions after he got into a fight, as well as their work to help him avoid further trouble in the future. Audrey and her husband felt this incident was serious and could potentially put Jamal in danger. She said:

> At school, Jamal made a comment about a girl to someone, that you couldn't trust her. He felt she was saying bad things about a friend of his. And someone else told that to the girl he made a comment about. Then the girl's brother came to find Jamal. He was in my son's face, being very threatening. He didn't hit Jamal. And Jamal didn't hit him. We've taught Jamal, you only hit when you're hit, but there was a lot of peer pressure for Jamal to score back.

This incident didn't end with the first altercation. Audrey reported that Jamal succumbed to ongoing pressure to continue engaging in conflict:

> Then there was a second time when the girl's brother made a negative comment to Jamal. Jamal did walk away, but as he did, he made a comment about that boy, who then yelled at Jamal and insulted him. Jamal turned around and walked back and took a swing at him.
>
> Fortunately, nothing more happened, Jamal didn't actually hit that boy, but we were really worried when we heard about that. You never know who someone knows. If he knows someone from a gang or is part of a gang— kids have weapons, kids die, they can die from some really stupid things, I was scared.

Audrey and her husband devoted considerable thought, time, and work to managing this situation, both interpersonal work with Jamal and logistical work to arrange transportation for Jamal to and from school to protect him from what they worried was ongoing potential for harm. She said:

> My husband and I had long talks with Jamal about what could have happened. He had a lot of emotional feelings about this and we had to help him adjust his feelings. We had to help him deal with his emotions. I told

him, "This one was your fault. Yes, the other boy hit, but you started this by what you said and by turning around and going back."

Audrey said she told the school counselor what happened and asked him to watch the two boys. "The counselor said he would," she said, "he was sympathetic, but we know there are not enough counselors and he can't keep a close watch on everyone." She continued:

My husband picked up Jamal at school for the next two weeks because we didn't know where he might see that other boy. Jamal usually goes to school on a city bus. But after what happened, we thought about what bus route he could take to school that would be the safest, that most kids in his school usually don't take. This whole thing got to my son, it affected him a lot, it affected him emotionally, he found it hard to concentrate and do his schoolwork.

This incident was the focal point of Audrey and her husband's life for several stressful weeks. She said, "We were all affected. My husband and I worried a lot, we still do." They did extensive emotion work, talking at length with Jamal to help him manage his anger and fear, and they made new transportation plans. Audrey feels like their work has paid off so far; Jamal has been staying away from teens with whom he could have conflicts and has continued to keep his grades up. Like some other African American mothers, however, Audrey believes it is an ongoing struggle to keep her teens from too much contact with "that street culture" and from contact with police that could occur in the wake of fights or at other times, contact that could put their teens at risk of harm.

"The Street" and Gangs

Middle- and upper-middle-class mothers in the city are able to live in neighborhoods that are considered fairly safe. Working-class neighborhoods can also be relatively safe, but families in the lowest-income neighborhoods with fewer resources can face challenges, including those presented by what some mothers call "the street," where there can be gangs, drug dealing, or other criminal activity.

African American mothers—because of the ever-present possibility of police harassment and violence toward their teens, especially their sons—have to be particularly vigilant about their teens' safety. However, they can also find themselves in a bind with regard to calling the police. While African Americans experience racial profiling on an ongoing basis, they also sometimes need the help of police in neighborhoods where local and state governments have failed to provide resources that would create safe conditions.

Ella, a working-class African American mother with two boys in high school, stated that the police sometimes don't respond to callers from her neighborhood, which can leave residents without protection. As she noted:

> The gangs in our neighborhood are getting worse. One time I called the police about five times. There were gangs on the corner, they were yelling and threatening to fight. Then I stopped calling. Everybody in the neighborhood stopped calling because you knew the cops wouldn't come.

Ella said that even if the police eventually come, they can just issue threats and tell the gang members to go away. She said, "One time, a boy in our neighborhood who was threatening other kids walked away laughing after his talk with the policeman, who was Black." At the same time, Ella, like other African-American mothers, is fearful that her teens could face harm at the hands of police, particularly white police.

Sexual Coercion

As noted previously, some mothers I interviewed said they fear their daughters could experience sexual coercion or violence. In 2021, 30 percent of high school students had ever had sexual intercourse and 21 percent were sexually active. Eight percent (14 percent of girls, 4 percent of boys) were physically forced to have sexual intercourse when they did not want to.[27] Catherine, a white middle-class mother, spoke with a great deal of sadness about a situation that remains deeply troubling to her and her husband, Jerry. Their older daughter, who did very well in high school, is a junior at a well-regarded

---

[27] Centers for Disease Control and Prevention, "Youth Risk Behavior Survey 2011–2021."

college. Things seemed to be going well for their younger daughter, Merry, a sophomore in high school.

However, starting in mid-November, Merry seemed depressed. She stopped talking much at home and spent most of her time in her room. Teachers contacted Catherine and said that Merry was missing some classes and was not handing in assignments. Catherine and Jerry tried to talk to their daughter, but she refused to respond to their questions. They finally told her she would have to tell them what was going on. Catherine said, "The only thing that made her tell us what happened is that we said to Merry if she didn't, we would take away her cell phone."

Over several evenings of painful discussion, Catherine and Jerry learned that Merry had been sneaking off to see her boyfriend after school. During the fall, Catherine and Jerry, who usually got home from their jobs at a local hospital between 5:30 and 6:00 p.m., thought Merry had been attending meetings of the school film club two afternoons a week and taking a photography class during the third afternoon. The other two days the plan was for her to come home and do homework. They trusted what Merry was telling them, that she was sticking to this plan, just as they had trusted their older daughter's reports of her activities.

However, Catherine and Jerry learned that earlier in the fall Merry had been leaving school and going to the house of a boy she considered her boyfriend, sometimes as many as three times a week. His parents did not return home from work until dinner time, by which time Merry had left. Merry said that recently, her boyfriend had started pressuring her to have sexual intercourse. Merry said she has tried to convince her boyfriend that she doesn't want to have sex, but her boyfriend has threatened to break off the relationship. He said that Merry must not love him and that he wouldn't see her anymore unless they had sex. Catherine said that at that point Merry was extremely upset and broke down crying. According to Catherine, "Merry said she loves her boyfriend, she says, 'He's the best thing that's happened to me, and now it feels like he's being so mean. I want to see him but he'll be angry if I keep telling him I won't have sex.' She was distraught, she said her life was 'a mess,' that she didn't want to go to school, and she wouldn't talk about it anymore."

Catherine said she and Jerry were shocked to learn that Merry had been sneaking off to see her boyfriend and that the relationship had become so problematic and had the potential to harm Merry. Catherine says they gave Merry a lot of sympathy but also told her they wanted her to end the relationship, that it was harming her, she was falling behind in school, and that her boyfriend could potentially force her to do something she didn't want to do, with very negative consequences. The conversation went on for some time. Catherine and Jerry also told Merry she would have to stop missing classes. If she needed to stay home for a short period of time to start feeling better before going back to school, they would see that she got her school assignments. Catherine says they will try to get Merry to agree to see a counselor as soon as possible. She says they also need to talk more to Merry about how she was concealing the fact that she was not going to activities after school but was seeing her boyfriend. Catherine concluded by saying, "This is heavy on our hearts, we are very sad and upset for Merry, and we will do everything we can to help her recover."

Drug Use and Abuse

A small number of mothers I interviewed reported that their teens had abused drugs. In what follows, I present the accounts of an upper-middle-, middle-, and working-class mother who had to manage their teens' drug problems. In these cases, mothers described their daughters' abuse. In each case, their teens engaged in serious drug use; all of the parents had done their best to prevent this, but their teens had continued using drugs, which parents found very upsetting. Responding to trouble requires time-consuming work: assessing the facts of what their teen did; determining how to best respond to their teen; working with law enforcement personnel; and overseeing punishments or legal actions taken against their teens. As they deal with trouble, upper-middle and middle-class families have more resources to deal with these problems, including more social capital, which enables them to access good lawyers and helping professionals, and more financial resources to pay for them. Good legal advice can help parents secure reduced penalties for their teens and also keep their teens' rule-breaking off their official records.

A white upper-middle-class mother named Edith described her daughter Anne's addiction, her subsequent arrest for drug use, and the resources she and her husband John secured to handle the situation. The incidents Edith described took place the summer after Anne finished tenth grade. Edith said one day that summer, she and John got a call that Anne was being arrested for drug dealing. They were shocked and frightened. She said:

Anne really got into trouble with marijuana. She got caught at the state park nearby with some friends; they had quite a bit so they were arrested and charged with dealing, they were dealing. She could have ended up in jail.

Edith said that she and John quickly mobilized to secure a lawyer for their daughter. She reported, "John works with a good lawyer who helped us find another lawyer who knew about these kinds of cases." Edith thinks this was important because she says "the courts were signaling that they were not going to be more lenient with better-off kids."

Edith says Anne was "incredibly lucky." Two years earlier, she and some friends had stayed in their town park after the curfew. The police found them and searched them; Anne had some marijuana in her pocket. Because it was her first offense, she was only charged with a misdemeanor. She was also fined $250 and ordered to do community service. This was put on her record but would be removed after a year if there were no further offenses. This previous offense had just recently been expunged from her record when Anne and her friend were arrested in the state park. Edith said that if that incident hadn't been removed from Anne's record, "I think there is no doubt Anne would have ended up with very serious charges against her. We were incredibly upset and worried and angry at her." Edith said:

> The lawyer provided great advice about how to handle Anne's court appearance. Her punishment was that she had to be under supervision by a social worker and do community service for a year. A therapist friend also referred us to a good counselor and we got Anne into therapy right away. The counselor was terrific. She got her going to NA [Narcotics Anonymous]. It turned out Anne was really addicted. We didn't realize that.

Anne was slowly able to overcome her addictions and is now in college. Interestingly, her community service experience has helped her find a direction in life. As Edith pointed out:

> Now looking back, Anne learned a lot. For her community service, she worked at a program for kids who age out of foster care. She learned about what can happen to these kids. Now she is motivated to go into the field of social services and help kids.

The following account of Margaret, a white middle-class mother, similarly demonstrates the importance of access to support systems in managing trouble and securing good outcomes. Margaret reported that her daughter, Beth, began using drugs, primarily marijuana, in ninth grade. Margaret said it was the school counselor who first alerted her and her husband, Rich, to Beth's drug use:

> At one point, the school counselor called me and asked if Beth was into drugs or alcohol. The counselor was very good, keeping track. My daughter had kind of gotten labeled because of the friends she was hanging around with. Having those friends made her under suspicion. And I think those friends were helping her get marijuana.

Margaret said that after the counselor called, "I began watching Beth really carefully and started to think she might be using drugs." Margaret and Rich arranged for private drug testing for Beth, and the school also tested her for drugs on a regular basis:

> The school actually tested Beth for drugs several times and one time she tested positive for marijuana. She was suspended for a week. After that, the school counselor kept having her tested. And we had her tested regularly at a clinic.

Margaret said that at first, Beth tried to resist her parents' attempts to address her addiction:

> One time, Beth tried to hide the fact that she was using drugs to pass the test. The school said that Beth had put vinegar in her urine sample so they rejected it. They made her do another test, which showed that she hadn't stopped using drugs.

Margaret said, "Ninth grade was really hard." Beth continued to lie about her drug use. Margaret said she and Rick kept saying to her, "Look, it's your life, your life is in your hands," but Beth continued to find a way to access drugs:

> One time a teacher found Beth in a school bathroom using drugs. Rich and I got calls at work and immediately went to the school. Both the principal and the counselor called. That time, Beth was suspended from school

for two weeks. We talked to the counselor a lot. The counselor has been a real ally.

Fortunately, Margaret said, things have now turned around. Beth agreed to see an addictions counselor and is not using drugs anymore and has new friends who do not use drugs. "This year, her junior year," Margaret said, "Beth has changed. Now she's back on track. Some of her friends are honors students, athletes too. She's dropped some of her old friends. A lot of them had a lot of dysfunction. One girl was expelled from school for being a heroin addict—she actually lived right near us. I could tell that Beth was scared about that."

Margaret said she and Rich are hopeful that this extremely difficult period is behind them and that Beth has a better understanding of the dangers of drugs. "So now Beth has seen what drugs can do, she has been through a lot. She's had the experience and the fear and she's seen friends expelled. Her friend who was expelled from school is in drug rehab. Seeing her friend I think helped turn Beth around. She said to me recently she doesn't want to be a 'loser.'" Margaret feels deeply grateful that Beth has recovered and is very thankful for the support of family, friends, and the school counselor. As she mentioned:

We were so worried, we could have lost her, it was really bad. Fortunately, we had the counselor, who was so important in all of this, I know we are lucky, many schools don't have such good counselors. And my family and others were really supportive. We have a very close family.

[Laughing] One of them said to me, "You should just take her and drop her in [a neighborhood with drug users in the nearby city] and leave her there. Then she'll see what it's like, where she's headed."

Margaret is relieved and very happy that she and her husband were able to help their daughter get through this difficult period. She also says she finds herself thinking about whether she and Rich could have prevented this:

Sometimes I think, should I have sent her to the Catholic school in this area where they are more strict, would that have been better? Maybe I should have done that. This all started in eighth grade and I could have.

I mentioned that to Beth at the time, but she said no, she didn't want to go there. She didn't want to leave her friends and go to a new place.

Margaret said that this two-year period has been very hard on her and her husband. They had never dealt with such a situation before, they never expected their daughter would become addicted to drugs. They were taken by surprise a number of times, and because they had no experience managing drug use, it was "learning as you go." Margaret said she and Rich experienced a great deal of emotional stress, worrying that they could "lose" their daughter. She reported that "I still go over and over all of this in my mind. I am so grateful that Beth's school has such a good counselor who helped us so much."

By contrast, Ruby, a working-class African American widowed mother was not able to get the assistance she needed to help her older son, Khalil. Ruby said her younger son has stayed "on the right track." He is finishing high school and thinking about his future employment, perhaps as an auto mechanic. However, Khalil is now in prison. Ruby said she "lost" him. As she phrased it, "the street got him," and he began using, and then dealing, drugs. According to Ruby, Khalil was caught by the police while selling cocaine to some young men in the neighborhood. He was charged with dealing and received a two-year sentence in prison.

Ruby movingly described her painful feelings about losing Khalil to the streets and reflected on how "the street" can gain control of someone like her son, despite a parent's best efforts:

> You can still control them, I've had somewhat control over my sons. But they're not going to let you control so much of them. So all you can do is control them as long as you can and give them your opinion on what life is about and raise them the best way you know how and hope they pick the right way to go.

Ruby asks herself whether she had a role in what happened to her son, but she said that it was her son who made bad choices, despite the fact that he knew right from wrong. She said:

> And sometimes it's a reflection on you and sometimes it's not. But most of the time like my oldest one, the street got more control of him than I did,

the fast money and dealing drugs. But he knows right from wrong. And when push came to shove, he knows what's what, but he picked the hard road. If it's out there to be done, they're going to do it anyway because that's what they want to do. They think they can get all that money on the street.

Ruby believes it's unfair to put all the blame on parents for what happens to their children. She said:

> You know, it's not the parent who has all the fault on how you turn out. Because you know you raised them the best way you know how and you gave them as much as you could and showed them how to survive and everything else.

Ruby is deeply hurt, because she said the judge who sentenced her son blamed her for what happened to him, even though he doesn't know anything about her life or how hard it is to raise a male teen in a poor African American neighborhood and counter the lure of "the street" and fast drug money. As she said:

> The judge said, "Well you can't parent him because he turned out this way," but they don't know about you, they're just going by what's on a piece of paper. A lot of times there's nothing you can do if the street got them. The street is cool, it's got real strong pull, and they get faster money out there so they all want to go that way. My son never did get much money anyway, it didn't do him no good to go that route, that's what his father taught him before he died.

Ruby believes that strangers who don't know what her life is like should not judge her:

> A stranger can't come up and say you're not a good parent because they don't know me, they don't know my son and they don't know what we went through in our lifetime. Only somebody like my mom or my brothers know what our family is like. A judge can't treat you like that, he just knows what's on that paper, that black and white. He doesn't know everything we did to try and keep my son off the streets.

According to Ruby, the judge who decided on her son's punishment or-
dered that her son be sent to a prison that is 50 miles away from where
she lives:

> The judge said my son needed a place away from home, that it would be
> better for him if they took him and put him as far away from home as pos-
> sible. So that's what they did.

Ruby says, "Now I have to spend a lot of time getting there to visit my son.
I don't have a car and the public transportation to that place is not good."
Ruby summed up her feelings in a sad and moving statement:

> It's a hurting feeling for somebody to tell you these things, but you know
> you did your best so you don't have regrets. It's just the idea of it, of some-
> body just telling you that, when they don't know anything about your life
> and all you've done for your child.

The judge's comments can be seen as reflecting the way that poorer African
American mothers are held in low regard by the wider society and are stereotyped by racist views that portray them as lacking motivation and the will to
discipline their children. Whatever Ruby did or didn't do to care for her son,
it is a revealing image, a white male judge, a man of privilege, lecturing a low-
income African American mother on being a good mother.

These cases show the kinds of advice and resources upper-middle-class
and middle-class parents can mobilize from counselors, therapists, and
lawyers to deal with trouble. While working-class parents also have resources
to draw on, including extended family members and members of their church
congregations who can help them secure professional assistance, they have
less money and less social capital to use in securing professionals who can
help them manage trouble and work to gain more favorable outcomes for
their teens.

Conclusion

Keeping teens safe, parents' highest priority, presents numerous challenges.
As one mother said, "our teens are always out ahead of us." Teens want to do
new things, be with their friends, and spend more time on social media. In

order to gain more autonomy, it is essential that they have experiences and go places where they can develop new skills, make new friends, and try on new identities. This means that teens are increasingly away from adult supervision, sometimes in environments adults view as presenting risks. To keep their teens safe, mothers talk to and lecture them, monitor them, and create rules about what they are and are not allowed to do. However, as mothers say, they can't be policing their teens all the time, they have to give them more autonomy. Ideally, mothers are able to trust their teens as they let go and allow them to do more things. However, the mothers I interviewed described developing trust in their teens and letting go as an ongoing, sometimes uncertain process. It can be difficult to get sufficient information about their teens' activities to assess their safety, and their teens don't necessarily listen to advice and warnings.

As adolescence progresses, mothers increasingly engage in letting go, renegotiating control so their teens can gain more autonomy and take more responsibility for their own decisions. This happens along different pathways. On an individual level, some mothers come to trust their teens; they see them make good decisions about their safety, and they give them permission to do more things. Others engage in extended negotiations with their teens about what they can and cannot do. Teens also gain more autonomy through participation in institutions—schools, sports teams, social clubs—which increasingly enable them to gain more freedoms as they engage in new activities and spend more time away from parental control. Finally, teens just stop asking permission and do things on their own.

These accounts from mothers also illustrate how those with more resources gain major advantages in keeping their teens safe. If they don't already live in safe neighborhoods, they can often move to such neighborhoods. One white middle-class family reported moving from a declining neighborhood in the city, where drug use was increasing, to a suburb that had good schools and extracurricular activities, where they felt their son began to thrive. Due to housing segregation and a lack of affordable housing, African American families have fewer choices about where to live. One African American family felt they had no other choice but to send their children to be with relatives who lived in a safer community in the South. They missed their children a lot but felt that this was necessary to ensure their teens' safety.

Some mothers described how their teens got into trouble. They described more minor trouble including underage drinking, using drugs, and receiving police citations for violating town curfews. A smaller number described more significant problems: problems with drugs, threats of violence, sexual coercion, and mental health challenges. Tragically, one mother reported that two of her young adult children died of a drug overdose. While all teens face risks, working-class and African American teens live in neighborhoods where there is more crime and gun violence, and African American teens and young adults are at risk of being profiled by the police. Upper-middle-class and middle-class mothers, especially if they are white, have social and cultural capital that enables some of them to obtain legal assistance that can reduce penalties their teens may face.

4

Promoting School Success and Preparing
for Postsecondary Education

Parents consider promoting their teens' success in school as one of their highest priorities. The stakes are high. In contemporary societies, educational credentials are critical for finding a place in the adult world and achieving economic independence. A high school diploma is essential for almost any type of employment, and in the current era, at least some postsecondary education is also needed to find work that will provide an adequate standard of living.[1]

Researchers have identified the central role parental involvement plays in children's schooling and its impact on their academic performance. They cite the importance of parents' helping their children and teens with homework and school projects, as well as with the work of "academic socialization"— providing encouragement, helping them create goals, and promoting their academic resilience. Researchers have also identified the value of parents' attendance at teacher conferences and their volunteering at their children's school.[2] Schools expect parents to invest significant time in promoting their teens' educational success, and they often fault parents if they think they are not sufficiently involved.[3]

However, while researchers have demonstrated the importance of parents' support to the success of their children, they pay less attention to the challenges mothers face in promoting their teens' educational success. The mothers I interviewed were highly motivated to do what they could to ensure that their teens gain the educational credentials necessary to move

---

[1] Currently, two out of three jobs require at least some education or training beyond high school. Fifty-six percent of all good jobs that provide an adequate standard of living require a BA degree. A. P. Carnevale et al., "Three Educational Pathways to Good Jobs" (Washington, DC: Georgetown University Center on Education and the Workforce, 2018).
[2] M.-T. Wang and S. Sheikh-Khalil, "Does Parental Involvement Matter for Student Achievement and Mental Health in High School?," *Child Development* 85(2) (2014): 610–625.
[3] Q. Allen and K. White-Smith, "'That's Why I Say Stay in School': Black Mothers' Parental Involvement, Cultural Wealth, and Exclusion in Their Son's Schooling," *Urban Education* 53(3) (2018): 409–435.

Letting Go. Demie Kurz, Oxford University Press. © Oxford University Press 2024.
DOI: 10.1093/9780190222482.003.0004

into the workforce and on to independent lives. They help their teen children with schoolwork as they are able, they search for good schools and school programs where they believe their teens will get the best education, they contact teachers when there are problems. Some volunteer or go to meetings at their teens' school.

At the same time, mothers report many challenges in this work. They told a more complicated story about supporting their teens' education than is typically presented in research and popular narratives. Some reported that their teens were not motivated to work hard in school; they were not applying themselves or working up to their potential. Researchers have shown there are high rates of student disengagement in school. Many students lack motivation because they don't feel challenged, don't enjoy schoolwork, or become bored. Even in high-achieving schools, about two-thirds of students are not fully engaged.[4]

Amy, a white upper-middle-class businesswoman, expressed frustration and worry at her inability to get her 14-year-old son, Adam, who is in ninth grade, to do his work. She said:

> Adam is this really smart boy, he tests high on aptitude and in school subjects, and he is wasting his good mind. He wants to get out of the advanced program he easily qualified for because he doesn't want to work that hard. We don't want him to do that; we know he can do the work.

Amy asks herself:

> What are my husband and I going to do? I can't duct tape Adam to his desk. I can't force him to do schoolwork. I can't nag my son about these things all the time. My husband isn't having any success either.

Amy's phrase, that she can't "duct tape" her son to his desk, is telling, and reveals the challenges some parents face in instilling motivation. For the moment, she is unable to persuade Adam to do his schoolwork and is uncertain about what to do next. "You know what they say," she said, "You can bring a horse to water, but you can't make him drink. Adam says school is boring,

---

[4] J. Moellera, M. A. Brackett, Z. Ivcevic, and A. E. White, "High School Students' Feelings: Discoveries from a Large National Survey and an Experience Sampling Study," *Learning and Instruction* 66, 101301 (2020): 1–15.

and when he had to attend classes online during the pandemic, he said they were really boring."

Other mothers reported dealing with teens who are experiencing stress. Over half of all high school students feel stress about their grades and about getting into college. Competition to gain acceptance at top highly ranked colleges is intense, although the average college acceptance rate in the United States is over 50 percent.[5] However, even students applying at less competitive colleges worry about whether their high school record will be strong enough to enable them to gain college scholarships. Stress can have negative consequences for students, including lowered engagement, trouble with concentration, poor academic performance, and an increased risk of dropping out of school.[6]

In addition to facing new issues of motivation and stress, mothers also described challenges in communicating with teachers about their teens' school performance. In junior high and high school, where classes are typically larger than in elementary school, it can be more difficult for parents to connect with their children's teachers and get information about their teens' performance in required schoolwork.[7] Ingrid, a white middle-class mother who works as a financial analyst at a bank, said that in elementary school, her children's teachers were a good source of information for finding out how her children were doing, something she doesn't find to be the case in her teens' junior high school. As she pointed out:

> I think the transition into junior high is a big thing—the transition to multiple teachers, from the one teacher who is almost like a parent figure. The school isn't a substitute home anymore, it's more like a workplace. As a parent, you lose a resource. The teacher only knows your child as a math student, or a history student. That's very limited.

[5] Sixty percent of 13- to 17-year-olds say they feel stress from pressure to get good grades, more than twice as many as feel pressure to fit in socially or look good. J. M. Horowitz and N. Graf, "Most U.S. Teens See Anxiety and Depression as a Major Problem Among Their Peers" (Washington, DC: Pew Research Center, February 20, 2019); Selective colleges typically have acceptance rates of 10 percent or less. For average college acceptance rates, see I. Bouchrika, "List of College Acceptance Rates in 2024," research.com, April 17, 2024, https://research.com/education/list-of-college-accepta nce-rates#2.

[6] M. C. Pascoe, S. Hetrick, and A. G. Parker, "The Impact of Stress on Students in Secondary School and Higher Education," *International Journal of Adolescence and Youth* 25(1) (2020): 104–112.

[7] M. Wang and S. Sheikh-Khalil, "Does Parental Involvement Matter for Student Achievement and Mental Health in High School?" *Child Development* 85(2) (2014): 610–625.

Another major priority for mothers in supporting their teens' schoolwork is securing schools and programs. Good schools and programs can not only provide a suitable education but can increase the likelihood of keeping their teens engaged in school. In their work to find good programs and schools, those parents who have more income and those who have more knowledge of their school system have a greater choice of schools that can help their teens remain engaged and provide more programs and activities, smaller class sizes, and better guidance counseling. Parents can customize their school choice, matching a school's character and resources to their teens' abilities and interests. Children in families with fewer resources are more likely to attend schools that are underfunded and sometimes short-staffed, with large class sizes and not enough guidance counselors to help students with issues of engagement and other problems. Only one in five high school students is enrolled in a school that has an adequate number of school counselors.[8]

At the same time, while many students experience stress and disengagement in their schooling, it is also the case that some teens like school and are able to stay engaged. Margo, an upper-middle-class white woman, is an education specialist with two daughters (ages 15 and 17). She reported that her daughters have been very successful in their suburban public school. "Our daughters are good students," she said. "They like their teachers, they are involved in sports and other activities. Now my daughter Sabrina is very excited about her class trip next month to (a Central American country) where she and her classmates will participate in service projects with a sister school." When teens are successful in school, mothers experience not only satisfaction but joy. One white working-class mother I interviewed, for example, reported that her daughter has always done well in school:

> When she was in third grade, her teacher recommended we have her tested for a mentally gifted program and she got in. She got involved in student council in grade school and went to a leadership weekend—like a four-day workshop for leadership— and ever since then, she's just, like, she's always been involved in school, she's a leader, we are so proud of her.

[8] L. Marrero, "Why School Counselors Matter" (Washington, DC: The Education Trust, 2019), https://edtrust.org/the-equity-line/why-school-counselors-matter/; M. Filardo, J. M. Vincent, and K. Sullivan, "How Crumbling School Facilities Perpetuate Inequality," *Phi Delta Kappan* 100(8) (2019): 27–31.

A working-class African American mother reported that her son is doing well in high school. "He's been a real good student," she said. "His high school loves him, they've recommended him for a special advanced program this summer, with computers. He likes school, he likes his teachers."

In this chapter, I present mothers' accounts of overseeing their teens' schooling during adolescence, including their work supporting their children's engagement in their studies, finding the best schools and programs for their teens, and helping them prepare for college or other post-high school training. Their accounts demonstrate the often-unrecognized challenges mothers face in working with their teens to promote their success in school, as well as the critical role resources play in this process.

Promoting Engagement

Mothers do important work to promote their teens' engagement in school and schoolwork. Students who are engaged in school and schoolwork not only perform their academic tasks better, they experience better mental health and fewer problem behaviors.[9]

Supporting Teens Who Are Stressed

As noted above, more than half of all high school students face difficulties completing their schoolwork due to stress.[10] Some students experience stress because they don't understand their schoolwork or they don't like their teacher. Over half of teens in the United States report that their biggest source of stress is their worry about getting into college. Over 60 percent report that they feel pressure to get good grades to get into college, more than twice as many who feel pressure to fit in socially or look good. Since more girls say they are planning to attend college, more of them report that they worry a lot about getting into the college of their choice.[11] Some teens can experience stress because they fear they won't be able to meet the expectations of their

---

[9] Pascoe, et al., "The Impact of Stress on Students in Secondary School and Higher Education."

[10] Horowitz and Graf, "Most U.S. Teens See Anxiety and Depression as a Major Problem Among Their Peers."

[11] Horowitz and Graf, "Most U.S. Teens See Anxiety and Depression as a Major Problem Among Their Peers."

parents, their teachers, or themselves.[12] During the COVID pandemic, many students experienced stress because they found online learning difficult. Some found the technology difficult to manage, some found it more difficult to learn on a computer screen, and many became sad or depressed because they were isolated from their friends.[13] Math and reading scores fell as a result.[14] Students can also feel stress due to bullying. Fifteen percent of students experience bullying—being made fun of, called names, insulted, or the subject of rumors; being pushed, shoved, tripped, or spit on; or being excluded from activities on purpose.[15] As described in the previous chapter, nearly half of US teens ages 13 to 17 report experiencing cyberbullying behaviors, being the subject of false rumors, being called offensive names online, and receiving unwanted explicit images.[16]

The upper-middle-class mothers in my sample reported that their teens are stressed about the college application process. Many of them hope their teens will be able to attend prestigious universities or liberal arts colleges, which they believe will help them gain acceptance to graduate school and secure the credentials they need to enter a profession. Research shows this to be the case. Compared with attending a flagship public college, attending a high-prestige college or university such as one in the Ivy League doubles a student's chance of attending an elite graduate school, gives a college student a three times greater chance of obtaining a job at a prestigious firm, and greatly increases their chances of joining the ranks of the top 1 percent of earners. The eight Ivy League universities are considered very prestigious and difficult to get into, as are the relatively small number of other prestigious universities and small colleges where admission is highly competitive.[17]

[12] J. O. Connor and D. C. Pope, "Not Just Robo-Students: Why Full Engagement Matters and How Schools Can Promote It," *Journal of Youth and Adolescence* 42 (2013): 1426–1442.

[13] D. Braga and K. Parker, "Most K-12 Parents Say First Year of Pandemic Had a Negative Effect on their Children's Education" (Washington, DC: Pew Research Center, 2022).

[14] M. Kuhfeld, J. Soland, K. Lewis, and M. Morton, "The Pandemic Has Had Devastating Impacts on Learning. What Will It Take To Help Students Catch Up?" (Washington, DC: The Brookings Institution, 2022).

[15] Bullying is defined as any unwanted aggressive behavior by a youth or group of youths who are not siblings or current dating partners. Bullying can be physical, psychological, or social, including cyberbullying online. Bullying is very likely to be repeated and can inflict harm or distress on those who are targeted. Centers for Disease Control and Prevention, "Youth Risk Behavior Surveillance System (YRBSS) Overview" (Atlanta: Centers for Disease Control and Prevention, 2023).

[16] E. A. Vogels, "Teens and Cyberbullying 2022" (Washington, DC: Pew Research Center, 2022).

[17] R. Chetty, D. J. Deming, and J. Friedman, "Diversifying Society's Leaders? The Determinants and Consequences of Admission to Highly Selective Colleges," *Opportunity Insights Non-Technical Research Summary* (Cambridge, MA: Harvard University, 2023).

Gaining acceptance at these competitive schools is challenging, the bar for admission to top highly rated colleges is high, even with excellent grades and high standardized test scores. Those from higher-income families have traditionally had an advantage in gaining admission to prestigious colleges over students with similar test scores. These colleges can also look favorably on students who are "legacies," children of alumni, who typically come from higher-income families, who are the children of donors, and who have engaged in athletics and extra-curricular activities at a high level, activities that require money to participate.[18]

Barbara, a white upper-middle-class mother with a 17-year-old son and a 12-year-old daughter, feels that her son, Michael, a high achiever, is pushing himself too hard. Michael attends a competitive high school and wants to go to a high-prestige university. Barbara is worried he could burn out, that his grades could fall, and that he would have to take a break from school, which she says would be very upsetting to him. Her description of her son fits the picture of an overworked, stressed high school student. She says he feels a lot of pressure to get into a top-ranked school, that Michael is "overextended, he's trying to do too much too well, he's so responsible." She continued, "Well, I might as well say it, he's very successful. He's president of student council, he's taking two Advanced Placement courses (courses that may qualify for college credit), he goes to some religion classes outside of school, he plays two sports—one each season, soccer and baseball—oh, and he does some volunteer work at a soup kitchen." Barbara said she wishes she could help Michael more:

> What I feel I can do is listen; my son needs to vent. He wants to process things and have me listen. I hope that takes some of the pressure off him, I'm not sure. I don't think I'm doing enough to deal with Michael's stress, but I don't know what else to do, I don't know how to slow Michael down.

---

[18] Students from the top 0.1 percent of households in income are two and a half times as likely to be admitted to a top college as students from less wealthy households with the same scores. Research shows that although attending an elite university doesn't increase a graduate's income on average, it does nearly double the chance of attending an elite graduate school and triples the chance of working at a prestigious firm. In this way, elite universities "amplify the persistence of privilege across generations." Chetty et al., "Diversifying Society's Leaders?" The 2018 Survey of College and University Admissions Directors found that 42 percent of admissions directors at private colleges and universities took legacy status into account in their admissions decisions compared to only 6 percent at public colleges and universities. See Inside Higher Ed, "The 2018 Survey of College and University Admissions Directors: A Study by Inside Higher Ed and Gallup," 2018, https://www.insidehighered.com/news/survey/2018-surveys-admissions-leaders-pressure-grows.

Barbara said she herself experiences stress as she supports Michael. This stress can be more difficult than what she experiences in her work as an administrator at a social service agency. She's hoping her younger son, a freshman in high school, won't experience as much stress. She said, "I think my younger son won't push himself so hard academically. He's active in the theater program at school, he might just want to go to our state university. That could be good, they have a strong drama program." Barbara concluded by saying she thinks teachers at her son's school give mixed messages. "They tell the kids, 'Just do your best' and, 'Go to a college that's a good fit, don't worry about prestige.' But then the expectations are extremely high, and those who get into top colleges are praised."

The mothers I interviewed experiment with different strategies to see what will help mitigate the stress their teens feel. They listen and work with them to create more manageable schedules. Several reported taking time off from work to help their teenager. Claire, a white middle-class mother, re-ported that her daughter, Jill, who is in the top academic track at her school, questions how smart she really is. Even though she is in ninth grade, Jill is already thinking about what she has to do to get into a highly ranked college and feels pressure to get good grades, knowing she will be applying for ad-mission to college in three years. Claire said that before upcoming tests, Jill starts talking about how she has to study more, how the work is hard, and how she doesn't think she'll do well on the test. Claire described using psy-chology to help her daughter deal with her anxiety:

> When Jill is anxious about a test coming up, one thing I do is to help her process what she's going through. I say, "OK, what's the worst case, what's the worst thing that could happen? Let's say you get a bad grade. Well, then what? You could talk to the teacher about doing some kind of extra credit." I try to get her to see there are ways to manage her stress.

Claire, a nurse, said she is glad that in her nursing courses, she learned how to help people think through a situation to deal with their fears and that this has helped her counsel her daughter. She noted, "A lot of it is their fear of the unknown and we talk it out and then Jill says she feels better, I hope so." Claire said she expects her efforts to help her daughter deal with stress will be ongoing. As she said, "So after we talk, Jill seems to feel better, but when she has another test coming up, she gets nervous again. I'll help her as I can."

Mothers reported helping teens with a variety of other kinds of stress as well. Teens may not like some of their classes, and they may feel pressure from their teachers. Mildred, a white upper-middle-class mother, reported that her 17-year-old daughter, Ruth, became overwhelmed by schoolwork and extracurricular activities and had fallen behind. Mildred said she and her husband didn't realize how much stress Ruth was experiencing until she got a call at work one day from Ruth's assistant principal, who said Ruth had left school without telling anyone. Mildred said, "I was really worried. I called Ruth's cell, and she didn't answer at first. But thank goodness she called when she got home, she was crying." Mildred said, "I left work and went right home. We immediately sat down and talked about what had happened." She continued:

A lot of things came out, like that she had just been given more assignments, that she had chorus rehearsals, that she didn't have anyone to go to the prom with. She said she didn't want to go to this school anymore, her teachers didn't understand, there was too much pressure, on and on.

Mildred said she and her husband talked with Ruth for a long time: "I said to her, 'Look, we'll help you figure things out.' We helped her prioritize the things she had to do for school, we got some ideas for the prom, I think she felt a lot better." Mildred said she will keep working with Ruth on managing stress; she sees this as an "ongoing project." She said this event was taxing for her too: "This was tiring, and I was stressed." As she went to work the day after this incident, Mildred said she continued to worry about her daughter and tried to think of more things she could do to help her. She also said she is planning to speak to her supervisor and request to work more hours from home so she can spend more time with Ruth when she comes home from school. She thinks this will be possible, that there are other administrators at her bank who are working more hours from home.

Johnetta, a working-class African American mother, reported helping her daughter, Latoya, with another source of stress, bullying. Latoya was "very stressed out" because she was being bullied, a problem that, as noted above, a fifth of all students in the US experience in schools. Johnetta said Latoya experienced bullying from some girls at her mostly all-Black school who started making demeaning comments about Latoya's clothes and hair, calling her "stupid," and excluding her from their friendship group. When Latoya's grades began to drop and she said she wouldn't go back to school and that she hated it, Johnetta reached out to the principal. Johnetta had a positive experience working with the principal. She reported, "I'm lucky, he got it. It all took some time and negotiations, but he was actually able to get Latoya transferred to a nearby school in the same school system." Johnetta said, "It's a smaller school, and the principal there says he'll make sure one of the counselors meets with Latoya and checks up on her, that makes me happy, I'm hopeful that Latoya will start to feel better about going to school."

Promoting Motivation

Researchers have found low levels of student engagement and excitement in American schools that begin in adolescence, with higher rates reported among boys. Before the pandemic, students spent over a quarter of their waking hours each week in school or school-related activities.[19] Some students become bored with classes they are not interested in. Some find it more difficult to connect with their teachers and feel a sense of belonging.[20] These issues were seriously aggravated during the recent pandemic, when remote learning and the closure of schools led a number of students to become more disengaged from their academic work and from the structure and routines of in-person education. Some found it more difficult to get help from their teachers, and as noted above, some found it difficult to learn on a computer screen, and had technical difficulties with their computer software.[21]

Students attending smaller, more personalized schools do better academically than students who attend larger schools that generally have higher student-teacher ratios and fewer counselors to help students with academic and personal challenges.[22] Boys do not perform as well in school as girls, spend less time reading and more time playing video games, and they are 8 percent more likely than girls to report that school is a waste of time.[23] Researchers have offered various explanations for why this gender disparity exists. Some have argued that boys are influenced by traditional norms of masculinity that discourage academic achievement; they may instead favor

---

[19] L. Steinberg, *Adolescence* (New York: McGraw-Hill Education, 2020), 159.

[20] Moellera et al., "High School Students' Feelings."

[21] Braga and Parker, "Most K-12 Parents Say First Year of Pandemic Had a Negative Effect on Their Children's Education."

[22] Connor and Pope, "Not Just Robo-Students."

[23] Organisation for Economic Co-operation and Development, "The ABC of Gender Equality in Education: Aptitude, Behaviour, Confidence" (Paris: OECD, 2015).

action-oriented activities, including sports, over academic activities. Others believe that the brain development of boys is two to three years behind that of girls, which disadvantages them when it comes to school performance.[24]

Mothers take a variety of actions to increase their teens' engagement in school and their motivation to complete their schoolwork. They cajole and pressure them to complete assignments. Some try reasoning while others lecture. Some resort to nagging, although they don't feel it is effective. Mothers pressure teens to get help from teachers, they quiz teens on material, and they help them with memorization. Some spoke of checking whether their teens have done their homework and other assignments. Mothers also help teens get material for research, taking them to libraries and talking with them about organizing and prioritizing their work. Depending on their time and comfort level with school topics, mothers may read a history report or help teens memorize a poem. They may also arrange for extra tutoring or alert teachers to their teens' problems. When their children don't do their schoolwork, mothers can apply pressure by denying them privileges until they do—for example, by preventing their teen children from socializing with friends until their assignments are done.

Sometimes mothers are able to see that their teens become more engaged. Meredith, a white upper-middle-class mother whose daughter, Cecilia, is a sophomore at a private school, reported that Cecilia recently stopped handing in schoolwork. Meredith didn't know why. As she said:

> Cecilia has always done well in school, but recently, things haven't been going well. We're having issues over her homework. We started to get notices from one of her teachers saying, "I didn't get Cecilia's project on [subject matter]," or, "This project was really late." We started asking Cecilia about it. She's always like, "I'll get it done."
>
> I don't know what's up. She's always done her homework, but I think this year, they have more projects where there's a deadline further along. Like she's always had no trouble just doing her homework each night.

Meredith proposed that she go with Cecilia and talk to her teacher, but Cecilia resisted this idea. Meredith said she insisted. She pushed her

---

[24] For the brain development of boys, see R. V. Reeves, *Of Boys and Men: Why the Modern Male is Struggling, Why It Matters, and What To Do About It* (Washington, DC: Brookings Institution Press, 2022). Lundberg argues that norms of masculinity discourage academic achievement. S. Lundberg, "Educational Gender Gaps," *Southern Economic Journal* 7 (2020: 416–439).

daughter, and they had the meeting, and it turned out to be productive. Cecilia's teacher was helpful; she explained what assignments were coming up and helped Cecilia organize a schedule for completing them. Meredith reported that Cecilia seems more organized now and is doing her work again. Meredith has not been receiving notices of late assignments from Cecilia's teacher.

Jane, a white working-class mother with two sons, one a junior in high school and the other who is 24, said that her younger son began getting poor grades in 9th grade. She said, "My younger son got Fs in ninth grade, and he was cutting class. My older son did the same thing." Jane reported addressing her son's failure to do his work in a more direct way than other mothers. She said:

> I yelled, I'm a yeller. I yelled at them, "You're wasting your life." I said, "You don't have to be like me, you can be anything you want—a doctor, a lawyer." I don't want him to be like people in this neighborhood. People here do nothing. There are 25-year-olds who hang around on the playground, who have no jobs.

But then Jane said, "In tenth grade, things got better. Now my younger son wants to go to college. Not like just the community college around here, he wants to go to [public university in another state]." She continued, "My husband credits us for encouraging our son and pushing him. I'm not sure that's what did it. I don't know what turned him around, but now he's doing his work."

The following cases show the kinds of efforts some mothers make to obtain more time to help their teens who are having difficulties with their studies by making changes in their work schedules and placements. In two cases, mothers reported that their daughters started doing poorly in school. In a third case, described below, a girl refused to go to school at all. Two of the mothers were able to work with supervisors at their jobs to rearrange their work schedules and get more time to help their daughters. In each case, these mothers' efforts helped their teens become more engaged with their schoolwork. Alicia, an African American working-class mother who works as an assistant to the manager of a small nursing home, recently learned that her daughter, Dairisha, a sophomore in high school, had started to fail several subjects in school. Alicia said she didn't know why. She pushed her daughter to do better in school but, as she noted, "None of it was working.

I told her it was fine if she thought I was too hard on her or she couldn't work with me, she could go work with one of my sisters." Alicia said, "I was so frustrated I just started yelling. I said, 'If you want to fail, you will. If not, you're going to have to work really hard to pull up your grades.'"

Alicia then tried another strategy to turn her daughter's school performance around. She said, "I took personal days off from work, the ones I had coming to me. I had saved some up so I was able to take some time with Dairisha. I worked with her at home. I had her read to me from her schoolbooks while I was cooking dinner, and then I had her repeat back to me what she had learned. I helped her make appointments with teachers to discuss her situation." Alicia said her daughter slowly started to do better and her grades went up.

Alicia was grateful she was able to use her personal days to help her daughter, but now she is left with another challenge. She had expected to use her personal days to care for her partner. She said, "He's got to have surgery. He got injured when he fell off a ladder at his construction job." But Alicia used up her personal days to help Dairisha, and she used up most of her sick days earlier in the year when she was recovering from her own surgery. Because she has already used all her sick days for this half of the year, she was hoping her supervisor would allow her to start using sick days for the half-year period that was coming up. Alicia said she is trying to arrange all this while helping another family member: "My grandmother is very sick. I go over to my mother's house where my grandmother lives, and I help them with shopping and laundry; my uncle does too. I have to say being at home is like being at work."

Nan, an upper-middle-class white mother with an 18-year-old son and 15-year-old daughter, who works as a full-time remedial Language Arts teacher at a large urban high school, also took steps to change her work situation to help her daughter, Suzanna. Suzanna, a sophomore at another public high school, started complaining that she didn't like school. Nan said she needed to step in:

> I realized I had to start spending more time with Suzanna—she needed more time from me, she wasn't getting enough. She was doing her schoolwork but her grades started to go down and she was acting out, getting a bad attitude, saying she didn't care about school, she didn't like her teachers.

Nan says she tried to spend more time with Suzanna at the end of the day and find out how things were going at school. However, time was limited and Suzanna did not necessarily want to talk about school at the end of the day. Suzanna's afternoons were busy with soccer practices. Nan's job required her to hold in-person meetings with students three afternoons a week after classes ended. She also had a 45-minute commute.

Nan says she loved her job, she hadn't been planning to leave it, but to help her daughter she decided she needed to. Before the end of the school year she met with the school superintendent to ask if she could be transferred in the fall to another school in the same school system, one that was much closer to where they lived. He agreed. It wasn't that difficult to arrange this, Nan said; she knows the superintendent and had worked with him before. She was lucky, she said; there was an opening in the school she wanted to go to. And Nan says that her job in the new school is going "OK" so far.

Now, Nan says, on some days, she can come home and pick up Suzanna at her school and take her to her soccer practices, which are at a different school, rather than her daughter having to take a long bus ride. During these times, Nan says Susanna will sometimes talk more openly when it is just the two of them together. She says Susanna has begun to talk to her more about what is upsetting her. "Susanna says she's been feeling bad, she feels a lot of pressure to do well in school, that it's really important to her to get good grades, but she's been having a really hard time with math, it was getting harder and harder." Nan said she urged Suzanna to talk to her teacher, but according to Nan, "She didn't want to talk to her teacher because she didn't want the teacher to think she wasn't smart or couldn't do the math. And she was afraid that if she did poorly in math, it would ruin her chances of getting into a college she wanted to attend." Nan says she tried to keep the conversation going over several days. She also told Susanna that if she wanted, they would get her a tutor. Susanna finally agreed to talk to her teacher and said she would think about whether she wanted a tutor.

Both Alicia and Nan are engaged in a significant amount of work to support their daughters academically. This work included not only spending more time with their teens to help them with schoolwork but also negotiating with supervisors and arranging their work schedules for more time to help their teens. They both felt fortunate they were able to arrange things to get more time with their daughters. However, Alicia has had to use personal days to help her daughter, and Nan has left her preferred job.

The case of Rose, an African American working-class mother who worked as a teacher's aide before leaving her job to care for her ailing mother, shows how difficult and stressful it can be to get a student back on track and the time and effort it can take. Rose reported that in the middle of eleventh grade, her daughter, Seraphina, refused to go to school. Rose engaged in extended efforts to help her and was ultimately successful in getting her back to school, though this was a lengthy, trying, process. She said, "I walked her to the bus every morning. We'd get there and Seraphina would say she didn't want to go to school and she'd turn around and come back." Rose said, "I tried to get her to go to all kinds of programs and she wouldn't go." She said she then insisted that Seraphina go with her to see the school counselor, but when they did, "Seraphina acted like she didn't care, you know, like she just didn't care." According to Rose:

> I wasn't getting anywhere with Seraphina. I don't know if it was depression or what, she wouldn't tell me. I tried to find out, but she wouldn't tell me. I kept saying, "Why are you so sad? What's wrong? What happened?"

Rose also noted, "I kept in touch with her teachers, I let them know I was doing everything I could think of to get Seraphina back to school. I talked to the counselor a lot, and I tried to get her into a special evening program."

After several weeks of trying to get Seraphina to return to school, Rose decided to pull back and stop trying to figure out what she could do. "I backed off for a while," she said, "Then I don't know what happened, but a little while after that, Seraphina agreed to go into the high school evening program. It's for kids who want to work at a job in the day and go to school at night." Rose said she still doesn't know why Seraphina decided to go back to school. She thinks she may have changed her mind because she had a friend who told her that the evening program was "Okay." Rose concluded by saying, "You never know who they'll listen to. They definitely don't always listen to their mother."

Limitations on Mothers' Ability to Help Teens

In some cases, the mothers I interviewed reported that they have spent considerable time trying to make their teens work up to their potential, but so far, their teens have not become more motivated to do their schoolwork. These cases involve boys who, as noted above, are more likely to become disengaged from school during adolescence. In each case, mothers said that their sons were capable of doing well in their schoolwork, and that their teachers had confirmed they did not have learning differences that might be hindering their ability to do schoolwork. Leah is a white middle-class mother with two sons (ages 15 and 13). She said that her older son, Ben, tests well and was accepted at a more competitive public high school. But she said that he is "a procrastinator" and can sometimes be lazy. As she phrased it, "He says that himself, he's very honest but it doesn't necessarily make things easier." She said, "My husband Arnie and I get really frustrated with Ben."

Leah said she engages in extensive negotiations with Ben to try and increase his motivation to do his schoolwork. She said she tries reasoning, a common strategy of middle-class mothers who engage in "concerted cultivation."[25] However, thus far this strategy has not been working. As she said, "I want to talk things out with Ben and reason with him, I don't use punishments or grounding or things like that, I don't think they really work. I talk, I argue—Arnie does too." Leah contrasted herself with friends who, she said, "act like helicopter parents. They go through their kids' notebooks and say, 'Did you do this, did you do that?'" But Leah said, "I think that's going too far."

Leah described a recent incident that shows the limits of reasoning as a strategy to motivate someone like her son. She had an extended talk with Ben after he came home from school and said that he had flunked one test and that he might have flunked another. Leah said she dropped everything, stopped cooking dinner, told Arnie to come to the kitchen, and told Ben to sit down. Building on their knowledge of their son and what they had learned from extensive negotiations with him in the past, Leah said she and Arnie argued with Ben for a long time. They tried to use persuasion to counter his arguments. Leah said, "Ben said that he hadn't studied very much, that that was reason that he had flunked the test." Leah said she told him, "You're talking on the phone too much, that's part of the reason you are not studying." And Ben said, "Well I'm a teenager." Then Leah said she told him, "Well, that doesn't carry much weight with me, I don't accept that. So you're a teenager, that might mean something, but it's not that you're really different."

---

[25] A. Lareau, *Unequal Childhoods: Class, Race, and Family Life Second Edition With an Update a Decade Later* (Berkeley: University of California Press, 2011).

Leah said that at one point Ben asked she and Arnie if there could be a reward for doing his schoolwork: "Like, if we could give him things when he
does well, like money or sneakers. Ben says, 'Then I'll be thinking that I have
to work on this to get better sneakers, I know I'll get sneakers if I do well.'"
Leah and Arnie have agreed they will not be giving rewards for schoolwork.
"I told Ben, 'First of all, you're talking about sneakers, the kind you like are
very expensive. If you want that kind of thing, you should be thinking about
your future.'" As Leah put it, she tried to convince her son that doing well in
school could help him get good things in the future:

> I told Ben, "We don't want to play games about rewards, that's an ex-
> ternal thing. This has to come from you. You're going to have to figure out
> what motivates you, we can't do it. Look, do well in school and get us off
> your back."

Leah said she also talks to Ben's teachers, who say they are doing what they
can to motivate him, but she says they are frustrated too.

The challenges Leah details indicate the limits of mothers' and fathers' influence and control when their teens refuse to apply themselves seriously to
their schoolwork. Leah said, "I feel like I don't want to be bitching at him all
the time, nagging. And sometimes I do find myself nagging at him—did you
do this, did you do that? I don't want to be doing that, I feel like I'm forced
to be that way, and I don't like it. It's not effective. My kids say, 'There she
goes, she's nagging.'" As Leah described the situation, for the moment, Ben
is not taking her and Arnie's advice and doing what they think he must do to
succeed. Acknowledging the limits of her power, Leah said that for now, she
and Arnie have done what they can: "I've asked Ben, 'So what are we going
to do now—what can we do to help you, what can the school do to help you?'
I haven't heard an answer." She said, "We have to pull back and let go of this
for a while." Leah said she hopes Ben will "come to his senses" and realize
that to meet his goals he has to do well in school. She said her son "will have
to figure this out on his own."

Like Leah, some mothers pull back on their efforts, letting go because they
no longer feel effective. Their strategies, including providing rewards for
doing schoolwork, aren't working. Trish, a white middle-class mother with
three children (ages 17, 15, and 13), said two of her children are very responsible about their schoolwork and usually get it done on time, but her son John
does not. She said, "John is smart, he doesn't have any learning challenges,

but he just doesn't study much for tests, he doesn't care if he gets C grades when his teacher says he should be getting A's, and he failed a course." Trish said that mostly she has to handle this situation by herself. "My husband," she noted, "is real helpful, we parent together a lot, but he is a manager at a construction site, he has to be out the door at 6:00 a.m. every morning, and at night he's really tired."

Trish has tried a variety of strategies to motivate John. As she said, "Every night I say, 'Okay, who's got homework? Do you need any help?' Every night John says no." Trish has also offered her son incentives to help him get into a program she thinks would interest him, if he will do his schoolwork.

> John is interested in sports—he's not athletic but he loves to watch sports. I saw an ad for a summer program for teens where they could learn about sports journalism. He could work with TV stations on sports. I've said to John, "We'll pay for you to go to that program but you need to do more schoolwork." But no, nothing.

Trish said she has thought about whether offering John a reward would make a difference. She even briefly considered whether or not to give him the Christmas present he wanted if he didn't pull up his grades but would have felt guilty not giving him a gift:

> I said to my kids, "What do you want for Christmas—just do well in school." So my younger son got very good marks and he got the drum set he wanted. John didn't get good marks. But he got a skateboard, that's what he wanted. I would have felt too guilty not giving a gift to him and giving gifts to the other kids. He's still my kid. But he'll have to get a kick in the butt. He's a tough one. Sometimes I think, what does he think we are, stupid?

Laughing, Trish concluded, "He needs someone to smack him in the face. Like the army, that's where he needs to go."

At this point, Trish said she has "run out of things to try," however. Like some other mothers I interviewed, she is going to let John suffer the consequences of not doing his schoolwork. She said she has "fought with him" about it long enough: "Maybe you can say this is a cop-out, but I've decided I've got to let go of this, he's just got to fail. Maybe that's a cop-out, but I've tried everything. He'll just have to fail and repeat a grade." Trish did say that perhaps John learned something recently. "He had an incident in school where a teacher failed him on a paper, and he was upset," she said. "He said the teacher hadn't really explained the assignment. Well, I'm sure it's not the teacher's fault. I'm glad he was upset, maybe that will put some sense into his head."

Maxine, a middle-class African American mother, reported that her daughter Zahara, who is in ninth grade in her local public school, has been perceived by her teacher (who is white) as being unmotivated. Maxine met with Zahara's teacher and pointed out that her daughter is doing her school-work. She said, "I met with Zahara's teacher. She told me she doesn't think Zahara is trying hard enough in school." Maxine feels her daughter has been unfairly perceived as not motivated. She said, "I met with the teacher and told her that Zahara does care about school and reminded her that Zahara has been handing in her assignments." Maxine said the problem is that Zahara feels pressure from classmates to show a tough exterior in school. According to Maxine, her daughter is not rude to the teacher, but she doesn't communicate with her much. Maxine says Zahara feels she can't be seen as liking school too much or she'll be labeled a "teacher's pet."

Maxine also worries about racially based perceptions of African American students. She noted, "Black mothers like me really have to watch that our kids are not stereotyped and treated differently. I'm afraid my daughter could be punished unfairly." Maxine's fears are realistic; African American students' behavior faces more scrutiny than other students, and they are disciplined for minor disciplinary infractions more frequently than white students.[26]

Trouble: Truancy, Suspension, Expulsion

Some teens break school rules, which can lead them to get into serious trouble. In my sample, for instance, two white teens from upper-middle-class families were suspended from school for 10 days—one for smoking mari-juana and one for what the school termed an incident of "excessive drinking of alcohol." Both incidents occurred on school grounds. A third student, who had previously been sanctioned for smoking marijuana, was caught doing it a second time and was suspended for six months. The two students were able to return to school. They were given makeup work to do while they

[26] J. D. Del Toro M. and Wang, "The Roles of Suspensions for Minor Infractions and School Climate in Predicting Academic Performance Among Adolescents," *American Psychologist* 77(2) (2022): 173–185.

missed their classes, so it did not take long for them to catch up. One of these students was a senior. The colleges he had applied to were informed of the suspension. As a result, although he did get into a college, he was rejected at his first choice.

Two other students, white middle-class teens, were suspended from their local high school for drug use and underage drinking. In one case, a high school junior invited a half dozen school classmates to her house on a Saturday afternoon when her parents were not home, and a neighbor saw them drinking beer in the backyard. The neighbor called the police, the school was informed, and the girl was suspended for two weeks and warned that there would be a more severe punishment if this happened again. As I described in the previous chapter, in another case, a school counselor discovered that a girl had become addicted to drugs. She was suspended for two weeks, and when she returned to school, her parents and the school counselor monitored her behavior closely and worked together to help her recover from her addiction.

While mothers from all social classes may face teens who are seriously disengaged from school, teens—and particularly boys—from lower-income and Black and Hispanic families have higher rates of truancy and are more likely to drop out of school.[27] They attend larger schools, where it is harder to get personal attention and solid academic preparation. As noted above, teens of color face the additional challenge of attending schools where racial bias—some unconscious, some not—can result in increased surveillance of their behavior and harsher penalties for infractions.[28] While boys and students with disabilities generally experience disproportionate levels of disciplinary actions against them, African American students, who account for

[27] Truancy is defined as a failure to reach school or stay at school in the absence of school permission or a valid excuse for 15 days a year. Rates of truancy rose during the pandemic and remain at high levels, although levels had been rising before the pandemic. The national average rate of chronic absenteeism increased from 15 percent in 2019 to 28 percent in 2022, and remained high in 2023. N. Malkus, "Long COVID for Public Schools: Chronic Absenteeism Before and After the Pandemic," American Enterprise Institute, January 31, 2024, https://www.aei.org/wp-content/uploads/2024/01/Long-COVID-for-Public-Schools.pdf?x85095. Students who are truant are at risk of dropping out of high school. In 2021, the average high school dropout rate for all 16- to 24-year-olds (those who are not enrolled in school and do not have a diploma or alternative credential) was 5.2 percent, with higher rates for Hispanic students (7.8 percent) than Black (5.9 percent), white (4.1 percent), and Asian (4.7 percent) students. This rate includes all dropouts, no matter when or where they last went to school. Students from poorer families, communities, and schools are also more likely to drop out than other students. See the Education Data Initiative at https://educationdata.org/high-school-dropout-rate (accessed February 28, 2024).
[28] A. E. Lewis and J. B. Diamond, *Despite the Best Intentions* (New York: Oxford University Press, 2015).

15.5 percent of public school students, account for 39 percent of the students who are suspended from school.[29] At the same time, in terms of overall graduation rates, 88 percent of African Americans earn a high school diploma, which is close to the national average.[30]

In my sample, two working-class mothers reported that their teens are not attending school. Not attending school can lead to dropping out permanently, which in turn can result in serious economic and personal challenges in adult life.[31] Alberta is a divorced working-class African American mother of two sons (ages 15 and 20). Her older son graduated from high school and is doing well in his job at a construction company. Alberta is very worried about her younger son, Shawn, a sophomore in high school, whom she no longer seems to have control over. It's not clear how the trouble for Shawn began, but he is now suspended from school for truancy and must meet weekly with a probation officer. Alberta said that he has been in trouble and cutting classes since he entered high school. She noted, "They cut in the building to meet with friends in places where it's harder to find them." She has continually been in touch with the school's assistant principal to try to get Shawn back on track. She said, "I keep asking him, 'Can't you do anything else about this?' He said they are trying but then he talks about how many kids they have to deal with. He doesn't sound optimistic at all." Alberta thinks it's a big problem that Shawn "hangs around with the wrong crowd," and she thinks that he and his friends "just go to school for socializing." Alberta said Shawn is currently repeating ninth grade, and she is worried that he will not pass again this year:

> The school keeps calling me. I have to take the bus all the way up there with me not feeling well and hypertension. My older son didn't get into trouble like this, he graduated from high school, but my younger son has always been into mischief since he was young. I've always had to stay on him. I don't know, maybe he has the traits of their father. His father is more carefree.

[29] US Government Accountability Office, "K-12 Education: Discipline Disparities for Black Students, Boys, and Students with Disabilities" (Washington, DC: US Government Accountability Office, 2018).

[30] Hanson, "College Dropout Rate," Education Data Initiative, 2023, https://educationdata.org/college-dropout-rates.

[31] J. Gubbels, C. E. van der Put, and M. Assink, "Risk Factors for School Absenteeism and Dropout: A Meta-Analytic Review," *Journal of Youth and Adolescence* 48(9) (2019): 1637–1667.

Alberta continues, "I've tried everything, I haven't been able to work because I have to deal with Shawn and try to keep him from getting into more trouble." She said, "I've talked to Shawn until I'm blue in the face, it's a power struggle. It was a lot easier when they were younger." Alberta also believes that "It's not just that a boy needs a male figure because my son spends regular time with his father." She said her ex-husband tells her he is concerned as well, "But his attitude is basically this is your job. He just wants our son to go to the racetrack with him." Alberta said, "I also went to the truancy office. They're down in [another part of the city]. I've been there, I've talked to them to see if there's anything they can do but nothing happens." Alberta concluded by saying, "I've had a lot of stress. Around the time I had the stroke, there was a lot going on. My father had prostate cancer and I was running back and forth helping him."

One white working-class mother reported that her son will not go back to school because he is afraid of experiencing violence. He says there are too many students who get into physical fights, a problem at some inner-city schools. She is angry because she says the school is not doing enough to curb the violence. She, her husband, and her son are looking for alternative schooling.[32]

A working-class single mother, who is white, reported that her son started missing classes when his school switched to remote teaching during the pandemic. As a nurse's aid, she had to spend long hours at the hospital where she works and only had limited time to help her son with his online courses, which he found difficult to follow. When her son's school opened back up, she went to see his teachers and explained that her son would need help catching up on his schoolwork. She is worried, she says he is still struggling to catch up.

Finding Schools and Other Resources

In addition to working directly with their teen children, mothers also said they work to find good schools and programs that can promote their teens'

---

[32] In 2021, 9 percent of high school students did not go to school because they felt unsafe either at school or on their way to or from school at least once during the past 30 days. Seven percent of high school students were threatened or injured with a weapon, such as a gun, knife, or club, on school property. Centers for Disease Control and Prevention Prevention, 2023, "Youth Risk Behavior Surveillance System (YRBSS) Overview."

success in school. They investigate public, private, and religious schools and try to find those that have a good reputation and that are more likely to keep their teens engaged with their schoolwork. In the United States, however, there are stark differences in schools and educational opportunities for teens based on their social class and racial background. Eighty-two percent of students in the United States attend public schools, which are primarily funded by local property taxes. Given that neighborhoods are highly segregated by class and race, the school systems that families in lower-income neighborhoods can access are able to pay far less per pupil than districts that are better off.[33] In the wake of the Great Recession, school district funding for schools decreased. Additionally, state and local governments, which provide some funding for schools, have made cutbacks, and in some cases, these have been severe.[34]

Among the mothers I interviewed, those with resources are able to customize their search for good schools and choose those that will fit their teens' particular needs. Parents who live in the suburbs can move to neighborhoods with more resources, where residents pay higher property taxes for schools that in turn spend more per pupil, have more counselors and qualified teachers, and offer more advanced courses. Upper-middle-class and middle-class mothers who live in the city can face more challenges, but they often see to it that their teens attend the better public schools. There are different levels of city public schools. There are neighborhood schools where all are admitted, citywide schools that require good grades and test scores for admission, and a smaller number of highly selective magnet schools. At the time of my interviews, most of the children of upper-middle-class families were able to gain admission to more selective schools based on their records.[35]

---

[33] In 2021, 81.9 percent of students were enrolled in public schools and 12.8 percent of K-12 students were enrolled in private schools. J. Fabina, E. L. Hernandez, and K. McElrath, "School Enrollment in the United States: 2021," American Community Survey Reports (Washington, DC: US Census Bureau, June 8, 2023). Funding for schools in the US comes primarily from state and local resources and is generally inadequate and inequitable. Levels of school funding vary widely, with high-poverty districts getting less funding per student than low-poverty districts. S. Allegretto, E. García, and E. Weiss, "Public Education Funding in the U.S. Needs an Overhaul" (Washington, DC: Economic Policy Institute, July 12, 2022). In the United States, the wealthiest school districts receive 7 percent more per pupil in state and local funding than the lowest poverty school districts. Funding for school districts with the fewest students of color is two times greater than funding for districts with the most students of color. I. Morgan and A. Amerikaner, "Funding Gaps: An Analysis of School Funding Equity Across the U.S. and Within Each State" (Washington, DC: The Education Trust, 2018).

[34] K. Shores and M. Steinberg, "Fiscal Federalism and K–12 Education Funding: Policy Lessons from Two Educational Crises," Educational Researcher 51(8) (2022): 551–558.

[35] Due to a recent change that occurred after the interviews for this book were completed, upper-middle-class families can no longer be sure their teens will secure a placement in one of the more

Upper-Middle-Class Mothers

The upper-middle-class mothers I interviewed want their teens to attend schools that will both provide them with a good education, and will also help them gain admission to more highly ranked colleges and universities and hopefully secure well-paying jobs. They can customize school choice to find a school that matches their teens' strengths and abilities. Upper-middle-class families in the city send their children to private schools or to the selective public schools. They have been able to secure schooling for their children at the elementary and middle school level that can help them gain admission to selective magnet schools. These schools in turn have the resources to give more attention to individual students, which increases the likelihood that their students will attend college. The private schools in particular often have attractive campuses, good science labs, and educational enrichment trips abroad. In interviews, upper-middle-class mothers noted that the cost of sending their teens to private school was high, but they had decided to make their teens' attendance at a private school a priority. Those who live in the suburbs have chosen jurisdictions with good public schools that are financed by high property taxes. They research a town's school system before moving, or if they know people in the area, they rely on their social networks to get information about local schools and their quality—their reputation, students' SAT scores, and college placement data, including not only a school's college acceptance rates but information about which colleges or universities graduates of particular high schools attend.

The ease with which upper-middle-class mothers spoke of choosing schools that would both provide high quality instruction and meet the particular needs of their teens was striking. Judith, a white mother, said her daughter is experiencing a lot of stress in her current school. Even though Judith and her husband live in a suburban district with a good public school, after consulting their daughter, they recently decided she would be better off enrolling in a nearby private school, where they hope she will experience less stress. Judith did not report financial considerations in making this decision:

---

selective city schools. The school system recently switched to a lottery system as a way to provide more equal access to the better schools. Students must still have some academic credentials to gain admission to a school they have been accepted at through the lottery system, but currently, no group is guaranteed access to the better schools. Many parents are not happy with the system. School system authorities say they will work to make improvements to the system.

Our daughter is a very good student. She studies a lot, she is shy, she has all kinds of wonderful interests in literature and theater. But she was considered a nerd in the public school. It was very hard on her, she was getting so stressed out.

Judith said it was her daughter who made the final decision because "the smart kids have to hide that they are smart. It's not cool to be smart in that public school, and it made my daughter anxious." Judith said her daughter chose a boarding school that offered advanced courses she was interested in.

Elaine, an African American mother of a 14-year-old daughter and a 10-year-old son, worked to find a less stressful school for her daughter and was able to find one. The family lives in a neighborhood with high taxes that fund several good public schools. Because the school system allows for some choice, Elaine was able to get her daughter moved from one public school to another as a way to help her daughter feel less anxious. She said:

The new school is so much better, it's night and day. I really, really didn't like the crowd in her other school. It was cliquish and too many girls were just interested in clothes and boys. The new school is much better, it has a diversity of kids from different backgrounds and it's not so cliquish.

Elaine said her daughter also has more motivation now. As she noted, "She says she is happier and is doing well in her classes. She kind of fell through the cracks at the other school, she just got Bs, she wasn't very motivated."

Lee, a white mother with a 10-year-old daughter and a 15-year-old son, Steve, said her son has become "bored" with his public school. She is helping Steve apply to a private boarding school. Lee reported, "Steve tells me he is getting less interested in school, and I think he's starting to slack off at his schoolwork. He says, 'I know it's supposed to be a good school, but the classes are big and I feel like some of them are really boring. I don't really like the school.'" Lee said, "I went to a few of his classes and I got bored [laughing]." She continued, "The boarding school Steve will be going to is wonderful, it has really interesting programs and smaller classes, I don't think he'll be bored." Lee did not mention any difficulties in paying for this boarding school.

In one case, a white mother spoke of switching her daughter, a freshman at a small private school, to a larger private school. She said, "My husband and I didn't think our daughter was putting enough effort into her classes because she wasn't being challenged." She talked with her daughter about this, and her daughter agreed to go to the larger school. Joy said her daughter is very bright, and Joy thinks she needs to be more challenged academically, which would happen in a school with a "bigger pool." At first their daughter was a little behind in the new school, but Joy and her husband engaged tutors who were suggested by the new school, and they helped their daughter catch up with her studies. Joy and her husband are very pleased. She said, "After she caught up, she started making the honor roll, and she made it for the whole year. She was pretty happy about this."

Lorraine, a white mother, was able to use her ability to secure good schooling to forestall what she saw as potential trouble by moving her son, Albert, who was in ninth grade, to a different school. She was afraid that even though her son was attending a public school with a good academic reputation, Albert had started to associate with "the wrong crowd." She said, "I could just see the changes happening. I got a call from the assistant principal, Albert had signed a letter from students criticizing a teacher who they thought was giving too much homework. I think one of Albert's friends had pressured him into it, I don't know, I don't think that was a good thing to do." After this incident, Lorraine and her husband moved Albert to a well-regarded private school. She said he might have been all right in his old school, though as she noted, "He might have gone the other way. He might have stayed with that group; you just don't know and we didn't want to take a chance."

In addition to providing advantages to their teens by customizing their selection of schools, some upper-middle-class parents are able to gain advantages for their children within schools due to their greater knowledge of how educational institutions work, and their willingness to intervene on behalf of their teens with school administrators and teachers and administrators.[36] Ellen, the mother of a ninth grader named Sarah, said she and her husband were very concerned that when their daughter entered ninth grade at her highly regarded public school, she was put in a middle track in math. Ellen said Sarah's grades in math went down in eighth grade because she was experiencing more fatigue than usual after contracting a mild case of mononucleosis, but by the school year's end, she had begun to

---

[36] A. Lareau and A. Cox, "Social Class and the Transition to Adulthood: Differences in Parents' Interactions with Institutions," in *Social Class and Changing Families in an Unequal America*, ed. M. Carlson and P. England (Stanford, CA: Stanford University Press, 2011), 134–164.

pull her grades back up. Ellen said, "We didn't want Sarah to get permanently tracked into a lower academic level, that can happen, she would have started to get behind." Ellen says she and her husband contacted the chairman of the math department and said that they thought their daughter should be placed in a higher track. She said:

> We explained that we were sure Sarah could perform well in the higher track, we had her grades and standardized test scores with us and we were able to show that her grades dipped while she was sick. We said we could get a tutor for her so she could catch up. The math department chair didn't seem completely convinced about what we said. I don't know if he saw us as interfering but he said, "All right, we'll give it a try." The thing is, we don't want to take any chances.

Ellen and her husband are very aware of the competitive requirements of the academic world they think Sarah might be entering. Looking into the future, Ellen said, "Sarah might want to go into science or medicine, you have to take top-level math and science courses. You can't fall behind in high school."

Middle-Class Mothers

Most middle-class mothers in my sample have some ability to choose schooling for their children and teens. Middle-class mothers who live in the suburban community whom I interviewed send their children and teens to their community's public schools, which they consider adequate. In some cases, there may be a Catholic school in a neighboring town that a few families send their teens to when they feel their teens need an environment they believe will provide more discipline. Middle-class mothers in the city have some school choice, including among some highly ranked schools. Some have the resources to send their children to Catholic schools, although they say that the more exclusive private schools are too expensive for them. Other mothers debate about whether to move to the suburbs, where they believe they will find better schools.

Sally, a white mother of three children, described having a good experience with the city public school system. She did a thorough search for schools she believed would most suit her children and was able to match her teens' interests to particular schools. She said, "I really like that in this city there are choices of schools that work for different kinds of kids." She said she tells people, "You have to go and find out, do the research." Sally reported that one of her sons is academically gifted; he is a senior who goes to the city's top magnet school. She said, "My son really likes it, and we just got good news. He got three scholarships to [well-regarded local university]."

Other mothers are able to find schools that have programming in the areas their teens are interested in. Evelyn, a white mother of two teens (ages 15 and 17) said that her son had some academic difficulties in junior high school. "But," she said, "I did some research and found a high school that has a really good program for preparing for careers in the media, a program my son would qualify for. My son was interested in that field." She said she and her son are excited because he has gotten a summer internship at a local radio station. Another mother, Maxine, was able to find a high school with a good sports program that suited her daughter. She said, "My daughter isn't so interested in academics, but she's really into sports, that is what really connects her to school. This school doesn't have that many Advanced Placement classes, but I think it's important that the sports program keeps my daughter really involved in school and hopefully doing well academically."

An African American mother named Bethany has two high school-aged children. She said she and her husband were very pleased with the Catholic school their teens were attending. They had searched for good schools and were pleased with this school. However, after two years, they realized they could no longer afford tuition for both of their children. They worried about sending their teens to public school, but their children successfully got into a magnet school, so they went there. Bethany and her husband had been very disappointed that they could no longer afford the Catholic school their teens were attending, but they were pleased that their children are having a good experience at the public high school they currently attend. Bethany said:

> Both of them go to [high-ranking public high school]. It's a wonderful school, a top school. We worried a little about how it would go. We heard there wasn't much discipline in the public schools, not like the Catholic school they went to. Sometimes you hear bad stories about what goes on in public schools, but they sought out kids like themselves and it was fine.

Working-Class Mothers

Working-class mothers have much less ability to customize their choice of schools for their teens. One white mother named Irene felt very fortunate that she lives in a neighborhood with a good school, a neighborhood that has been gentrifying. The school has gotten grants to improve their facilities and install up-to-date instructional technology. Other mothers, however, reported that the public schools their teens attend lack resources. Some spoke of overcrowded classrooms and overburdened teachers who have less time to invest in individual children. In the poorest schools, as in poorer schools in the United States more generally, equipment and amenities, including sports facilities, arts programs, and educational technologies, are inferior.[37] As one mother complained of a particularly underresourced school, "The computers in my son's classroom are old, there aren't enough for everybody, and sometimes the furnace breaks down in winter."

Some mothers who are not pleased with their neighborhood school try to find a better one within the larger school system that their teen will be able to get into. Mothers described how it can take time and effort to understand what choices are available. Some find a school they are satisfied with. One African American mother, Doria, researched schools her son could attend and helped him gain acceptance at a public magnet high school where there was a lot of competition for admission. She said her son is very bright. She went to see one of his eighth-grade teachers and urged her to help her son apply to this school. She believes that the teacher's help meant that her son was able to submit a competitive application to the school and be accepted there.

Gayle, a working-class African American mother of three high school-aged sons, could not find a public school that she felt would be good for her sons. However, she feels very fortunate that she found a private boarding school for children of veterans, one that gave each of her three sons full scholarships. The school is several hours away by car. Gayle says: "I don't worry about my three older boys because they are not here in this environment. There are kids in this neighborhood who do bad things. Now," she reported, "My kids are studying, they are getting their work done." She said:

[37] M. Filardo, J. M. Vincent, and K. Sullivan, "How Crumbling School Facilities Perpetuate Inequality," *Phi Delta Kappan* 100(8) (2019): 27–31.

I feel secure now about where they are, you know what I mean? They have what I've been wanting for them. I am so happy I found this school. I feel comfortable and secure where they're at, and I know they're going to do well and graduate.

Unlike upper-middle-class and middle-class mothers, Gayle doesn't believe she has many choices. She can't afford private schools, and she doesn't have the option of moving to a neighborhood with better schools. As she said, "We can't afford to move, it's just as plain and simple as that. If we could afford to move or put them in private school here, they'd be home in a flash." She continued:

I love the school where they go, we're very fortunate they can do there, but if I could, I would have them home. If I had my choice, I'd rather have them home with us than away, but it's because of this environment here. If I could move to a better neighborhood where they wouldn't have so many distractions and they could do well here in a school in the city, I would do it just like that. But we can't do that.

If they can afford to, some working-class mothers send their teens to Catholic schools, where they believe there will be more supervision of students and their teens will be less likely to get into trouble. Aline is a white mother of three children, two who are already in college and one who is in junior high school. She is trying hard to comply with her younger son's wishes to go to a particular Catholic school but she is worried about how she will pay for it. She is also not sure he will get into the school he wants to go to, there is a lot of competition for admission, so she spends a lot of time worrying about what school he will attend if he doesn't get into the Catholic school. She has made a backup plan in case he doesn't. As she said:

He wants to go to this very good parochial school for ninth grade. It's pretty expensive and competitive but if he really, really wants to go and he can get in—which is another thing, it's not that easy—then I guess I'll see if we can make it work out, financially I mean. If he doesn't get into that, we will try for one of the good public schools, and if that doesn't work, then I'll find a small parochial school, I have one in mind.

Aline continued, "This is so stressful. I've been worrying about this for two years. All the calls and forms, it makes me tired and I worry about what will happen. But we have to have a backup plan."

Families with the lowest incomes cannot afford Catholic schools, and many fear that public schools will not provide a good education for their teens. One mother, whose daughter is a freshman in high school, said, "If I had the money, [daughter] wouldn't have to go to the public school, she would go to a Catholic school. The public school system today is not what it should be, the teachers are overloaded." Some mothers, like the middle-class mother quoted above, have to take their children out of Catholic school because they cannot afford the cost. One African American mother said her son really liked the Catholic school he was attending but, "I was unable to keep, you know, the tuition up." She believes that this had a negative impact on her son's education:

> That Catholic school was good with the smaller classrooms and other things. I know how it is once you get out because when my son got out of the Catholic school after sixth grade, he had too much independence in the public school—they weren't checking up on him, he wasn't learning. He felt he could do whatever he wanted. He's been promoted each school year but he doesn't do as well as he did in Catholic school.

A few working-class parents tried to get their children into a public school in another district. Most cannot afford to pay the fees for schools in other districts, however, so they have to find a person who resides within the district who will allow them to use their address illegally to register their teen for school there. One white working-class mother reported that she has been trying to get her high school-age son into the school district where his aunt lives, a district where there is a school she believes would be very good for her son. But she said that now her aunt plans to move to another district, so even if she were able to arrange this transfer, it would no longer be possible. And, she says, they cannot afford to move to a neighborhood with a better school.

Preparing for Post-Graduation

As mothers work to promote the success of their high school students, they also provide valuable help in applying to college or some post-high school training. Today, a postsecondary credential is essential for gaining a place in the labor force. As noted above, two-thirds of jobs require that a person have some education or training beyond high school, and a college degree is required for most better-paying jobs.[38] Those without postsecondary education or training are at risk of experiencing unemployment for some period as adults, or at worst, permanent unemployment, which can result in unstable personal relationships, substance abuse, and higher rates of mortality.[39]

Parents provide essential help for their teens as they apply to college. The application process can be very demanding, and many students, as well as parents, find it stressful. For parents, it not only involves determining what kind of college would benefit their teens but also deciding whether attending college is financially feasible. There are many steps in this process—taking the appropriate college preparation courses, researching and visiting colleges, filling out applications, and applying for financial aid. Parents must also continue the work of managing their children's stress and keeping them motivated so they do not miss deadlines. Mothers who have not attended college are often less aware of all the application requirements, and their teens may attend schools without adequate guidance counseling for applying to college. The fact that low-income and African American students attend schools with the highest student-counselor ratios creates a big disadvantage for them, as students identify counselors as important sources of information about college attendance.[40]

Mothers must also invest considerable time in figuring out how to pay the high cost of attending college. Over the last 40 years, tuition and student loan debt have risen dramatically. Parents often make great sacrifices to help pay for college, and many young adults who complete their degree are saddled with large amounts of debt after graduating. If parents and young adults consider the financial help that parents have given as loans, questions arise as to when and how students will pay back the loans.[41] If young adults fail to finish

---

[38] Carnevale et al., "Three Educational Pathways to Good Jobs."

[39] A. Deaton and A. Case, *Deaths of Despair and the Future of Capitalism* (Princeton, NJ: Princeton University Press, 2020). Deaton and Case argue that drug overdoses, suicides, and alcoholism have fueled an increase in what they term "deaths of despair."

[40] D. Vega and A. M. Puff, "It Takes a Village: How Counselors and Psychologists Support the College Aspirations of Students of Color," *Phi Delta Kappan* 102(4) (2020): 40–45.

[41] More than half of students leave college with debt averaging $28,950. This includes 55 percent of students from public four-year institutions and 57 percent of students from private nonprofit four-year institutions. A. Hahn and J. Tarver, "2024 Student Loan Debt Statistics: Average Student Loan Debt," *Forbes Advisor*, July 16, 2023. J. Mazelis and A. Kuperberg, "Student Loan Debt, Family Support, and Reciprocity in the Transition to Adulthood," *Emerging Adulthood* 10(6) (2022): 1511–1528.

college, they are set back in their ability to achieve a middle-class life, and their parents, who have contributed financially, lose their investment.[42]

Upper-Middle-Class Mothers

As noted earlier, many parents want their young adults to attend highly ranked colleges or universities, which they hope will provide the credentials they need to secure prestigious professional jobs or gain acceptance to a graduate school that will prepare them for those jobs. As more young people obtain college degrees, a graduate degree has become increasingly necessary for obtaining a professional-level position in some fields, creating an even greater premium on getting an undergraduate degree from a prestigious college.[43] As parents provide assistance to their teens in applying to college, the atmosphere can be competitive and stressful for both them and their children.

Many upper-middle-class mothers in my sample are knowledgeable about which colleges and universities are viewed as prestigious; many went to these colleges themselves. They may provide advice to their teens to help them gain admission to these colleges and universities, including how to choose courses that will increase their children's chances of being accepted at these colleges. Many of the high schools their teens attend also provide helpful information about the college application process. One mother said that the college guidance counselor at her son's small private school told parents he would carefully monitor their teens' progress in applying to college and that parents didn't have to worry about their teens failing to complete the required application materials or missing deadlines. In addition to the better counseling their teens receive in school, many affluent parents hire college admissions consultants, whose fees can range from $200 per hour to $2,000 per hour, depending on the number of services provided.[44] Some upper-middle-class families also have money to pay most of the cost of college; those who cannot are able to manage the process of applying for the financial aid that is available at elite colleges and universities.

[42] C. Zaloom, *Indebted: How Families Make College Work at Any Cost* (Princeton, NJ: Princeton University Press, 2019).

[43] F. Torche, "Intergenerational Mobility at the Top of the Educational Distribution," *Sociology of Education* 91(4) (2018): 266–289.

[44] J. Moody, "What to Look For When Hiring a College Consultant," *U.S. News and World Report*, April 4, 2019, https://www.usnews.com/education/best-colleges/articles/2019-04-04/what-to-look-for-when-hiring-a-college-consultant.

As the mothers I interviewed work to help their teens with the college application process, they also provide emotional support to their children who may be experiencing a lot of pressure to excel academically. Claudia, a mother whose daughter is in tenth grade at a private school, said she is trying to help her daughter deal with "the pressure of this system." "The pressure starts in ninth grade, and it's very stressful" she said, "Especially if you are thinking about early decision," an application with an earlier deadline that can give a student increased chances of acceptance at a college if the student applies only to that school. Claudia said, "I worry about how all this will go for my daughter and whether she will be able to get into the college she wants to go to. But I'm not like some parents who worry about this all the time; they seem to be living for their children."

As noted earlier, acceptance at high-prestige colleges not only requires an excellent academic record but also participation in extracurricular activities. Several mothers spoke of teens who worry they don't have enough extracurricular or other qualifications that make them competitive candidates at top-ranked schools. A mother named Deborah said her daughter, a high school junior, is worried she is not a strong candidate because she isn't participating in enough extracurricular activities. She noted, "My daughter said to me recently, 'For these top schools I need things that make me look really good, and I'm worried that being managing editor of the school newspaper is not enough. But that job takes up so much time plus I'm in two Advanced Placement classes with a ton of work, how can I fit other things in? Should I start doing a service project or join another club?'"

Deborah has questioned whether she and her husband should continue to support their daughter in her goal of trying to get into a high prestige college. She said, "Like me, my husband thinks this whole system is crazy. But it's hard to go up against the system. Should I tell my daughter it's not worth all this stress, we have a good state college she can go to? If I do that, will I regret that?" Another mother, Georgette, said that her daughter, who is a junior in high school, is very "stressed out" about applying to college and has complained to her, saying, "Mom, why didn't you go to an Ivy League school so I could be a legacy for getting in there?" Georgette said, "This whole legacy thing is incredible, how fair is that?"[45]

---

[45] In the wake of the 2023 decision of the Supreme Court limiting the use of affirmative action in college admissions, a debate has grown over the legitimacy of legacy admissions. E. Cochrane et al., "The Legacy Dilemma: What to Do About Privileges for the Privileged?," *New York Times*, July 20, 2023.

Mothers also talked about how they try to manage their teens' expectations to reduce the degree of disappointment their teen could experience if they are not accepted at the college that is their first choice. Marilyn, an upper-middle-class African American mother, supports her daughter's wish to attend a high-prestige university but thinks her daughter doesn't understand the challenges of getting into this school. "She wants to go to [Ivy League school], but like 14 kids from her high school—it's a private school—are applying there. With that kind of competition, I think it's ridiculous for her to think of even getting in there. She's also going to probably apply to three other Ivy League schools."

Marilyn said the application process is making her daughter "so stressed out. I think she should go to [smaller liberal arts college that is less competitive]." Marilyn has engaged in negotiations with her daughter and has pressured her to pick a backup school (a college where a student is more likely to be accepted). She said, "My daughter finally agreed to choose one, but she really doesn't want to go there." Another mother, Irene, is also trying to help her son prepare for the fact that he may not get into a highly competitive college. She said, "It's going to be hard for my son to accept that. I want to support him. My son is trying to tell himself it's okay whatever happens, but he's stressed. I've tried to tell him there are lots of good colleges out there, but he says all his friends at school want to go to an Ivy League college."

In helping her daughter choose the colleges she will apply to, another mother, Simone, reported having to negotiate with her daughter over what field she would study. Her daughter wants to apply to a well-regarded university to pursue a degree in the music school, which has a prestigious program within the university with its own application process. Simone and her husband are worried that a degree in music would limit their daughter's options for a future career. They are trying to pressure her to apply to the university and get a university degree. They are telling her that she could still take a lot of music courses and maybe major in music. Because Simone and her husband will be paying some of her college costs, they believe they have the right to pressure their daughter to make this decision.

While most teens from upper-middle-class families are highly motivated to apply for college, a white mother named Emma reported dealing with her daughter's failure to be motivated. She said, "Our younger daughter is procrastinating, she hasn't started filling out her college applications, she could miss the deadlines." Emma thinks that the process "makes her too anxious." She said, "I've read the application, I'm getting everything organized for her and getting the information she needs." Emma said, "I will not do my daughter's college application though," but she can't take a chance that her daughter would regret not applying so she is "keeping on her, trying to get her motivated, trying to figure out how hard to push." She said her daughter could wait a year and apply "but all her friends are going to be getting into college, probably good colleges, and she would be miserable if she didn't go, she isn't talking about any kind of alternative." But Emma says, "if she doesn't start working on her application soon, she will have to suffer the consequences, I'm not going to do any more for her."

Mothers not only deal with their teens' stress but their own. Attendance at a high-prestige college or university, in addition to being an important means of attaining a good professional position, is a status symbol that confers symbolic capital. Upper-middle-class mothers feel pressure from their social group to have their teens attend high-prestige colleges. One mother reported that when she told a friend her son had been accepted at a high-prestige college, he said congratulations to her as if she were the one who had achieved the acceptance. In part, this is certainly true. Without the extensive help and resources of their parents, most teens would have difficulty getting into college, particularly a high-prestige one. However, it was her son, not her, who was accepted. The friend's congratulations illustrate how acceptance at this college signals a prestigious status for parents.

Caroline, whose son is a senior who is applying to college, acknowledged that if he attended a high-prestige university, it would be a mark of status for her as well. Her statements reflect her disappointment that her son is not applying to a top college, he says he wants to go to the state university where his friends are going. She said:

> I just think that he'd get more of an education at these Ivy League schools, although I don't know if that's really true, you can probably get a good education other places. Maybe it's snobbery that I want him to go to an Ivy League university because that gives you prestige, for him and I guess for my husband and me.

Caroline's comments reveal that she also feels pressure indirectly from her family to have her son attend an Ivy League university:

> Many people in my family have gone to Ivy League schools. They won't look down on my son if he doesn't go to an Ivy League school, but privately,

they may think that where he goes just isn't as good. Or maybe that he's not as smart as they are or he just didn't try hard enough. And—this is hard to say—that he has let the family down. But he works so hard.

Caroline also acknowledged her feelings of competition with others whose young adult children go to Ivy League universities. She said, "It's like a feeling that, 'My child could go there too.' I hate to say it but maybe, like, 'My child is just as good as yours.'" However, she says she is trying to be understanding of her son and support his choices of less prestigious schools.

As they advise their teens, some mothers talked about how they can help their children gain admission to prestigious colleges. Audrey has two sons, one who is entering eighth grade and one who is entering his junior year of high school. She scaled back her work as a consultant at a software company to accompany her older son, a top tennis player at his high school, on college visits so he could see which ones he liked and which ones he would have a chance of being admitted to. She and her son were visiting high-prestige colleges around the country that had contacted her son based on his strong high school record as a tennis player and his good academic record. Audrey said the purpose of the visit was not only to give her son a chance to see which college he liked best but also to show the colleges that her son had a strong interest in applying to their school. As she said, "We wanted to make an impression, that if they know my son is really interested, they will consider him more seriously." Her husband is a lawyer with a good salary, so cutting back on her work time did not pose any financial difficulties. Audrey does not anticipate problems in returning to her work as a consultant.

Another mother, Charlotte, described helping her daughter gain advantages in applying to college. Her daughter is anxious to attend the high-prestige college that Charlotte went to. She advised her daughter to apply for early decision, knowing this could confer an advantage in the admission process. Charlotte was also very aware of potential advantages her daughter could gain based on her own alumnae status. She and her daughter went to visit the college together. Before arriving, Charlotte made appointments with staff in the admissions office, and made sure to inform them that she was an alumna. She also arranged for her and her daughter to visit the academic department of the field her daughter was interested in. Charlotte said that during the visit, she accompanied her daughter and always introduced herself as an alumna. It's unclear if this made a difference in her daughter's chances for acceptance, but as noted previously, legacy applicants have traditionally been favored at prestigious colleges and universities.

A white upper middle-class mother named Sandra gave an account that shows both the emotional work some mothers do if their son or daughter is rejected or waitlisted at a college, as well as the ability of upper-middle-class parents to gain advantages for their teens in the higher education system through personal connections. Sandra's son Jonathan, a senior at a private school, really wanted to go to a prestigious liberal arts college. He applied to be considered for early decision but was put on the waiting list. He was extremely disappointed. Sandra's account reflects the anxiety and stress that can occur when students aren't accepted at the colleges they have applied to. She said:

> A few weeks ago, my son was feeling really down. He found out that many of his friends were getting into the places they had applied to early decision, but he was only on the waiting list at the college he applied to.

Sandra said that after this happened, she and her husband talked with Jonathan about other options, including taking a gap year, a year between high school graduation and starting college, telling him that if he found a really good opportunity, it could strengthen his resume if he reapplied to this college. Sandra said this experience has been stressful for her and her husband as well as Jonathan. "My husband and I have been angry at it all," she said. "The whole system, all the stress and pressure our son feels. He's a good student and contributes so much to his school."

As she continued to talk, however, Sandra's story took a more positive turn. She used her social capital, or her "privilege" as she said, to get more information about where her son's chances for acceptance stood. She said:

> So I was feeling really bad about my son's situation. And then I decided, okay, this is privilege, I have it. I once worked with someone who is in the administration at the college. I decided to call her and tell her the situation. I was able to learn from her that Jonathan was very high up on the waiting list. Also, I told her more about Jonathan's accomplishments because I was hoping she would put in a good word for him.

Two weeks later, the college informed Jonathan that he had been accepted at this college.

Middle-Class Mothers

The middle-class mothers I interviewed are very aware of the need to have a college degree to get good jobs and achieve a middle-class lifestyle. They believe they have benefited from their college education and are hopeful that a college degree will further their children's chances of success in life as well. A white mother named Susan said she is very thankful that she has a college degree. She said, "It's opened up doors, I love being a 5th grade teacher and I wouldn't have this career without it. It was hard on my parents financially, but it was one of the best investments they ever made. Actually, I got scholarships too but they had to pay some."

Middle-class parents face challenges in considering college for their children, however, particularly when it comes to paying for college. They worry a lot about cost. A white mother named Amelia spoke about her daughter Emily's good fortune in getting scholarships. She said:

> Six years ago I would have been telling you, "We don't know how the heck we are going to get Emily through college, look at what it's going to cost." But thank goodness she's such a good student, she got a lot of scholarships and she won't graduate with much debt and we didn't have to pay much either.

However, Amelia also noted, "Now [groaning] we can start to worry about how we're going to pay for our son's college. He's going to be a junior next year."

For many middle-class parents, cost is a major factor that determines where their children will attend college. In negotiations with their teens about what colleges they will apply to or attend, mothers take their teens' wishes into account, but as the ones who provide at least some financial support for them to attend college, they may decide they are the ones entitled to make the final decision. One mother said that because of the cost, her daughter cannot attend a well-regarded local university where she had been accepted and where she really wanted to go. As this mother noted, "They did not give enough financial aid, it was not enough, she didn't really have the choice of going there. She had to go to [small local Catholic college] because they gave her a full scholarship." She said, "My daughter was really disappointed."

Other mothers have a different concern. Their goal is for their young adults to attend college to gain preparation for a field or career, and they wonder whether going to college is worth the cost if their teen doesn't know what kind of work they want to do in the future. Ingrid, a white middle-class whose daughter is a high school junior, said, "People have told me it's good to go to college when you know what you want to do. My daughter doesn't know yet." She continued:

> We told her she has to wait for college. She has to decide what she wants to do. [Hesitating] I'm a little disappointed that she can't figure out what she's interested in, but [working to sound more confident] she'll figure it out.

If their teen doesn't know what kind of work or career they want, mothers' may advise them to attend a local community college, where they hope they will find a direction for their future. A white mother named Kathleen described her daughter, a second-semester high school junior, as having little sense of what she might want to study or what field she might want to pursue. Kathleen has tried to help her daughter develop ideas about a future career. She persuaded her to take a volunteer job at a healthcare clinic, hoping it would give her daughter a better idea of what occupation she might be interested in. However, it turned out her daughter was not enthusiastic about that type of work. Kathleen said:

> At this point, my daughter doesn't know what she wants to do, so she shouldn't go to a four-year college now. If we forced her and she didn't want to be there, it would just be a waste of time and money. She should go to the local community college; that will help her figure out what she wants to do.

Lenora, a middle-class African American mother whose son is a first-semester high school senior, stated that she and her husband will insist that their son to go to a college in their state because the tuition will be lower but also because "he doesn't know what he wants to do." She said, "If he really knew what he wanted to do and there were a good program somewhere else we would say, 'Okay, we'll see if we can help you pay for that.'" Lenora said that at one point, her son wanted to go to a highly ranked public university in another state and, "We asked him why. He said he heard it was a good school." Lenora said, "We told him, 'No, that's not a good enough reason, you would need a reason to go there.'"

In selecting colleges to apply to, some middle-class parents said the high schools their teens attend do not provide much assistance. Maryanne is a white mother whose son is a junior at the local high school, a large school which she says is considered to be "a pretty good school." But she said she and her son cannot count on the guidance counselor for help. Maryann has talked to the college counselor at her son's school who is "very nice," but she noted, "My son's guidance counselor only seems to know about local colleges and sometimes state colleges but just in our state. My son would like more choices; he might want to go out of state." Maryann said her friend's son goes to a local private school, and he is getting much more help working through the college admission process:

> My friend told me that the counselor at the private school was spending her whole winter break helping kids find colleges that would be good for them to apply to and then helping them with applications! My son certainly doesn't get that kind of help. I'm going to have to get information about colleges from my friend.

A white mother named Terry was very upset that her son has not gotten more support from guidance counselors at his school. She said, "I thought it would be okay to rely on the school to advise my son about applying to college." However, she is now feeling very badly that she didn't realize that her son, a senior at a large public high school, wasn't receiving the advice he needed about applying to college. She said:

> Before Christmas, I went to talk to one of the counselors I thought was assigned to seniors. But he didn't seem to know who my son was. I said to him [with feeling], "Do you know who my son is?" He said, "Well, he has to come and talk to me." [With anger] I couldn't believe it. My son is a senior and he didn't know him! He didn't have a clue. If I hadn't gone to the school, I don't think the counselor would have signed the right papers so my son could attend college.

Terry had been calling the counseling office to get information for her son on applying to college but hadn't gotten a call back. Her son told her that he wasn't getting information about applying to college from the high school counselor's office and hadn't been able to make an appointment with the college counselor. Terry said, "It's a good school but it's understaffed, the counselors have too many students. I know they have too many students, but they shouldn't let anyone fall through the cracks." As noted above, only one in five high school students is enrolled in a school that has an adequate number of school counselors. It's likely that most upper-middle-class mothers would have acted sooner than Terry did to make sure their teen's school counselor was helping them with the college application process. Now that she understands what the counseling office can and cannot do for her son in applying to college, Terry is trying to make sure the school counselor fills out the necessary paperwork for her son's application. She is also trying to get her son to work on his college applications, and she is working to gather all the information parents must submit when their son or daughter applies for financial aid. Like many mothers, she finds her part in the college application process burdensome:

> I'm so tired with these college applications. There are all these deadlines for applications and for the standardized tests, the juniors have to take all these tests. I have this long application I have only half-filled out for [local university]. I have to take time out from work to finish this. I wish the schools would make things easier for you.

Working-Class Mothers

Some working-class mothers I interviewed also place a high priority on their young adults' college attendance, particularly as a way to gain better work opportunities in the future. Several mentioned that they believe they have missed opportunities because they do not have a college degree. A white mother named Annemarie—who has a daughter who is a senior in high school and a son who is a freshman—feels this particularly keenly. As she said:

> My husband and I have known that our kids were going to college since the day they were born because we know how we lost out because we didn't. At our jobs, we work just as hard as people with college degrees and we do the same kind of work, but we make a lot less money.

Annemarie said she has been pushing her kids: "We've talked about college for a long time—it's always been, 'You will go.'" She continued, "I did well at school, but I was never pushed to give it my full, you know, by my school or by my parents. I mean graduating high school, I wanted to go to college." But Annemarie said she didn't know about the college application process or how to apply for scholarships or grants. She added, "My parents didn't take the initiative to look into it for me. That's why I feel I need to do this for my kids."

Working-class mothers cited cost as a major factor in where their teens can apply to college. Marla is a divorced African American mother who works as a medical technician. She reported that her daughter wanted to go away to college. She said, "We had to discuss that a lot. She wanted to go out of state, she really wanted the college life." Marla said she wanted to help her daughter experience college life and live on campus, but that her salary isn't good enough to help her daughter do that and her ex-husband was not going to contribute to their daughter's college tuition or expenses. Plus, she has three other children who may want to go to college. She said:

> My daughter was sad. We argued, we talked it through, I tried to tell her there were good things about [a local college], I helped her get loans, but she didn't get a scholarship for an out of state school. So no, out of state, we couldn't afford that. I'm sorry for her, I know she's really disappointed, I told her I was sorry.

Like many middle-class mothers I interviewed, working-class mothers want their teens to have an idea of what they will study before they go to college so they will graduate prepared for work or a career. For example, Ava, a white working-class mother whose daughter is a high school sophomore, said, "My daughter should get a job when she graduates from high school and wait for college. She has to decide what she wants to do before going to college and she doesn't know yet so she'll have to figure that out. She says that's okay with her. Actually, I don't think she really wants to go to college yet."

Since they have not been to college themselves, most working-class mothers have less knowledge of how the college application process works and often rely on school personnel or, in some cases, their children to complete the process. Marion, an African American mother, has tried to reach people at her son's high school to get help advising him about how to apply to college. She said she's been trying to schedule a phone conversation with one of her son's teachers about which local college would be best for her son to apply to. Marion thought it would be easier to get through to her son's teacher than the school counselor. "The line is always busy there," she said. "But even with teachers, it's much harder to get ahold of teachers when your kids are in high school." She said, "I think schools should be more supportive of parents. Before high school, like in eighth grade, the schools were more supportive. You could get hold of a teacher; they would call you." Marion finally got through to one of her son's teachers who did have some information about the local colleges her son was interested in. But in the end, Marion said, her son chose his college by "looking in one of those books that tells you about colleges. He was accepted at three colleges."

Several mothers believe it is their teens' job to apply to college, that preparing for the next stage in their teens' lives, turning 18 and continuing their education, is their children's responsibility. Some of these mothers, like Marion, also assume that their teens are receiving adequate help applying to college from their high schools. One mother says leaves this process up to her daughter. She said her daughter has begun researching colleges:

> She's talking about college now, she's definitely talking about college. The school helped her get a book about different colleges, she showed me she's made a list of [local colleges]. I know she'll figure this out, she's become much more responsible.

Another mother said, "My daughter applies for all the scholarships, I'm not sure which ones. It's her job to figure this out, I can't pay. But I'm supposed to fill out paperwork about how much we can pay. Well, we can't pay anything, so that should be an easy job."

Mary Catherine, a white mother of two teens in junior high school and a daughter who is a first-semester freshman at a local college, reported that her husband became involved in the college application process in what she describes as a somewhat unusual way. Mary Catherine said her daughter was thoughtful and organized as she applied to college. She wanted to attend a local college, she chose the colleges she was interested in, visited them, and made a top choice. She was accepted at all the colleges she applied to and got a full scholarship to one; however, she only got a partial scholarship to the college she had her heart set on, which, along with the loans she had access to, did not provide enough money for her to attend.

Mary Catherine then described her husband taking action to help their daughter get a full scholarship to the college she really wanted to attend. She said, "I had no idea my husband would do this, he's a little nervy, but I'm glad he did." She continued:

> There was a function for students who were accepted at the college my daughter really wanted to go to. It's a very good college. When my husband realized we were going to this function, he took the letter from the college that was giving my daughter a full scholarship. As I said, he's kind of nervy. He walked up to one of the college officials at the function and said, "This is what [the other college] is giving my daughter but she really wants to come here." And lo and behold, we heard soon after that that they gave her a full scholarship and she went to that college!

While Mary Catherine spoke as if her husband's actions were something unusual and "nervy," it is likely that some upper-middle-class or middle-class parents would contact a college and argue forcefully for a full college scholarship if their teen needed more financial aid.

When there is no parental involvement in the college application process and a parent relies on the school for college guidance or on the teen to manage the process, as a previous example indicates, there can be negative consequences. Julie, a white working-class mother whose son, Jason, is a senior at a local high school, reported, "My son Jason is very smart, but he's lazy and doesn't work all that hard in school." But she said now Jason has become more motivated. This is happening in part because of positive feedback he recently received for his school performance. This past year, Jason has done well in computer science classes and has recently been told he has a special aptitude for computer programming. He then became excited about applying to a local university that is strong in computer science and where there is also a lot of competition to gain entry. However, Jason recently went online and found that he will not be able to apply. Julie said:

> I'm furious, just furious. Jason started applying to [university] on the web and he figured out that for what he wants to study they require more math or science courses than he has taken, and it's too late for him to register for more. [With great feeling] I'm really going to speak my mind tonight at the parent-teacher association meeting, I want people to know that the

counseling office is not doing its job, or maybe it's just way understaffed. But it's too late for my son to be able to go to this college.

It is difficult to imagine that this would have happened if Jason attended a well-resourced school with adequate college counseling.

Another group of working-class mothers I interviewed believe their teens should get jobs after their high school graduation and work toward financial independence. As one mother, who is white, said in response to a question concerning what her goals were for her teen, a junior in high school: "To get his diploma, to get a job, to take care of himself." An African American mother was similarly focused on her son getting a job after high school. She noted:

> When they graduate high school, they should be independent and get a good job and stick with it. They need to be responsible, they should take opportunities to improve themselves. Maybe take night classes. I want my kids to save too. My daughter needs to learn how to save money, she's not good at that.

In her account, this African American mother, a widow with two sons, is not focused on the possibility of her sons attending college, but rather on how to pay her living expenses. To make ends meet, she is working full-time at a hardware store and part-time at a local grocery store. She said:

> I just want him to finish high school, succeed, and meet all the goals he can, get a good job. And don't do as much trouble as his mother did. He should find himself a good-paying job and pursue his goals. I think he will, I think he will go into automotive technology.
>
> But right now we just have financial things to worry about, you know. It's tough paying his Catholic school tuition and all. And I'm thinking I have to drop my part-time job—it's too much, it's bad for my health, especially my blood pressure problem.

A few mothers want their young adults to get job training, although one white working-class mother I interviewed was not very specific about how her daughter will get the training. In response to the question, "What do you think your 16-year-old will do when she graduates from high school?" she said, "Some kind of training. She's into computers, it's a good field."

Finally, the account of an African American mother, Collette, reveals the hard work that can be involved in getting a teen to go to college. Her extensive efforts to motivate her son Damien, to get him out of his neighborhood environment and into college, and to pay for his education, like the efforts of some other working-class mothers, are not typically recognized by schools or the wider public. Working-class and poorer mothers are often viewed as insufficiently supportive of their children's school performance. However, they may in fact be supporting their teens in ways that are very important for their postsecondary education.

Collette applied enormous pressure on Damien to apply to college. She lacks the cultural capital that upper-middle-class and some middle-class mothers can use to promote their older teens' college acceptance, but her work pushing her son to go to college has been invaluable and has paid off. Collette said that when Damien was a junior in high school, she would continually ask him, "Are you going to college?" She said Damien would tell her, "'I think I'm just going to go to trade school here in [hometown].'" Collette then said that one day when she came home, "Damien was out there messing with some bad boys. I said, 'Let me tell you one thing right now, you got your choice—either you go to college or you go in the service, but you're not going to a trade school in this city and then hang out on the corner with those boys.'" She continued:

> I told Damien "I mean what I say, either that or I'm going to pack you up and you're going to be a homeless child. I'm going to put you out on the street." I kicked that in the butt before it got started.

Perhaps responding to his mother's pressure, in the spring of his junior year, Damien remembered that he had received a letter from a college in a nearby state. Collette said, "They wrote him about college, so he contacted them and said he might be interested in their college. Damien was on the football team in high school; he was actually quite a good running back. Then," she continued, "We had some good luck. A man from the admissions department of that college was from here and he was home visiting his family in the summer, and he came and interviewed Damien. By him being home visiting, he said he would come and visit Damien." So Collette said, "While he was here I gave the man a check for the application, and I said, 'I'll give you a check every month if you take this boy.' And that's what I told my husband. If he's accepted there, we're going to give them a check every month." Damien was accepted at the college, and Collette followed through on her commitment, even though this was a heavy financial burden for her and her husband. She said, "It was big money and I paid every penny he didn't get through his scholarship, which wasn't much at all. I paid all that money, and it was a hassle—it was really a hassle. I had told my husband, 'We just have to do without.'"

Collette said Damien successfully completed college and is now grateful that she pushed him to apply. Without Collette's efforts, it is certainly possible he would not have gone to college, at least not right after high school; he didn't have the motivation. And it's not clear what college advising his high school counselor was providing, or if the counselor was providing advice at all. However, it appears that when Collette decided to put serious pressure on Damien to go to college or enlist in the military, he remembered that he had gotten a letter inviting him to apply to a college and finally became motivated. There was also luck involved when it turned out that a representative of the college who lived in another state was visiting his family in the city and was able to meet with him. Collette said, "Now Damien thanks me all the time. Like I tell him, 'You could be dead or in jail or someplace like that.'"

Popular accounts of parenting give little attention to the kind of important work that Collette did to push Damien to go to college. Likewise, the advantages of those with resources are also often invisible in current narratives and public discussions. Meredith, a white upper-middle-class mother, gave an account in which the role of resources that have helped promote her daughters' success is absent from view. Meredith supervises special education teachers in her county and has two daughters (ages 15 and 22). She reported that she is very proud of her daughters' successes in school. Her comments reflect the view that children and teens' school performance is the result not only of students' ability and effort but of parents' actions. She noted:

Our daughters are growing into mature, responsible people, into young leaders, it is just wonderful to watch. They work hard and they are successful. They are everything I would want them to be, I couldn't be more pleased. Each of them is unique. They are very strong academically and one is a really good athlete and the other one is active in the drama club at her school.

Recently, Meredith's 15-year-old daughter, Melanie, was recognized for her academic achievements. She was listed in the local newspaper as having received honors for the spring term at her school. In reflecting on her daughters' successes, Meredith noted:

> I credit everyone for this, of course my daughters. But I know that my husband and I have played a major role, and I give a lot of credit to my parents, as well as myself and my husband. We've given our daughters a lot of encouragement, and they've taken up challenges, done extracurricular activities. They are joiners, they are outgoing, it's so rewarding to see them.

As Meredith indicated, in addition to seeing Melanie's achievements as a product of her hard work, she views her daughter's success partly as a reflection of the efforts of her and her husband, and her parents. Without a doubt, these efforts have been critical to the success of Melanie and her sister. What we don't see in Meredith's account, however, is the role resources have played in enabling her daughter to stay engaged, to prepare for her future, and to be successful. Meredith and her husband have chosen to live in a suburban area known for having good schools, which are paid for by high taxes. All the schools their daughters have attended have experienced teachers, up-to-date facilities and technology, and appropriate class sizes, resources many working-class families do not have access to. In the US, securing a good education is dependent not only on students' efforts and intelligence, but on the ability to live in a school district with high taxes that can fund good schools or the financial resources to pay for private school.

Conclusion

As teens work to gain educational credentials, the stakes are high. Today, securing a high school diploma is essential for gaining even low-wage employment, while a college degree is necessary to achieve an adequate standard of living. Parents are expected to see that their teens succeed in school and gain the necessary credentials to move on to independent lives. School officials urge parents to become involved in their children's schooling, attend conferences with their teachers, and volunteer at their child's school, actions which researchers have found contribute to teens' educational success.[46]

Researchers have paid less attention, however, to what it actually takes to help teens succeed in school and the significant challenges parents can face. Helping teens with schooling is not a straightforward process. Some teens are engaged in their schoolwork—they like school, participate in extra-curricular activities, and plan for college or future training. As one mother noted, her daughter, who is in high school and in a program for academi-cally gifted children, has been a school leader as well as an excellent student. As she put it, "She's always been involved in school, she's a leader, we are so proud of her."

At the same time, however, large numbers of students find school boring and have trouble staying engaged. Schoolwork is more difficult in junior high and high school and the transition to high school creates new challenges for students. High schools are large and students receive less attention from individual teachers. To keep teens motivated, mothers provide encourage-ment, they assist with schoolwork as they can, and they help with problems, including those students may encounter with teachers. Mothers who believe their teens are not sufficiently motivated push their children. They negotiate with them, they argue, and they nag. But mothers find it difficult to force mo-tivation. As several mothers said, yelling and haranguing their teens to do schoolwork doesn't work. As one mother who is quoted in Chapter 1 said, "I can't duck tape my son to his desk." Some mothers stop pushing their teens. They let go and decide their teen children just have to fail a class or a school grade when they are not applying themselves and hope that this experience will motivate them to apply themselves in school later on.

Large numbers of students also experience stress. They may have trouble understanding their schoolwork, they may find it too difficult, or they may feel there is too much of it. Teens who plan to go to college experience stress in trying to get good enough grades to gain acceptance to college. Teens who wish to attend prestigious schools feel particular pressure to perform at a high level in a very competitive atmosphere. Mothers expend a lot of effort to help their teens manage the stresses of high school and applying to college.

---

[46] Wang and Sheikh-Khalil, "Does Parental Involvement Matter for Student Achievement and Mental Health in High School?" *Child Development* 85(2) (2014): 610–625.

They talk with their teens about their schoolwork as they can, they listen, and they give them encouragement, hoping that their efforts will help their teens do well in school although they cannot guarantee that this will be the case.

Resources are also critical for promoting teens' success. Good schools with smaller classrooms, experienced teachers, and adequate numbers of guidance counselors, provide students with academic advantages that help them gain entrance to college. They can also help teens with issues of engagement and stress. Mothers with resources can often "customize" their teens' education. They not only have financial capital, they also have cultural capital, including knowledge of how to gain advantages for their teens in school. They can choose to switch their teens to different schools—including those that will better match their teens' interest in the sciences, the arts, or technology—where they think they will be more motivated to succeed. They can help their teens gain entrance to schools where they will experience less stress. The schools they are able to choose can also increase a teen's chances of acceptance at highly competitive colleges, which in turn can lead to higher-paying professional careers.

While resources are critical in helping teens succeed academically, however, mothers support their teens' education in a highly unequal system. In my sample, the ease with which many upper-middle-class mothers reported being able to secure programs and schools that provided adequate and often good resources was striking. Most mothers engage in extensive work trying to ensure their teens' success in school. Their efforts, however, are constrained by a system that favors those with more resources. The fact that wealthier districts can provide much more funding for their schools creates a tracking system that makes it difficult for students in lower-income districts to catch up with their peers as time goes on. It reinforces the distance in the social class and racial positions of different groups of teens. After their high school graduation, some teens head off to highly ranked colleges and universities, some go to state colleges and universities, and some enroll in community colleges. A few enter the military. Others, including a greater number of boys, have a difficult time finding a direction for their future and remain uncertain about their next steps.

5

Parenting Young Adults and Letting Go

At age 18, older teens enter a new stage known as "young adulthood," a period of development that most researchers see as taking place between ages 18 and 25 (and sometimes beyond). Earlier in the twentieth century, reaching the age of 18 was considered an important milestone in achieving adulthood. At that age, children were expected to find jobs, become self-supporting, enter marriage, and have children. In the wake of major social and economic changes, however, reaching the traditional markers of adulthood—finishing high school, leaving home, starting work or a career, getting married, and having children—has become an extended process. In the current economy, one in which more jobs are based on knowledge production and intellectual capital, in order to become financially independent and secure employment that provides an adequate standard of living, young adults need to gain more educational credentials, attend college, do an apprenticeship, or receive some other type of training.[1]

The lengthening period of young adulthood has led to major changes in the relationships between parents and their young adult children and new questions about letting go. In the past, young adults were expected to assume major responsibility for their lives at age 18, but in the current era, the majority of high school graduates remain dependent on their parents for a longer period of time. Forty-four percent of young adults between the ages of 18 and 34 received financial help from their parents in the last year. Forty-five percent say they are financially independent from their parents.[2] Young adults continue to need significant financial assistance from parents to pay for college or additional training. While college costs have risen sharply, a college degree is necessary to attain what many people consider to be "good jobs."[3] In the United States, paying for college is seen as a largely private

[1] F. F. Furstenberg Jr., "On a New Schedule: Transitions to Adulthood and Family Change," *The Future of Children* 20(1) (2020): 67–87.

[2] R. Minkin, K. Parker, J. Horowitz, and C. Aragão, "Parents, Young Adult Children and the Transition to Adulthood" (Washington, DC: Pew Research Center, January 2024).

[3] In 2021, the median earnings of 25- to 34-year-olds who were working full time and had a master's or higher degree were $74,600, which is 21 percent higher than the earnings of those who whose highest level of attainment was a bachelor's degree ($61,600). And the median earnings of

Letting Go. Demie Kurz, Oxford University Press. © Oxford University Press 2024.
DOI: 10.1093/9780190222482.003.0005

responsibility. State funding for higher education has decreased, leaving parents and young adults personally responsible for higher college costs. Many parents, as well as students, take out loans and go into debt to pay for their education.[4]

In this extended period of young adulthood, parents face new questions about how much financial and other support they should provide their young adults. They continue to face the challenge of how to provide assistance while simultaneously letting go and promoting their young adults' autonomy. In wider public discourse, there is debate over whether parents are "overparenting" or "helicopter parenting" their young adults. Many people believe parents are too involved with their young adult children, that they are "coddling" them. These parenting styles are presumed to be widespread and harmful to young adults as well as children, creating anxiety and low self-esteem. Surveys show the majority of adults think parents are doing too much for young adults and that young adults should be financially independent by the age of 22, although parents think they themselves are providing the right amount of assistance for their young adult children.[5] Young adults who are believed to have become too dependent on parents are said to have more difficulty developing the skills they need to make decisions about their lives after college.[6]

The majority of parents give their young adults at least some financial assistance.[7] They provide "scaffolding" to help their young adults secure

those with a bachelor's degree were 63 percent higher than the earnings of those who completed high school as their highest degree ($39,700). V. Irwin et al., "Report on the Condition of Education 2023 (NCES 2023-144)" (Washington, DC: US Department of Education, National Center for Education Statistics, 2023).

[4] Rates of student loan debt vary by state. In 2023, the average student loan debt was $28,950. A. Hahn and J. Tarver, "2024 Student Loan Debt Statistics: Average Student Loan Debt," *Forbes Advisor* (New York: Forbes, 2024).

[5] Fifty-five percent of adults say that parents are doing too much for their young adult children, 10 percent say they are doing too little, and 34 percent say they are doing the right amount. Sixty-four percent of Americans think young adults should become financially independent by age 22. A. Barroso et al., "Majority of Americans Say Parents are Doing Too Much for Their Young Adult Children" (Washington, DC: Pew Research Center, 2019).

[6] L. T. Hamilton, *Parenting to a Degree: How Family Matters for College Women's Success* (Chicago: University of Chicago Press, 2016).

[7] In 2018, 59 percent of parents reported giving their young adults at least some financial support. Barroso et al., "Majority of Americans Say Parents are Doing Too Much for Their Young Adult Children." Those who helped pay for college gave substantial amounts of money. In 2022–2023, the average amount paid for college was $28.026. Forty percent of the cost was covered by parental income and savings; 29 percent was covered by scholarships and grants; 11 percent by student borrowing; 10 percent by student income and savings; 8 percent by parents' borrowing; and 2 percent by friends and family. Sallie Mae, "How America Pays for College 2023" (Newark, DE: Sallie Mae and Ipsos, 2023).

additional education and training. Their support serves as a safety net when their young adults encounter difficulties and need financial assistance. One out of three 24-year-olds live with their parents.[8] If their young adult children attend college, some parents help pay for tuition and fees, although given the high cost of college, many of them have to take out loans to support their young adults, which can strain their finances in the future. Parents with lower incomes may provide room and board at home for college students or young adults who are working or engaged in a training program.

Parents support their young adult children in other ways as well. As they did for their secondary school students, those who have been to college continue to share institutional and cultural knowledge to help guide their young adult children as they navigate the requirements of higher education and decide on a career.[9] Parents also continue to provide emotional support for young adults who may become anxious about their futures, their performance in college, or their search for a job. Some help their young adult children who may experience other kinds of challenges. Rates of alcohol and drug use and abuse rise in young adulthood. Many mental health disorders also appear around the onset of young adulthood. Almost one in four college women experience sexual assault or misconduct. Although young adults ages 18–24 represent 9.5 percent of the US population, they account for 23 percent of all arrests. They are also more than twice as likely as the general population to be the victim of a serious violent offense.[10]

[8] T. T. Swartz, "Safety Nets and Scaffolds: Parental Support in the Transition to Adulthood," *Journal of Marriage and Family* 73(2) (2011): 414–429. J. Hatfield, "Young Adults in the U.S. Are Less Likely Than Those in Most of Europe to Live in Their Parents' Home" (Washington, DC: Pew Research Center, May 3, 2023).

[9] L. Hamilton, J. Roksa and J. Nielsen, "Providing a 'Leg Up': Parental Involvement and Opportunity Hoarding in College," *Sociology of Education* 91(2) (2018): 111–131.

[10] Alcohol consumption: in 2022, 49 percent of full-time college students ages 18 to 22 drank alcohol and 28.9 percent engaged in binge drinking in the past month (defined as consuming 5 drinks or more on one occasion for males and 4 drinks or more for females). Twenty-two percent of people aged 12 or older used marijuana in the past year with the highest percentage among young adults aged 18 to 25 (38.2 percent), compared to 20.6 percent of adults 26 or older. The 2022 National Survey on Drug Use and Health (NSDUH). Mental health: among adults aged 18 or older, 23.1 percent had a mental illness in the past year. The percentage was highest among young adults aged 18 to 25 (36.2 percent), followed by adults aged 26 to 49 (29.4 percent), and by adults aged 50 or older (13.9 percent). Six percent of adults aged 18 or older (or 15.4 million people) had serious mental illness in the past year. The percentage of adults aged 18 or older with serious mental illness was highest among young adults aged 18 to 25 (11.6 percent), followed by adults aged 26 to 49 (7.6 percent), then by adults aged 50 or older (3.0 percent). Substance Abuse and Mental Health Services Administration, "Key Substance Use and Mental Health Indicators in the United States: Results from the 2022 National Survey on Drug Use and Health" (Rockville, MD: Center for Behavioral Health Statistics and Quality, Substance Abuse and Mental Health Services Administration, 2023), https://www.samhsa.gov/data/report/2022-nsduh-annual-national-report. Sexual assault: D. Cantor et al., "Report on the AAUW Campus Climate Survey on Sexual Assault and Misconduct"

While providing this support, the mothers I interviewed described facing questions about how much financial and other types of support they should provide for their young adults and what they referred to as letting go and pushing them to take more responsibility for their lives. If their young adult children are in college, mothers may negotiate with them about paying for college expenses. Parents may want their children in college to pay more, but their children may resist taking on extra paid work, which could reduce their time for studying and enjoying their social lives. Parents and young adults can disagree over whether young adults are putting enough effort into preparing for a career or finding suitable careers to pursue. When young adults live at home, mothers must engage in negotiations over how much their young adult children should contribute to household work as well.

As they engage in these negotiations, mothers don't have control over their young adults' decisions in the same way they typically had when they were teens. They face young adults who have begun to make many more of their own decisions. If mothers disagree strongly with a decision their young adult child makes regarding a social matter, there are fewer privileges they can take away as a means of pressuring their young adult. While young adults are still in a dependent position financially, reaching age 18 brings newfound freedoms in their social lives. At age 18, young adults reach the "age of legal majority," a major marker of independence, and they become legally responsible for their actions. They become eligible to vote and join the military without parental consent, they can serve on juries, and they can be drafted into the military. While it remains illegal for them to purchase alcoholic beverages or drink in public until age 21, at age 18, it becomes legal for young adults to get a full-time job, manage their own finances, marry, and have a baby. If they engage in criminal behavior, they can be tried as an adult as well, which means they could face more serious punishments.[11]

During this stage of life, young adults also gain a great deal of freedom in their social lives. They can go where they please, keep their own hours, and make important decisions on their own. The comments of Norma, a white working-class mother, reflect this change. Norma's daughters (ages 19 and

(Rockville, MD: Westat, 2020). For arrest rates, see R. Pirius, "The Legislative Primer Series for Front-End Justice: Young Adults in the Justice System" (Denver: National Conference of State Legislatures, 2019).

[11] T. Spengler, "What You Can Legally Do When You're 18," Legal Beagle, December 12, 2018, https://legalbeagle.com/4744720-can-legally-do-youre-18.html.

21) both live at home while attending college. The family lives in a lower-income neighborhood that has recently experienced several robberies. Like other mothers whose college students live at home, Norma said she sometimes worries about her daughters' safety:

> My daughters go out on weekends with friends, and many times they stay out really late. Before, I could enforce the rules if they stayed out too late, I would ground them for a weekend or two, they had to stay in the house. I did that a few times.

"But," Norma said, "That's kind of over now, when they turned 18."

However, while mothers' ability to exercise control over their young adults' actions, and particularly their social lives, diminishes when their children turn 18, mothers and fathers can continue to exert leverage over their young adults' decisions through the provision or withholding of financial support. When they are contributing money to their young adults' education or living expenses, mothers reported that they feel they have the right to set some conditions for their continued support and to refuse to pay for things they don't want their young adults to have.

While all parents face similar challenges, there are significant differences in how they view their involvement with their young adults and in the resources they can access to assist them. Many middle- and working-class mothers are eager for their young adults to achieve financial independence as soon as possible. They provide funding for their young adults as they can by contributing to college costs—including by taking out loans—but their ability to financially support their young adults has limits. Working-class mothers whose young adults are not going to college provide some financial support while their young adults look for work, primarily room and board, but as is the case with working-class parents more generally, they believe that their young adults should begin assuming more responsibility for their lives at an earlier age than most upper-middle-class parents do. Upper-middle-class parents believe it will take longer for their young adults to gain financial independence. They can more easily pay the costs of college, and many can also continue supporting their young adults financially with postgraduate education and internships that will promote their success going forward.

As young adults reach the age of 21, their pathways continue to diverge. In 2021, 62 percent of recent high school graduates ages 16 to 24 were enrolled in college.[12] Those from upper-middle-class families have benefited from the private resources of their parents, which have enabled them to attend well-funded secondary schools and "good" colleges. They are on track to finish college prepared for a career, and many of them have the credentials to obtain jobs or pursue further training after college, which their parents will also help support. Middle- and working-class young adults who have graduated from college also have the opportunity to get a good or adequately paying job, though they may be paying back college loans for some time. Some of those who have not attended college have acquired a postsecondary credential through the military, some additional training, or a certificate program.

For those without a college degree or further training, securing a job that pays a living wage can be difficult. In the United States there are not many institutionalized routes to employment or a career for young adults who do not attend college.[13] Some face a future of low-paying jobs and lower rates of marriage or long-term partnerships. In adulthood, as noted in the previous chapter, some of these young adults can go on to experience higher rates of drug and alcohol abuse and higher mortality rates, which have been called "deaths of despair." This group includes young adults from lower-income families who are disproportionately male and disproportionately African American.[14]

Given the increased length of young adulthood, mothers and fathers ask themselves how long to support their young adults and when to push them toward independence. Mothers I interviewed ask what their role should be at this point in the lives of their young adults. What is enough support? When does adulthood begin? Some, primarily upper-middle-class mothers, continue to support their young adults financially if this is what is necessary for them to gain advanced educational credentials. Most middle- and working-class parents I spoke with, however, do not expect to continue financially supporting their young adults into their twenties.

As their young adults move into their twenties, mothers reflected on how things have turned out for them. Some are pleased. They feel their young adults have found a path forward to a good future. As one upper-middle-class

[12] National Center for Education Statistics, "Immediate College Enrollment Rate," *Condition of Education* (Washington, DC: US Department of Education, Institute of Education Sciences, 2023).

[13] F. F. Furstenberg, "Becoming Adults: Challenges in the Transition to Adult Roles," *American Journal of Orthopsychiatry* 85(5S) (2015): S14–S21.

[14] A. Deaton and W. A. Case, *Deaths of Despair and the Future of Capitalism* (Princeton, NJ: Princeton University Press, 2020).

mother said, "Now it's like we're at a play. Our older kids are on the stage and we are in the audience. As long as things are going well, we can step back a little and enjoy the play." One African American working-class mother said, "I feel like I'm out of the woods now. They all have a good base to live their life on. I think they are going to be all right. I'm very proud of them, it makes me so happy." These mothers credit their teens and young adults, and themselves, for what they have done to promote their children's success.

At the same time, there are other mothers I interviewed who are uncertain about whether their young adult children will reach a point of occupational or financial security. Even if their young adult children have a college degree, many parents are concerned about how they will find good jobs in an ever-changing, uncertain economy. Those whose children have only a high school diploma worry about whether their children will be able to find work that enables them to become financially independent. Parents of young adults with physical or mental disabilities that prevent them from obtaining gainful employment may also need to support their young adults for an extended period of time.

Post-High School, Ages 18–22

College

In the United States, of the 62 percent of high school graduates ages 16 to 24 enrolled in college in 2021 after graduation. Forty-three percent enrolled in four-year colleges, and 19 percent in two-year colleges. More were female, and more were Asian students.[15] Most of those from the fifth highest-earning families go to selective, elite colleges, while the majority of students attend public institutions of higher education, including 37 percent of students who attend community colleges.[16] Students of color and low-income students

---

[15] In 2021, the immediate college enrollment rate after high school graduation in two- and four-year colleges was 70 percent for females, 55 for males, 84 percent for Asian students, 64 percent for white students, and 58 percent for Black students. National Center for Education Statistics, "Immediate College Enrollment Rate."

[16] Attendance at selective, elite colleges: R. Chetty et al., "Race and Economic Opportunity in the United States: An Intergenerational Perspective," *Quarterly Journal of Economics* 135(2) (2020): 711–783. Almost 79 percent (78.9 percent) of undergraduates attend public institutions; 21.1 percent attend private ones. See National Center for Education Statistics, "College Enrollment & Student Demographic Statistics, US Integrated Postsecondary Education Data System (IPEDS) 12-month Enrollment component, 2018–19 Provisional data" (Washington, DC: US Department

are more likely to attend community colleges, and some attend for-profit institutions.[17] Most of those attending four-year colleges are enrolled full-time, while the majority of students at two-year institutions attend part-time. Twenty-five percent of students attend residential colleges. Half of students live at home while they attend local colleges and universities.[18] In my sample, all the young adult children of upper-middle and middle-class families, and a little over half of young adult children from working-class families, were attending college. Upper-middle-class students, like many upper-middle-class students in the wider population, go to the kinds of selective, elite residential colleges they have been preparing for, colleges they hope will enable them to gain admission to graduate and professional school and enter well-paying professions. The majority of middle- and working-class students go to state colleges and universities that are closer to home.

Parents provide valuable support to their young adults in college. Some provide important financial support, and many provide emotional support. Some offer help when their young adult children get into academic or personal trouble. However, as they provide this support, mothers face a variety of constraints. It is more difficult to gain information about their college students' academic progress than it was in high school. The federal Family Educational Rights and Privacy Act (FERPA) mandates that unless a college student gives permission, parents cannot access information about their college academic record, including their grades or their academic status. Some colleges require students to make a decision when they enroll as to whether

of Education, 2020). In 2018–2019 a third of college students attended community colleges. S. Craft, ThinkImpact, December 18, 2021, https://www.thinkimpact.com/community-college-statistics/ Sandra Craft.

[17] Students of color and lower-income students are more likely to attend community colleges. See The Education Trust, 2021, https://edtrust.org. One in 10 students from low-income families attends for-profit institutions. See R. Howarth and W. Barkley-Denney, "New Stats on For-Profit Colleges by State Show Continued Poor Outcomes and Disproportionate Impacts" (Durham, NC: Center for Responsible Lending, 2019).

[18] Almost 61 percent (60.9 percent) of all students, graduate and undergraduate, are enrolled full-time. Among first-time, first-year college students, 83 percent are full-time students. M. Hanson, "College Enrollment & Student Demographic Statistics," Education Data Initiative, last updated January 10, 2024, https://educationdata.org/college-enrollment-statistics. Twenty-five percent of students in the United States attend residential colleges. J. Johnson and J. Rochkind, "With Their Whole Lives Ahead of Them: Myths and Realities About Why So Many Students Fail to Finish College," 2020), Public Agenda, prepared with support from the Bill and Melinda Gates Foundation. Before the pandemic, half of students lived at home while they attended local colleges and universities. Students from low-income families were more likely to live at home or with family while attending college (51 percent) than middle-income families (48 percent) and high-income families (25 percent) are. Sallie Mae, "How America Pays for College 2020."

or not they will allow their parents to see their academic records.[19] It is also more difficult for mothers to learn about their college students' social lives. They can be in frequent contact with their young adults by cell phone, or in person if their children live at home while attending college, but young adults conduct their own social lives at college and may or may not share information about their activities with their parents.

Upper-Middle-Class Mothers

Young adults of upper-middle-class mothers attend college in demanding, competitive environments and typically live on college campuses. Upper-middle-class mothers described providing their children with various kinds of help, including academic support, emotional support to deal with stress and mental health challenges, and, for a small number, help managing trouble. These mothers and fathers see their young adults' path to independence as an extended process. They know that not only a bachelor's degree but a graduate degree is now required for many higher-paying professional positions.[20] The colleges and universities their young adults attend are very expensive. Some parents can provide a lot of financial assistance, some can provide less or very little but help their children apply for loans and financial aid. Some mentioned providing funds for their children to take additional advanced classes, enriching trips abroad, or unpaid internships that could help further their careers.

As they provide academic support, some upper-middle-class mothers can act as unofficial college advisors. Based on their social and cultural capital, their knowledge of particular subjects, and their understanding of how colleges operate, they can offer valuable advice and take part in decision-making with their young adults about how to succeed in college. They help their young adults choose coursework that will enable them to move on to graduate and professional training and prepare them for successful careers. This type of assistance can increase the likelihood that their college students will go on to graduate school or secure a good job.[21]

---

[19] US Department of Education, "The Family Educational Rights and Privacy Act Guidance for Eligible Students" (Washington, DC: US Department of Education, 2011).

[20] F. Torche, "Intergenerational Mobility at the Top of the Educational Distribution," *Sociology of Education* 91(4) (2018): 266–289.

[21] Hamilton et al., "Providing a 'Leg Up.'"

The upper-middle-class mothers in my sample, who were primarily white, did not speak about monitoring their college students in the more intensive way that is often associated with the term "helicopter parenting," which is used to describe the micromanagement of college students' decisions. However, based on their social and cultural capital and their personal knowledge of how colleges operate, they feel comfortable giving some academic advice and support. Some reported that they help with academic work when their young adult children request it. They described proofreading term papers, discussing the merits of various college majors, and advising their college students about going abroad for a semester. They offer advice about coursework, although several mothers I interviewed seemed a little defensive about appearing to be a "helicopter mother." One mother stated:

> I'm not a helicopter mom. When my daughter asked me during her sophomore year in college to look over a paper she was writing, I said sure. I did that once or twice for her in high school too. The way I see it, it's a natural thing to do, it's what happens in the real world. I'm a journalist, I edit things all the time. I'm editing, I'm not writing her papers for her. And she wouldn't let me anyway.

While she doesn't see herself as a helicopter mom, this mother certainly provides her daughter with valuable academic assistance.

Upper-middle-class mothers can help with planning a college major as well. Since they have professional positions as lawyers, doctors, professors, and business executives, they can provide advice about a course of study that will prepare their young adult children for those fields. One mother, a medical doctor, whose son had a pre-med major in college (a major designed to prepare students to enter medical school after graduation) helped her son get summer jobs at a hospital, which provided him with experiences that she and her son hoped would strengthen his medical school application. Another mother, an African American lawyer in private practice, said her daughter wanted help deciding what college courses would best prepare her for law school:

> I told her they want to see that you take demanding courses and get good grades and of course that you do well on the LSAT [law school admission test]. We talked about different kinds of advanced courses like in economics

and political science. I gave her some advice about how to prepare for the LSAT. She said it was helpful.

There are, of course, limits to the academic help mothers can provide, limits imposed by college and university requirements as well as by young adults themselves. Elaine, a mother of two teens in high school and a daughter, Sasha, who is a sophomore in college, described how she and her husband tried to help Sasha as she was planning to study abroad for a semester. Sasha, who is majoring in chemistry, is planning to go to graduate school in that field, but she didn't want to miss the opportunity to study abroad. Elaine went abroad in college herself, so she offered to help Sasha with the application process. Elaine said their conversations back-and-forth went on for several weeks. She wanted to help her daughter, but it became tiring. Her comments demonstrate how involved some parents can be in their college students' academic choices, even while there are limits to the assistance they can provide:

> Sasha is trying to decide about going abroad. She's having trouble figuring out about the credits. The courses she wants to take in Italy would give her fewer course credits than she needs to stay on track for her chemistry major, and she doesn't know if she wants to do additional coursework to make up the difference after she gets back from Italy.

Elaine said she and her husband disagree about how much to support their daughter's decision-making, that her husband rolls his eyes and says their daughter is "making this into a big issue and she should figure this out on her own." However, Elaine believes it's fine to help their daughter figure out how to get the credits she needs. She said, "College is different now, there are so many choices, things are more complicated, I think it's okay to help." Thinking further, however, Elaine spoke about the limits of her ability to assist Sasha:

> I can't make this happen for her, I can't control the college's rules on how many credits different courses count for. There's nothing I can do about that, she's going to have to figure this out herself.

Mothers also provide emotional support for their young adult college students who are experiencing stress in their competitive, high-prestige college environments. As noted earlier, in recent years, increasing numbers of college students have experienced anxiety and depression (see note 10). Students at prestigious colleges and universities in particular arrive at college having gone to competitive high schools where there is a lot of pressure to excel in academics. Mothers reported that their college students worry about keeping up their grades and continue to feel pressure to perform at a high level in order to be accepted into graduate or professional school and increase the chances they will be admitted to more prestigious professions.

Mothers sympathize when their college-age children are stressed. They listen, they push their college students to get help, to go to office hours, to talk to their professors. They also do emotion work to suppress their own anxieties. But in the end, they are not sure how helpful they can be. Rebecca, an upper-middle-class mother who is white, for example, worries because her son Aaron, a college junior, is "stressed out" about his academic work at a highly prestigious liberal arts college. She said he called recently and was very upset and said, "Mom, I can't do this. It's too hard and there's too much work, I can't finish it all, I'll never get into the grad school I want for [economics]. I've been trying to keep up all semester, I'm always behind. Rebecca said she listened for a long time, and then, as she said, "I took a deep breath." Trying to conceal her own anxiety, she told Aaron he should remember how well he has done in college up to this point. Rebecca said she then asked her son, "Are you talking to your professors, going to office hours?" She said, "I wanted to push on that because I know he doesn't want his professors to see that he's struggling. I stressed sorting out priorities and making a schedule for completing his assignments." She continued:

> I was just trying to think of whatever I could. I was trying to help him get back on track and feel better—and help myself feel better but not to push him too hard, I don't want him to flunk any courses. That would be very bad for him, his self-esteem would tank, and I guess I'd be pretty upset too.

However, reflecting on the difficulty of motivating her young adult child, or pushing him, as Rebecca called it, she noted that strategically pushing too hard has a downside. As she said, "I don't want to push so hard that he says I have to stop telling him what to do and stops listening to anything I say. I'm telling him he has it in him, I know he does, but he has to figure this out, I can't do this for him." Rebecca said that as their phone conversation continued, Aaron calmed down and said he would try harder to prioritize his tasks. Rebecca said she then had to work on her own emotions; it was hard for her not to worry. "I checked in with Aaron in a few days," she said, "of course I wanted to know how he was doing—and I guess I have to say, to deal with my own feelings. I needed to know he was okay." Rebecca reported that Aaron now sounds calmer and said he is slowly catching up on his assignments.

In addition to reflecting on the stress students experience in competitive college environments, Rebecca acknowledged that she too has a lot at stake in her son's success in college. She said:

> I know I have to stay calm. It wouldn't be the end of the world if Aaron took a little time off from college, although he would feel terrible about that— he would see that as a failure. If he actually had to withdraw from [prestigious college], or god forbid flunk out, it would be a huge blow to him, and I have to say, I guess it would hard for me. All the families around here have kids who go to high-prestige colleges and everyone would know what happened.

Rebecca's comment about other families reflects the high priority some mothers and their social groups place on attendance at a prestigious college as a symbol of social status in their community, both for their young adult children and for themselves, as well as a stepping-stone to graduate or professional school.

Students can also become stressed about their participation in social clubs and activities. Social clubs of all kinds are a central part of college life for many, they can provide important friendship groups and valuable networks for career building. But joining some clubs can also involve a competitive, stressful process of applying, being evaluated, and potentially being rejected by peers. Once accepted, students must work to fit into the group, which can be challenging for minority students and others.[22] Anita is an African American mother of a 19-year-old daughter in college and a 23-year-old son who is a college graduate. Her daughter, Christina, is experiencing stress about her application to a prestigious debating club at her college. Anita said, "Christina really wants to get into this club. She said it will help her get into law school. She said, 'I absolutely need this for my resume.'" Anita continued,

---

[22] B. R. Silver, *The Cost of Inclusion: How Student Conformity Leads to Inequality on College Campuses* (Chicago: University of Chicago Press, 2020).

"I just don't know where Christina comes from sometimes. First she wants to be in the club, but then she says she's afraid she won't be accepted so she is not going to apply, then she says she doesn't care about it anyway." Anita reported that this time was stressful for her as well. Christina called her every evening for four days. Anita told Christina to stop calling so late in the evening, that she often had trouble getting to sleep after their conversations. Finally, Christina called to say she had applied for membership in the club, and Anita said that two weeks later Christina found out she had been accepted.

A white mother named Patricia is dealing with a son who may drop out of college, although not because of stress. She is worried that her son, Andrew, may not graduate, even though he has only one more semester to complete. Patricia said she is "pushing as hard as I can. I talk with Andrew on the phone when I can get a hold of him but he keeps saying, 'What's the point of college anyway?'" According to Patricia:

> Andrew is really involved in the environmental movement, the eco-justice movement he calls it. He says, "How can I just keep studying, stick my head in a book, when we're destroying the planet every day? I'm studying for a future that may not exist. We're organizing conferences here, there might be a sit-in soon, I could get arrested."

Patricia said, "I try to tell him he's just got to hang on one more semester, that it can be hard to get back to college life when you get off track, that a college degree makes a big difference in your life, it can help him with his environmental work." She then concluded, "But I don't know what he's going to do. I really worry, I don't know what else to do, I feel kind of powerless in this situation. I just have to learn to live with whatever he decides. It's his life, I know."

Some mothers also have to deal with situations where their teens get into trouble at college, situations that can be difficult to manage and cause mothers stress—academic trouble, trouble with alcohol and drugs, or encounters with law enforcement. In one case, a white mother named Stephanie used personal connections to get a legal charge against her son Jared modified after his encounter with the police. Jared attends a small college several hundred miles away, the same college Stephanie attended. One evening Jared borrowed a friend's car to go to a restaurant with his girlfriend, and on the way back to campus, he drove through a stop sign. Two police officers immediately stopped him and told him he had broken the law. According to what

Jared told Stephanie when he called her later that night, he argued with the police and told them that he was driving carefully but it was dark out, and the stop sign didn't reflect the light from his headlights very well—you couldn't see the stop sign—so this wasn't really his fault.

Stephanie said, "It seems as if Jared probably argued too long with the police." She said she and her husband have always told Jared not to argue with the police; however, she reports that "Jared can be stubborn." The officers told Jared that since he was challenging them, they should go discuss this further at the police station. Stephanie said she thinks that made Jared calm down and stop arguing because the police did not take him to the station. The police did say that because Jared had continued to challenge them, they were giving him a $200 ticket and that he could also be given a point or two on his driver's license, a penalty which could increase the amount he would have to pay for car insurance and increase the risk of his losing his license if he should accrue more points. The police then let him return to campus.

According to Stephanie, Jared was very upset when he and his girlfriend got back to campus. Jared went back to his dorm room and talked with his roommate, who told him to call the office of the Dean of Students. The Assistant Dean, who was on duty after hours, told Jared to come in at 9:00 a.m. the next morning. Stephanie said:

> Jared called me after he left the Dean of Students' office. He was really upset and worried about the money this was going to cost but especially about the points he was getting on his driver's license. He admitted that he had argued with the police for too long.

Stephanie and her husband provided Jared with invaluable help, moving quickly and activating their social networks. Stephanie contacted one of her college friends—she correctly remembered the friend knew the president of the college. Her friend called the college president, who got in touch with the college's lawyers. According to Stephanie, the lawyers contacted the police, and because Jared had no record of prior offenses, they secured an agreement that he would have to pay the fine but he would not be given any points on his driver's license.

Stephanie, her husband, and Jared were relieved that Jared hadn't gotten into more serious trouble. It is not hard to imagine how things could have turned out differently if Jared were African American, given that incidents of police harassment and violence toward African American men have occurred in similar kinds of situations. After this incident was resolved, Stephanie said she told her son, "We're sorry you got in trouble, but you screwed up, you have to handle yourself better if you get stopped by the police. We definitely need to talk more about this." Stephanie said, "I feel like, geez, come on Jared, grow up, don't argue with the police." Without a doubt, in this situation Jared benefited from his mother's connections but also from the student services the college provided, services that may not be available at all colleges.

Middle-Class Mothers

The young adults of the middle-class mothers I interviewed were for the most part attending colleges and universities nearby, either in the city where they lived or at a location a few hundred miles away, including state colleges and universities, Catholic universities, technical universities, and a community college. Several were living at home while they attend college. Middle-class mothers provide financial, academic, and emotional support for their college students, and they sometimes help when trouble arises. As they provide this assistance, they focus on the need for their young adults to become more independent and take more responsibility for paying for their college expenses. These mothers also urge their young adult children to choose a major in a field that will enable them to start earning money after graduation, something undoubtedly all parents do, but middle-class and working-class mothers in my sample identified this as an immediate priority. A white mother who has a son who is a college junior and is majoring in biology, said, "When our son was accepted at college, he wanted to do astronomy for his major." She and her husband told their son not to do that, suggesting that because they are contributing money to their son's college education, they have a say in what he can choose as a major:

> He always liked looking through telescopes. But my husband and I looked online at career possibilities for different majors, and we didn't think astronomy looked too good. So we said, "No, you need to choose something more practical, you need to start earning real money when you graduate. We're paying money for you now so you will be able to support yourself." Maybe he can have a minor in astronomy.

Most middle-class mothers do not get as involved in the details of their college students' academic choices as upper-middle-class mothers. They urge their college-age children to take responsibility for their academic work and believe that colleges are there to ensure that their children do that. While providing less assistance in academic matters, however, these mothers can provide other valuable support to their young adult children, help that is often not visible to others. Those who monitor their young adults' progress in college can ask questions and listen for problems. They largely depend on what their young adult children tell them about their own academic progress. Some of their college students tell them when they are having trouble, while some do not.

Ellen, whose son, Anthony, is a third-year college student who lives at home, reported that things are going well for her son. She is pleased that he is in the business school at a local university, "so he will be prepared for a job when he graduates." Ellen, who is white, said she does not ask much about Anthony's college life. As she put it, "He's making his own decisions about college, he likes his major and his professors—he's done well. He's more independent now." She later said, "When I ask, Anthony will tell me about things at college, but I don't ask too much, I don't want him to think I am interfering." Presumably, Ellen believes that if Anthony thinks she is meddling, this could irritate him and make communication more difficult. Ellen's use of the word "interfering" also seems to reflect a belief that her son's college affairs are his private business because he is now, as she said, more independent. She said she trusts Anthony, and she noted, "If he has a problem, he'll tell me." Because he is not reporting any difficulty, she assumes things are going well.

While middle-class mothers on the whole may be less knowledgeable than their upper-middle-class counterparts about navigating the details of academic systems of higher education, they can and do provide valuable assistance in dealing with academic problems if their college-age children share information about their problems. Adele, an African American mother, reported that her daughter, Rashida, who was living on campus at a local university, was facing academic difficulties. At first, Adele did not know this because Rashida didn't tell her and because, due to FERPA, colleges do not send information about students' academic records to parents. During the fall and into the spring semester, Rashida had been telling Adele that everything at college was fine. However, in the middle of the spring semester, Rashida told her mother she had been put on academic probation. Adele said she could tell Rashida was distraught. "She was ashamed and scared," she noted. Rashida had worked hard to get into this university and had chosen a computer engineering major. She was one of only a few women and a few African American students in the major. After Rashida gave her this news, Adele demanded to see her daughter's report card. "But," Adele reported, "My daughter said, 'Mom, I don't have to show you my grades because I'm a college student now.'"

However, using the fact that she is contributing some money for Rashida's college tuition as leverage, Adele still considers herself "the boss" and succeeded in getting Rashida to tell her grades. Adele said she told her daughter, "Oh, yes, you do have to show me your grades because I'm paying real money for you, so I'm the boss here. You will show me your grades because I need to understand more about what the problem is here." Rashida relented, and Adele saw how her grades had dropped in her field of concentration. Adele pushed Rashida to get more help. Rashida had consulted a graduate student advisor in her major who told her she was not strong enough in computer engineering subjects to remain in this field and should consider switching to the Arts and Sciences College. Adele said this news was devastating to her daughter.

In a phone conversation she had with Rashida shortly after Rashida's meeting with the graduate student advisor, Adele reported that her daughter broke down sobbing and said, "'It's all over for me, Mom.'" Adele said Rashida was immobilized. She knew her daughter would feel like a failure if she could not be in some type of engineering or computer science field. "So," Adele said, "I pushed Rashida, I pushed her hard to talk with someone else before making a decision that would end her ability to major in her chosen field, I said 'Look, you have to investigate this more, you don't just go on what one person says, you have to talk to more people. Push yourself.'" Rashida took her mother's advice. She consulted a second advisor, who recommended that Rashida switch her major to the field of networking and communication in the Engineering School. Rashida had taken a few courses in this field and done better than in her computer engineering subjects. She was able to make this switch and continue in an area of study that interested her without leaving the Engineering School.

Throughout this time, Adele provided emotional support for her daughter. She texted her encouraging messages, telling her what a good student she had always been and how she had overcome academic challenges in the past. She took Rashida out to dinner and brought food to her at her dorm to supplement the normal college fare. As Adele said, "I was trying to boost her self-esteem." This case raises the question of whether if Adele had tried to monitor Rashida's academic progress more closely, she would have been able to intervene and help her sooner. However, students are expected to manage their own lives at college and Rashida was not sharing information about her academic work and was telling Adele that everything was fine. Once Rashida told her mother that she had been put on academic probation, Adele acted quickly and provided advice to her daughter that was certainly valuable.

Mothers described facing decisions about how much financial support they should give their college students and how much financial and other kinds of responsibility they believe their young adult children should take for paying for their own college expenses. They also worry about how much debt they and their young adult children should take on. For these mothers, paying for college not only requires filling out a lot of paperwork and writing checks; it also involves negotiations with their young adult children about how much they will contribute to paying for their college expenses. Some families require that their college students work for pay to help cover their expenses, either at regular jobs or work-study jobs (on-campus jobs that students do in return for financial aid)."

Chantel, a middle-class African American mother, pushed her daughter to start paying more money for her education. She said, "My daughter is living off campus now—we pay her rent and food. She covers her spending money and her phone payments from what she's saved from her summer job. She thinks she's contributing enough." But now, Chantel said:

> My husband and I finally got across to our daughter that she has to take more responsibility for things, that college isn't a given. This summer I told her we want her to pay for her books now and she agreed. There was a lot of back and forth. But of course she had to agree, she has to have our financial support, we've got the leverage here.

Mary Louise, a white middle-class mother whose daughter Stacey is a sophomore in college, said she and her husband contribute some money to their daughter's college expenses to make up for what her scholarship and her loans don't cover. But she said they need to be saving more money; they have two other high school-age children who will be attending college soon. Mary Louise and her husband are pressuring Stacey to start contributing more to the cost of her college education. They have recently had a difference with her about dropping a course, something they believe will cost the family more money. The actions of Mary Louise and her husband show once again the central role financial support can play in decisions about young adults' college attendance and the question of how much responsibility their college students should take for paying for their college education. As Mary Louise noted:

> Stacey is a sophomore now. The other day she called and told us she was going to drop a course. She said she was worried about her grade in the course and she had to drop it soon or she would miss the deadline for dropping a course.

Mary Louise said it was clear Stacey hadn't thought about the financial implications of this decision. She and her husband used the fact that they were contributing to Stacey's college costs as leverage to pressure her to take more responsibility for the cost of her college education. As Mary Louise said:

> After she told me about dropping a course, we had a heated discussion. I said to her, "You can't just drop that course, who's paying here? This would mean you would have to stay at college longer or pick up a course somewhere, and that would cost even more money!"

She said they talked some more, and Stacey agreed to get help from her professor and try to do better in the course so she would not have to drop it. Mary Louise concluded by saying, "Stacey's not happy about this. She'd still like to drop the course, but she has to understand that there are financial consequences to a decision like this. We're working hard to support her and she's got to do her part."

Miriam, a white middle-class mother, has a son, Paul, who is in college, and a daughter in high school. Miriam said she and her husband are conflicted about how much Paul should contribute financially toward his education at a nearby state college. They are trying to balance the goal of making Paul take some responsibility for college expenses with their desire to give him enough time to focus on his studies:

> We paid for Paul's college costs up until now, what his scholarship didn't cover, we had a little savings. He hasn't been working at school. We decided

that was okay because Paul has been struggling with some of his classes, that we would support him so he didn't have to have a job.

Miriam also said she had been hoping her children wouldn't have to work as hard as she did in college. "I had to go to college part-time and work part-time," she said:

> I want to give a better experience to my kids. I had to work like a dog to pay for college, I want to give my son and daughter better than that. And then I have to say, being an adult isn't a whole lot of fun, so why shouldn't they have their youth?

However, at this point, Miriam said she and her husband are going to make Paul take more responsibility for his college costs:

> My husband and I made our decision. We're going to tell Paul that now that his sister is going to college, we will be paying less money for his college next year, that we paid for him for two years, that we can't pay all the costs for both him and his sister so he's got to start earning money and cover the rent at his off-campus apartment. We will pay for the tuition that his scholarship doesn't cover, but he has to pay the rest.

Miriam concluded by saying, "I think Paul is going to be upset. He'll push up against us, but we won't back down, he's not the only one who needs our financial help to go to college."

Mothers of college students who live at home reported negotiating over another set of issues, household work, particularly with their daughters. These mothers support their young adults financially by providing room and board, and most want their young adults to take some responsibility for household work. Rachel, a white middle-class mother, said things are going smoothly with her two daughters who live at home while attending college. It has been easy to negotiate new agreements about how much responsibility they should take for their own lives. They don't pay rent, but they have started paying for personal expenses. They have part-time jobs and pay for their clothing and car insurance. Rachel said she has a different relationship with them now, that "they are more independent." She noted:

There are no rules for them now, they come and go as they please. And it's been easy for us to negotiate new agreements with our daughters. Now they do their own laundry, I used to do a lot of that. They cook their own meals. And they have their own cars. We bought them old cars because they have to get to their college classes.

Rachel said, "Things are working well. My daughters are pretty easy to be around. Sometimes we eat together or watch TV together, it's nice."

By contrast, Norma, a divorced white mother with two college student daughters living at home, feels as if she has failed to negotiate new terms of agreement about household chores with them. She said, "I feel like I am still stuck being 'mother,' you know, the one who has to do everything":

They need to take responsibility for their own lives now, but I don't think they are. They don't do dishes, and I still do their laundry. I should have had them do more chores when they were younger. I have a neighbor who didn't work outside the home when her kids were younger like I always have, but she still had her daughters do chores. Now they go to college and live at home and they still do their chores.

Norma said, "I don't know why I didn't push them harder to do chores when they were younger. I was going through a divorce, I was thinking about other things." She feels torn about whether to ask her daughters to do more now because they have part-time jobs and are very stressed about their college work.

Middle-class mothers' accounts also reflect a changing personal relationship with their young adult children, a distancing along with times of closeness. One mother said, "With my daughters now, I guess I'm more their friend than their mother. It's not the same—you're not as close as when they were younger, they have new friends. I'm glad for this, this is what's supposed to happen, but I liked being a mother the old way too, when they were coming up." As they negotiate over issues of responsibility and independence with their young adults, some mothers report continuing to be sensitive to how they talk with them. They issue directives when they feel they are necessary. However, they may also negotiate on a more equal basis, respecting their young adults' right to make more of their decisions and also fearing pushback, that their young adults could react negatively to being told what to do.

Jean-Marie is an African American mother, a widow whose son, Simon, lives at home while attending a local university. She described developing a new relationship with Simon, who is a senior. She said her son has become more independent, he has good judgment, and he's chosen good friends. "He's real solid," she said. Jean-Marie also said she is careful how she speaks to him and that she's been "backing off":

> I purposely try not to be overbearing so he has room to breathe. He's older, he's more independent, he comes and goes himself, I sort of let him figure out things for himself before I jump in and say what I'd like him to do. I think he has a foundation and that he's real level-headed.

Simon still consults with Jean-Marie, although it sounds as if Jean-Marie does not offer much advice and Simon mostly relies on his own opinions. "Simon checks things out on his own," she said, "then he runs things by me, he thinks of what he wants to do and then he says, 'How does this sound?' I usually say, 'Sounds feasible, as long as you looked into it.'" While Simon likes to run things by her, Jean-Marie also said, "He can't be talked into doing things he doesn't want to do."

Finally, Marianna, a white mother who works as an accountant, described how she is managing a situation that arose when her 19-year-old son, Steven, developed mental health problems. Marianna reported that Steven has developed a serious mental health problem at the public university he attends in another state and must leave college for now. The onset of mental illness often occurs during adolescence and into the early twenties.[23] A dean at the college called Marianna and her husband and told them that Steven had stopped attending his classes and that they needed to bring him home. Steven had told Marianna and her husband that he was depressed, and Marianna said they were keeping in touch with him, but Steven was insisting that he was "doing OK" and that he was getting better. He had not told them he was skipping classes.

Marianna and her husband have brought Steven home and have found a psychiatrist who has prescribed medication for his depression. Marianna said her son sleeps a lot and doesn't want to leave the house. However, she is hoping the medication will have a positive effect so that Steven can take a class or two at a local university before too long, although she said the priority now is for Steven to get better. The process of handling this situation

---

[23] B. J. Hibbs and A. Rostain, *The Stressed Years of Their Lives: Helping Your Kid Survive and Thrive During Their College Years* (New York: St. Martin's Press, 2019).

has been emotionally draining for the whole family. Marianna and her husband are trying to remain hopeful about the future. She said, "Steven is such a good student and a good person, I hope he can get through this pretty soon. It's really hard on him and it's really hard on us, worrying about when he will get better."

Working-Class Mothers

The working-class mothers I interviewed reported that a little over half of their young adult children are going to college. They attend local colleges, including two-year colleges. One mother reported that her daughter was going to a private, for-profit college. Half of these working-class mothers said their young adult children are living at home while attending college. Like other mothers, they provide their children with advice on their college planning, emotional support, and help with trouble. They also spoke frequently about money and the difficulty of providing financial help to their college-age students.

These mothers view their young adults' college attendance as a way to prepare for a career or a job that will provide them with more opportunities and a better standard of living than they have had themselves. They take pride when their college students are successful. One mother said that her daughter "loves her courses and her professors. She wants to go to graduate school for teaching kids with disabilities." Her daughter has a full scholarship to a local college. She, her husband, and their daughter have all been able to avoid taking out loans.

Like other mothers I interviewed, working-class mothers urge their college-age children to choose courses of study that will enable them to gain marketable skills while they are in college. Gladys, an African American mother, has two sons who are college graduates and one who is currently in college. Gladys said she has pushed her sons to pursue fields of study that will provide an adequate standard of living. She has taken on a bit of a role as a college advisor and feels she has been successful. Gladys has based her advice on her own experiences and her observations of her sons and what she thinks they would be good at. She said:

My goal was to make sure they would have a good skill when they graduated. [Chuckling] Actually I told them what to do in college and they did it, and that makes me feel good! I saw the field of physical therapy when I had physical therapy, and I told my oldest son, "You should do physical therapy, you're strong, you were a high school athlete and you can work with people."

Then, with the next one, I told him he should be a math teacher, I said, "You're good at math, and you're good at talking." And that's what he is. I knew my younger son would be good at computers, I encouraged him, and that's what he's majoring in at his college. So they all have good skills.

Working-class mothers I interviewed hope their young adults will do well in their courses, but they are typically not involved in the specifics of their college students' academic planning. They believe their children will get academic advising at college and should manage their college education themselves. In some cases, these mothers said that because their college students don't report problems, they assume they are doing well. They expect their young adult children to take care of their academic affairs on their own, although if their children tell them they are experiencing academic or other kinds of trouble, working-class mothers work to help as they can.

Sandy, a white working-class mother, held back on advising her daughter Samantha about a major, thinking she should be responsible for her own decisions in college. However, now that Samantha is having trouble with her academic work, Sandy wonders if she should have intervened in her daughter's decision-making. Samantha has chosen a specialization in the university's business school, risk management, that Sandy said Samantha was excited about. But this subject proved too difficult for her, and she dropped several courses. Now Samantha has to take extra credits and spend more time in school. Sandy said, "I sort of thought this field would be a little too hard for her and the program she is enrolled in has a reputation for being tough." Now Sandy is asking herself, "Should I have said more ahead of time and pushed her to get into another field?" "But," she said, "I'm trying to get her to think for herself, to be more independent. You don't want to tell your child what to do—I think she has to learn to make her own decisions." She also wondered, "If I had pushed Samantha to pursue another field of study, would she have listened?" As she noted, "Samantha has a mind of her own."

More working-class mothers than other mothers reported that their young adult children get into serious academic trouble. The dropout rate of college students in the United States—the rate of students who do not complete their program—is 33 percent (32.9 percent).[24] Students may drop out for a variety of reasons: they may have difficulties connecting to campus life, they may face academic challenges, they may need to attend to family problems at home, or they may experience financial difficulties. In trying to address their college-age children's problems, some mothers said they felt effective, while others said they did not.

Sue Anne, a white mother, is worried about her son's academic performance. She is upset that her son, Bill, has received a failing grade, and she is trying to pressure him to do better in college. She finds her son frustrating. He doesn't communicate with her much about his academic work, but she sees his college grades, which she said were average. When Bill enrolled in college, Sue Anne insisted that he give permission for his grades to be sent to her and her husband, thus bypassing the FERPA restrictions. However, Sue Anne recently received Bill's midterm marks and saw that he had received a grade of F. She said:

> I called Bill immediately when I got his midterm marks and saw that one was an F. I said, "Why did you get an F?" I just really lost it. I said, "What are we paying all this money for?" Bill said, "Don't worry, I'll bring it up." I said, "What grade are you going to bring an F up to, to make it worth the money we are paying?" He said, "I'll bring it up, don't worry about it." He's just like that.

Sue Anne questioned how much influence she has with her son. She said, "Bill is pretty even-keeled, laid-back really, nothing bothers him. Sometimes that's okay, it can even be good, but at times it can be really exasperating!" Sue Anne said she feels that so far, she hasn't been able to pressure Bill into working harder to get better grades. She said she and her husband have considered telling him they are going to reduce the amount of money they pay for his college education to pressure him to work harder in school, but they haven't decided whether to do this because Bill would have to get a second job and that could hurt his studies.

Some working-class mothers reported providing emotional support when their young adult children are having academic difficulties. Regina, a white

---

[24] Up to 32.9 percent of undergraduates do not complete their degree program. White students have a dropout rate 33.4 percent, and Black students have a dropout rate of 14.4 percent. M. Hanson, "College Dropout Rate," Education Data Initiative, last updated October 29, 2023, https://educationdata.org/college-dropout-rates.

mother, said she was worried about her daughter Shelley, who is struggling academically at the local college where she is pursuing a degree in occupational therapy. Shelley lives at home while taking college classes. Regina wants to support Shelley because she is experiencing a lot of stress. She is behind in her academic work and has to make up two incompletes she received for not finishing her work in two courses during the past semester. Shelley feels her high school didn't prepare her well for college. Regina said, "I talk to her a lot and try to support her. I don't want her to give up and then look back and feel like she regrets not finishing her degree." But Regina said she feels helpless in this situation. She said, "I didn't go to college, I can't help her with her courses. All I can do is encourage her, I don't know what else to do." Regina concluded: "I pray every night that Shelley succeeds and gets her degree and a job. She is really struggling with the occupational therapy courses. I hope she can make it."

In addition to concerns about their college students' academic performance, working-class mothers, more than other mothers in the sample, were very concerned about whether or how they would be able to help their young adults pay for college. Some cannot provide any financial help; some push their young adults to pay for more of their own college expenses. In addition to jobs on campus, some of their young adult children have off-campus jobs—bartending, waitressing, caring for young children as a nanny—and sometimes they work at more than one. This work, however, doesn't cover all of their college costs. Cheryl, a white working-class mother, said she and her husband are "very stressed" about money and are trying to decide how much their young adult children should contribute to their college expenses. They have two children in college and two in junior high school. Cheryl said they wanted to live in the city to be near her parents, and she and her husband knew this meant they would have to pay for private schooling because they didn't want to send their children to public schools. But as a result, they haven't been able to save much money for their children's college education.

Cheryl has two children who are enrolled at state universities and receive only small scholarships. She and her husband pay the remainder of their tuition and require that their young adult children pay for living expenses. She said:

We're just trying to keep our heads above water and it's not working. This is the third year with two in college. It's not working and I get so stressed out because we don't have enough money and we have to take out loans. And it's not fair to the other kids who are still at home.

Cheryl said she and her husband continually negotiate with their son about who will be responsible for various college expenses. She reported, "Part of our deal to make this work is that our son Sam who is a junior in college has to make good money in the summer. He works in construction and uses what he makes for spending money and dorm fees, including his meals. And he has his work-study job." However, she said:

I always forget that things come up. I think we have figured out how to cover everything and then there are all these extras. Sam's soccer team is going to play in a tournament in [another state] next month. He has to pay for some of the expenses for the trip; the university will only contribute a little.

Cheryl said she and her husband are talking about whether Sam will have to get a part-time job. She said, "I don't think he will like that. He's got a lot of schoolwork, he has soccer practices all the time, his team is doing well and they are hoping to win a lot of games and reach the championship."

Cheryl also stated that "We're always giving out money. We're helping pay our daughter's college expenses too." Their daughter is at a college two hundred miles away and has a job as a part-time nanny but still needs more money for rent and living expenses for the apartment she shares with roommates. Cheryl said, "Her bank statement is sent here. She and I have to talk more—I've gotten statements that say she has a $2.00 balance! She and I have to communicate better about this. She always waits until the last minute to say she needs money." Decisions about paying for college can affect the whole family. Cheryl said, "We have to help our college kids, but this is cutting into the money we are saving for our younger children." She said, "And my daughter who's 16, she keeps asking for money—and I'm always saying, 'No.' I feel badly because her two best friends seem to get handed the things they want. From time to time, I find myself yelling at her that she can't get all these things, and I feel badly about that too, it's not her fault."

Some parents have to take on extra work to pay for college. Jolene, an African American mother whose husband passed away several years ago, has a son and a daughter who attend a state college, spoke of needing to work additional hours. Her son and daughter have some scholarship money, and they have part-time jobs as restaurant servers while attending college, but the schools they attend require that Jolene contribute some modest funds for their tuition. As someone with a low-paying job as a nurse's aide, Jolene speaks anxiously about college bills. While we talked, she kept looking down at the college bills on her kitchen table and shaking her head. She thought the college made a mistake in sending her another bill, saying it seems like, "I'm always having to pay more":

> I am so frustrated. The kids get loans and grants, but then the forms say "contribution from the family." They have that line and I have to pay. They say I make too much money. And then I just got this new bill for $500. [With real agitation] I'm calling them. I'm going to call them to find out what is going on. I just paid $500, I thought I was done.

To pay for her young adults to attend college, Jolene said, "I'll have to work more because they keep raising the cost of college. I work full-time now, but I figure I'll have to work at least 10 hours a week more."

Students from working-class families can also face a lot of pressure because in order to afford college, they often have to work more hours at paid jobs than other students do. Forty-five percent of students in four-year colleges work at paid jobs for more than 20 hours a week. Sixty percent of students in community colleges work more than 20 hours a week, and more than a quarter of them work over 35 hours a week. When students who have jobs drop out of college, the majority say the difficulty of taking classes while working to pay for college is the primary reason they drop out.[25] Some college students not only need money for their own expenses; they also try to give some money to their families when they know they are struggling financially.[26]

Like other mothers, some working-class mothers provide help when their college students find themselves in trouble. This assistance, while often invisible, can be very valuable for their college-age students. Cora, a working-class African American mother, provided invaluable help to her daughter

---

[25] Johnson and Rochkind, "With Their Whole Lives Ahead of Them."

[26] L. Napolitano, "'I'm Not Going to Leave Her High and Dry': Young Adult Support to Parents During the Transition to Adulthood," *Sociological Quarterly* 56(2) (2015): 329–354. Elena van Stee describes how working-class college students who returned home during the pandemic made significant contributions to household work and childcare. This was in contrast to upper-middle-class students, whose parents worked to ensure that their college students were able to study at home without having household or family responsibilities. E. G. Van Stee, "Privileged Dependence, Precarious Autonomy: Parent/Young Adult Relationships Through the Lens of COVID-19," *Journal of Marriage and Family* 85 (2023): 215–232.

Shannon, who dropped out of college due to academic failure. Cora's older daughter graduated from a local university, earned a master's degree in library science, and has a good job in the city library system. Her younger daughter Shannon, however, went away to college in a state nearby and according to Cora, "messed up." Through a somewhat lengthy process, Cora held Shannon accountable while helping her get back on track:

> I had to go and get my daughter Shannon at college, she messed up. She had a meltdown, she was overwhelmed, she was behind in her work. She fell in love and went to live off campus. I think she partied too much. She didn't tell me about any of this. Shannon didn't learn how to manage her time, she had a new boyfriend and that wasn't going well, she was a mess.

Cora said, "This was very stressful for her but definitely for me too." When Shannon returned home, Cora took action and demanded that she take responsibility for her failure and get a job. She reported that, "When Shannon felt better, I said, 'You're not going to go to school, you have to work, that's what you have to do. And you have to help around the house.' Fortunately," Cora said:

> After a while, Shannon could see that she needed to go back to college to get a decent job, so she came to me and we talked about it and she said, "Mom, are you going to help me?" After I saw that she had straightened herself out and saved some money, I said, "Yes, I'll help you pay some of your tuition, only some."

Cora insisted, however, that Shannon take most of the responsibility for paying for her college expenses because she had not only "messed up" by getting too far behind in her college work to catch up, she had also lost her college credits and tuition for the semester. Cora said:

> Shannon asked me, "Am I going to have to use my money to go back to college?" I told her, "Yes you are, every last bit of it you're going to have use, yes. Because I did it for you, but you messed up. I'm going to help you but your money, yes, you're going to have to use it."

Shannon certainly paid a price for messing up. However, once she had left college, she was fortunate to have a mother who took charge of her situation and helped her find a path forward, with conditions. As Cora said, "I wasn't going to just bail her out. She had to learn how to take responsibility for her decisions and mistakes." One could ask in this case, as in a case cited earlier, whether Cora could have identified her daughter's problems earlier. She said she was in touch with Shannon at college by phone and text, but Shannon didn't mention having problems. Cora thinks her daughter was hiding things from her about how serious she was about her boyfriend because Shannon believed Cora wouldn't have approved of the relationship. Perhaps if Shannon had been living at home while attending college, Cora would have been able to intervene sooner. Cora reported that responding to this situation required a lot of work on her part handling the emotional, social, and practical issues that arose for herself as well as Shannon.

Isabel, an African American working-class mother of two daughters ages 23 and 15 faced an additional set of tasks helping her older daughter, Malika, get a college degree. Isabel reported that Malika is doing college "the hard way." She became pregnant while attending a local community college and living at home. She took a break from college to take care of the baby and then moved in with the baby's father. Malika did return to college part-time and recently married the baby's father, who is currently unemployed. She has a part-time job while attending college and taking care of the baby. In the coming summer, she will take a break from college and work full-time to save for next year's tuition. Isabel tries to help Malika on the weekends. She regrets that she cannot help her daughter pay for college and that her daughter's life is so stressful. A number of college students (more than 20 percent) and community college students (30 percent), the majority of them women, are attending college while raising children.[27]

Graduation rates of college students vary according to their social class, gender, and race. Three-quarters of all beginning college students start college at age 20 or younger. Sixty-four percent complete college within six years; 36 percent drop out. Seventy-five percent of those in high earning brackets earn bachelor's degrees compared to only 10 percent of students in the bottom income-earning bracket. Those who attend nonprofit four-year colleges earn a degree at higher rates than students who attend other types of

[27] B. Williams, "Many Determined College Students Are Also Dedicated Parents: A Preview of the Student Parent Affordability Report" (Washington, DC: The Education Trust, 2022).

institutions. More females than males graduate from college after six years, as do more white than African American students.[28]

Post High School: No College

In my sample, a little over 40 percent of working-class mothers reported that their young adults did not attend college. Some don't plan to go at all, some are not attending at present because they are undecided about what to study, and some are not attending because they don't have the money to enroll. Some mothers reported that their young adults who don't attend college are taking steps to plan for their future. They have entered the military, enrolled in a training program for computer programming, hairdressing, or automotive repair, or joined a police academy. Still others have started at low-wage jobs as hospital aides, demolition workers, or salesclerks. Two enlisted into the military. However, another group of mothers are worried that their young adult children are not finding a clear direction forward; they are not enrolling in training programs or taking steps to prepare for jobs that will support an adequate standard of living. As noted above, in the United States, there are few institutionalized routes that help young people who do not attend college gain job training and transition to adulthood. And those who do not gain an educational or work-related credential during this time or in the future can potentially face serious disadvantages, including uncertain work lives, the inability to form long-term stable relationships, and problems with substance abuse.[29]

As they provide assistance for their young adults who are not attending college, mothers are very concerned their young adults take steps to become independent. Using their knowledge of job possibilities and their personal networks, they provide advice to their young adult children on how to find jobs. Some believe their children are finding a path forward, and some worry about how they will become financially independent. They push them to

---

[28] Almost 65 percent (64.5 percent) of all students entering four-year colleges in 2015 graduated within six years. Sixty-six percent (66.4 percent) of all women had earned a degree within six years compared to 60.4 percent of men. "The Significant Gender Gap in College Graduation Rates" (Bartonsville, PA: Women in Academia, 2022). Seventy percent of white students earned a degree after six years, compared with 51.5 percent of Black and Latino (51.5 percent) students. A. H. Nichols and M. Anthony Jr., "Graduation Rates Don't Tell the Full Story: Racial Gaps in College Success Are Larger Than We Think" (Washington, DC: The Education Trust, 2020).

[29] A. Case and A. Deaton, "The Great Divide: Education, Despair, and Death."

find jobs and take more responsibility for their own expenses and living situation. Some use money as leverage to encourage their young adult children's independence. Others ask themselves not how much money they will give their young adults but how much their young adults should pay them.

One African American working-class mother reported, "Our son is living at home now, he got an internship at a bank through a high school program and then they offered him a position at the bank when he graduated. He's living at home to save money. We're only asking him to pay a small amount of money for rent so he can build up some savings." She said she and her husband are happy to have their son at home and that he gets along well with the family and helps around the house.

Sandra, who is white, is pleased that her daughter Alisha, now 21, is a police officer. When Alisha graduated from high school, Sandra said she pushed her to find a career and become more independent. Alisha lived at home after high school and worked part-time at a convenience store while attending the police academy. Sandra said she required her daughter to pay some money in rent because she was working, but only a nominal amount because Alisha was working at a minimum-wage job. She noted, "When I told Alisha she had to pay some money for rent, she said 'Why?' I said, 'Cause that's the real world, get ready for it, you have to be more independent.'" Sandra and her husband did help Alisha buy a car by cosigning a loan. She said, "Alisha needed a car to get to her job, and we didn't have an extra one to give her. She has to pay car expenses and repairs herself. I don't pay any of that."

Lucille is a white mother whose daughter Tyla Anne recently graduated from high school. She and her husband have developed specific conditions for Tyla Anne to meet in order to continue living at home. Lucille reports that Tyla Anne doesn't want to go to college yet; she has gotten a job in a doctor's office scheduling appointments. Lucille said she and her husband don't want any "bums" in the house, and they want their daughter to start paying rent and taking more responsibility for household tasks:

> Our position is we won't cut our children off when they are 18, but we don't want any bums in the house either. They are free to stay, but then they will start paying. Trisha will be 18 next month. I've told her she'll need to start paying 40 dollars a week. Then, as she gets settled, she will need to pay more.

She'll also have to keep up her responsibilities—helping get dinner on the table, taking care of the animals, the garbage, clearing the table. It's all over there on the calendar.

Theresa is a white mother of a 20-year-old daughter who works in a shoe store. She reported that last year, she and her husband also put conditions on providing room and board for their daughter, who had moved out of the house but then moved back in when she had a conflict with a roommate. This included the stipulation that their daughter had to begin saving money. Theresa and her husband didn't charge her rent but took steps they hoped would persuade her to start taking more responsibility for her own affairs:

> I told her, "We don't want any rent but what you have to do is you have to save." We said, "You move in with the condition that you have to save money for a deposit and first and last month's rent on an apartment for when you move out. And save money for things you need in that apartment."

Theresa was firm with her daughter, telling her, "If you don't save, you're out of here." To enforce this rule, Theresa said, "When she got her pay every two weeks, she had to give me the money to put aside, she had to hand it to me, and I put it in a bank account I opened for her, except for some money for personal expenses."

Another group of mothers worried that their young adult children are falling behind, not getting the training they need to find jobs that can provide an adequate standard of living. Several mothers believed that at the current time, there is not much they can do to promote their young adults' successful transition to adulthood. Bettina, an African American mother of a 9-year-old daughter, an 11-year-old son, and a 19-year-old son, Richard, feels badly that Richard cannot get a better-paying job. Bettina provides room and board for him while he is trying to save enough money for college. Currently, he works as a dishwasher at a fast-food restaurant. When he was in high school, Richard couldn't decide if he wanted to go to college, but now he wants to go. Bettina said Richard did "pretty well" in high school and is a hard worker, but for now, he is "in limbo." She said, "He is still not sure what he'd like to do for a career. What he would really like to do is go to school, but he has to figure out how to get the money, that's the problem." With disappointment in her voice, Bettina said, "People say they are going to help Richard get a better job, but some people don't follow through. They promise things, but they don't do what they say they're going to do. I really hope he can make it to college, he's motivated, he's a good kid." Of course, with only a high school diploma, Richard faces significant challenges in getting a better-paying job and saving money. And Bettina does not seem to have social connections that could help Richard find a better job.

Joan is a white single mother who feels that her son Jeremy is also in limbo, stuck for the time being because he can't afford further training. Jeremy was diagnosed with a learning disability in high school but was able to graduate. However, he found community college too difficult. Jeremy then said he wanted to be a musician. Joanna said she "worked on him" and convinced him he had to get some practical skills before trying to become a full-time musician. Joan paid for him to take a class in a training program for heating and air conditioning, and Jeremy said this is what he will do now. But Joan can't afford to pay for any more of the classes Jeremy needs in order to be cer-tified, and he is not making enough money at his job in a local pet store to afford the classes himself.

While more female than male young adults attend college, mothers can also worry about their daughters. In a few cases, mothers were worried that their young adult daughters lack the motivation to move forward. They have pushed them to work harder to find a job or enroll in a training program but have not been successful so far. A white mother named Madeleine has had a very frustrating experience with her 19-year-old daughter, Christy. Madeleine did her best to get her to enroll in college; she pushed her but was not able to persuade her to go. Christy had received a full scholarship for her freshman year at a local university but refused to attend. Madeleine said:

> I begged, I mean I pleaded, I talked with her, I kept pushing her, I said, "Go to college, try it, just go for the first year, it's paid for, and then if you don't like it, you still have all the credits." I actually begged, but that didn't work. She insisted she did not want to go to school anymore, she just couldn't.

Madeleine continued, "I told her, 'If you don't go to college, you're going to wind up working at a minimum-wage job, is that what you want to do?' She didn't know what she wanted, she was stuck." Christy continued to live at home, and Madeleine insisted she get a job:

> Then I said, "Now that you're not going to college, you have to get a job, and it has to be full-time, none of this part-time stuff." She had worked at

a drug store part-time when she was going to high school. I told Christy, "Get a full-time job and you're paying rent while you're living here." Christy said, "Why are you so mean?" Then her boyfriend got her a job at the store where he worked, a clerical job, and she went to live with him.

Madeleine concluded by saying, "I don't know what the problem is. Maybe her boyfriend doesn't want her to go to college? He didn't go." She said it is extremely disappointing that her daughter turned down a college scholarship, and that she feels very frustrated that she was not able to persuade her daughter to take advantage of the scholarship and go to college. Madeleine worries about how her daughter will manage in the future.

Laura, an African American mother of three biracial children, has grown very frustrated trying to figure out how to deal with her 19-year-old son. Two of her young adult children are attending a local community college, and she expects they will graduate. However, she said her 19-year-old son, Travis, who graduated from high school six months ago, has no motivation. His case seems somewhat extreme. Laura said, "I think Travis is depressed." She is trying to make him enroll in a job training program:

> He has no motivation, he doesn't get up and go do things. Through his school, he qualified for a summer job at the school's day camp. I went and signed him up and he got the job. But he wouldn't go. He didn't care, he just stayed at home all summer and played around on the computer. I had to go pick up his high school diploma at school, he wouldn't even do that.

Laura thinks Travis could be "a computer person, he's smart enough." She said, "I want him to go to community college, he doesn't have the track record to go anywhere else." Laura said this is taking a toll on her. "I'm so tired, and the thought of trying to make him do things gives me a headache," she said. She has tried to use money as leverage in her negotiations with Travis but hasn't been successful. She said, "Sometimes when he won't do his chores or make a plan about getting a job or taking some classes, I tell him I won't buy him things, but then he just does without. He just wears someone else's old sneakers. I do buy him glasses and medical things. Sometimes I can get his father to talk to Travis—he doesn't live too far away—but he isn't having much success either."

Laura has not given up, however. She said, "I don't feel powerless. Actually, I've decided to change my approach. I shouldn't be so stubborn, I shouldn't just keep insisting that Travis do things my way, that shouldn't be my only approach." She will negotiate with him, using her willingness to drive him places as leverage:

> I don't like it, but I'm going to have to start making deals even though I feel there are things he should just do at his age. Like when he wants to go some- where, I'll have to sound positive and say, "I'd be happy to drive you but I also need some help from you with mowing the lawn." He never offers to help with anything. I always have to ask, it's very exasperating.

Laura concluded by saying, "Travis says he wants to be a computer pro- grammer, so if he wants me to give him any money to do that, I will negotiate more with him, although I just want him to be motivated to take responsi- bility for himself!"

Shirley, an African American mother with six children ranging in ages from 6 to 22, has been trying to help her 21-year-old daughter, Kayla, who lives at home, to get some type of job. So far, Kayla has not heeded her advice. She dropped out of high school but then did get a GED. Shirley said, "I've been trying to figure out how to get her settled. Kayla was a checkout person at a supermarket and she's done telemarketing." She continued, "Kayla also did hair on the side, but she decided that was too much work." Realizing she wasn't able to make much money without a college degree, Kayla did decide to enroll at a for-profit college. Shirley said, "I didn't want her to do that, I told her not to go there, those for-profit places cost too much money." Enrollments at for-profit institutions have grown at a much higher rate than at private nonprofit and public institutions. However, nearly 80 percent of students don't graduate, and those who do are less likely to find an ad- equately paying job. Students who attend for-profit colleges graduate with more debt and default on debts at higher rates than students at nonprofit and public colleges.[30]

Shirley said Kayla did get an associate's degree from the for-profit col- lege, "But she's still paying loans from that school. She's looking for another job now. She found a job as some kind of assistant at a bank but she's not making much money." Shirley expressed sympathy for her daughter and tries

---

[30] R. Howarth and W. Barkley-Denney, "New Stats on For-Profit Colleges by State Show Continued Poor Outcomes and Disproportionate Impacts" (Durham, NC: Center for Responsible Lending, 2019).

to help her. She said, "I understand that she's unhappy about her situation, and I try to give her advice and reassure her. She can live here without paying anything, but I can't afford to give her any money. She should never have enrolled in that college." Shirley said that providing emotional support for Kayla "gets tiring, and I get anxious about whether she's going to get her life together."

Finally, two mothers reported that their young adult daughters had babies at the age of 17. They had repeatedly advised their daughters to be careful and not get pregnant. They worry about the burdens early motherhood is placing on their daughters, whom they fear will have difficulty supporting their families. Melanie, a white mother with two daughters (ages 23 and 17) and a son (age 22), wishes her daughters hadn't had children at such a young age. Melanie and her second husband, a plumber, are struggling financially to pay their own bills. Melanie's 23-year-old daughter has two children (ages 3 and 4), and her 17-year-old daughter has just given birth to a son. To help her daughters, Melanie is hoping to be accepted into the program of a local social service agency that would pay her a stipend for doing full-time day care for her daughters. Melanie said, "I need to get a paying job, we need the money, and I would be very happy if my job could be caring for my grandchildren."

Melanie said that on numerous occasions, she and her husband told their daughters that having a baby is a very big responsibility, that it's hard and they should not get pregnant. But, she said, "Somehow they didn't get the message." She continued:

You can't explain to somebody what it's really like, they don't understand. Kids don't listen. I didn't listen to my parents. Our daughters' friends were having babies. "Oh, how cute, how cute." But when they're not cute, you can't give them back.

Melanie said she and her husband tried but couldn't stop their daughters from having sex. She said, "We knew they were doing it—what are you going to do? You can't stop them. We did our best to teach them about safe sex, you know, and protected sex." Melanie said that with their older daughter, the first pregnancy wasn't planned. "Our second daughter wanted to have children. She didn't care about the father, she wanted babies. She thought it was easy, all her friends were doing it. Bingo." Melanie said, "Both of them are missing so much of their lives for their age." In what sounded like an effort to reassure herself, Melanie said, "But they are doing okay. They learned a lot."

Helen, a working-class African American mother, has just learned from her 18-year-old daughter that she is pregnant and wants to have the baby. Helen did not discuss birth control with her daughter, fearing that talking about it would lead her to believe it was all right for her to be sexually active. Helen is deeply disappointed. She said, "I told my daughter over and over that if she got pregnant and had a baby, it would make her life much more difficult." Her daughter, who has been a good student, has told Helen she really wants to go to college, that she can raise a child and "do college." But Helen is worried. She thinks it will take her daughter much longer to finish college now. She also thinks she will have to spend a lot of time supporting her daughter just when she was thinking she could pull back from parenting and focus on her own priorities.

At this stage in their lives, young adults need to gain credentials- a college degree, some vocational training and certification, or a good record of military service- and parents' support remains critical. Parents provide financial support if they can, and mothers report that they often provide valuable emotional support and encouragement for their young adults to help them gain these credentials. This can make the difference as to whether their young adult children can attend college, secure training for a skilled trade, or take advantage of a promising work opportunity. Of course, mothers' ability to help their young adults gain credentials is enabled and constrained by their access to resources. As young adulthood proceeds, those young adults who go to college are on a path to achieving work and careers that will support an adequate standard of living. Upper-middle-class young adults who attend highly ranked colleges can expect to enter well-paying careers. Working-class youth who are not in college face real-life issues earlier. Some have obtained jobs, while others lack direction and have not found a path toward an adequately paying job.

After 22: Emerging Adulthood: Launching and Letting Go in a Time of Uncertainty

Twenty-five of the mothers I interviewed (21 percent of the sample) were parenting a young adult between the ages of 22 and 25. While they are a much smaller and less representative group of mothers, their accounts illustrate some of the challenges of parenting children after they turn 21, the age at which young adults gain the final rights of adulthood in all states, including the ability to purchase alcohol and tobacco products and drink alcohol in public establishments.[31] While they gain these rights, however, in contrast to the past when young adults were expected to be financially and socially independent at age 21, in the current era, most 21-year-olds are not able to support themselves financially. Some parents, particularly upper-middle-class parents, continue to provide financial support to their young adult children, as well as career guidance and connections. Other parents can't afford to provide financial support for their young adults, and still others believe it is time for young adults to make their own way and become financially independent. In recent years, more young adults have begun living with their parents for longer periods of time. Currently, 57 percent of young adults ages 18–24 live in their parents' home.[32]

Upper-Middle-Class Mothers

Upper-middle-class mothers view attaining independence as a longer-term process that can extend well into young adulthood. They provide critical assistance to enable their young adults to find a path towards a well-paying job or enter the professional class, or to go to graduate or professional school and become doctors, lawyers, businesspeople, or academics. Young adults with degrees from prestigious colleges have increased chances for acceptance at top-ranked professional and graduate schools.[33] They can receive valuable guidance through their college career counseling offices, networks of professional alumni of their colleges and universities, and their parents' professional connections. Once they are enrolled in a highly ranked graduate or professional school, they have a more certain pathway to prestigious, well-paid positions.[34]

Some upper-middle-class parents whose young adult children are attending graduate and professional schools continue to provide financial support. One white upper-middle-class mother reported that her son who

[31] T. Spengler, "Things You Can Do at 21 Years of Age, But Not at 18," December 26, 2019, Legal Beagle, https://legalbeagle.com/8649600-things-age-but-not-18.html.

[32] Minkin et al., "Parents, Young Adult Children and the Transition to Adulthood."

[33] R. Chetty, "Diversifying Society's Leaders? The Determinants and Consequences of Admission to Highly Selective Colleges," Opportunity Insights Non-Technical Research Summary (Cambridge, MA: Harvard University, 2023).

[34] L. Rivera, L. Pedigree: How Elite Students Get Elite Jobs (Princeton, NJ: Princeton University Press, 2015).

just graduated from college has been accepted for a prestigious two-year fellowship at a well-regarded British university. She is very happy for him and expects this opportunity will help him to gain acceptance at a highly ranked graduate school in the United States when the fellowship ends. Another mother reported that her daughter received a fellowship to teach English in Nepal. Both sets of parents will pay whatever expenses are not covered by the fellowships. Some parents provide financial support for enriching experiences. One white mother reported that her daughter has been accepted at the graduate school she wants to attend but has deferred her acceptance for a year so she can have the experience of traveling in Asia. The family will provide financial help so she can have this experience.

Some young adults choose to look for jobs after college. Given the uncertainty of the job market, even those with a degree from a highly ranked college or university typically need financial assistance, which some of their parents will provide until they find paid employment. Tamara is a white upper-middle-class mother with two sons (ages 23 and 19). Her older son, James, graduated from a top-ranked college a year and a half ago and went with a friend to live in a different city and look for work. Tamara reported, "It took James quite a while to find a job. At one point he called and said he had just looked at his bank account and realized he had almost no money." Tamara said she and her husband then sent him money. They did this because they knew he would keep looking for work and were hopeful that given his credentials, he would find an adequately paying job.

A few months later, James called and said he had gotten a job, although not the kind of job Tamara and her husband were expecting:

> When he told us about getting a job we said, "Oh great, you got a job, that's terrific." He told us about the company, it was trying to make organic produce available at affordable prices to lower-income communities. It sounded like a good one, and then I said, "So what's your position," and he said, "Delivery." Oh, I said to myself, oh my god, this is the job you can get after your education which cost us thousands of dollars! [Laughing and groaning]

James did keep looking, however, and after some months, he was happy to find a job at a tech company that was more in line with his educational credentials. "But," Tamara said:

Even this job, they said at first they couldn't hire him at this time. So he asked if he could be an intern, good for him! They said yes. Actually they are paying him at the lowest rate. Then they'll review his situation in a few months.

Tamara and her husband will support James until he makes enough money to live on. They continue to assume James will get a good job, although they worry this may take a while.

If a son or daughter follows their passion and chooses a field where work is more insecure, mothers worry. Judith, an upper-middle-class mother who is white, worries about her son Levi, a recent college graduate who majored in film studies and is now trying to make a living in the film industry. He has had a few low-paying jobs working on films. He also has a part-time job in a retail store to make money to pay his rent. Judith and her husband pay for his health insurance. Judith says:

> I still worry about my son Levi. Will he have work? Like we were all together this weekend for a wedding, and I wanted to say to him, "So do you have work for next week?" And then at the end of the ceremony, Levi got a call on his cell phone and it was the guy he's been doing some work for who told him that he had work for him all next week. I was so relieved to hear that!

Judith would be happy to have her son come and live at home to save money, although she said things would be different now that Levi is older:

> I told my son he could come home and live for a while. I said to him, "Of course you couldn't just walk in the door and say, 'What's for dinner Mom?'" That's over! But it would be nice if he did move back, I would like it—for a little while anyway.

But Judith said, "When I told my husband what I'd said, he said no. He doesn't want Levi to come back home to live. He's said it's time for him to become more independent and be on his own, although if Levi has a difficult period, of course we'll help him." While her husband does not appear to be ready to have his son return home to live, Judith reflects the sentiments of those who are happy to have their young adult children at home for a longer period when they can develop closer relationships with them.[35]

[35] F. F. Furstenberg, "Becoming Adults: Challenges in the Transition to Adult Roles," *American Journal of Orthopsychiatry* 85(5S) (2015): S14–S21.

Parents can also put limits on their financial support and pressure their young adult children to get a job and earn money. Imani, an African American mother, has a 22-year-old daughter, Keisha, who recently graduated from college. Imani said her daughter doesn't have any concrete plans:

> Keisha just graduated from college and now she's been home for a few months. We're happy to have her here while she makes plans. She doesn't have a job yet and she doesn't know yet what she wants to do. Actually, she said she wants to go into finance. That was a surprise to my husband and me, she's never said that before.

Recently, Keisha told Imani and her husband that she is going to move out soon: "She said she's going to live with a high school friend in the city which is nearby." Imani said, "I immediately told her, 'You can't move until you get a job.'" Imani said she and her husband put this condition on their support to drive home the point that Keisha has to start taking responsibility for her own expenses. She concluded by saying, "I told Keisha, 'We are not paying your rent in the city.'" While it is the case that upper-middle-class young adults like Keisha face an uncertain job market, the education and training they have received, along with their parents' guidance and financial support, will undoubtedly enable them to find higher status, better-paying positions than those with less education.

Middle-Class-Mothers

The middle-class mothers in my sample generally want their young adults to become self-supporting as soon as they are able. Their young adult children who have attended college are beginning careers in teaching, nursing, library work, or business. It may take some time for them to find a job, they may start at a low salary, and some may need additional training or a graduate degree. At this time, mothers ask themselves when they should provide financial assistance and when their young adults should instead take responsibility for their own expenses. Some parents will provide financial support if there is a compelling temporary need, although this aid may be limited. Others cannot afford to provide any financial help. Still others are able to provide valuable guidance, including ideas for possible jobs or careers or contacts through their own jobs. Anne, a white middle-class mother, is proud of her daughter, who has graduated from college and wants to get a master's degree in special education. Anne said, "She's looking at graduate school now. She's not sure if she's going to get a job and go to school at night." Anne said financing her graduate program is up to her daughter:

> She'll need financial aid because we have told her we can't give her any financial support. We have three other children—she's the oldest. She's looking into getting a fellowship or—what did she call it?—an assistantship. There's an information night next week at the university she will be attending for her master's degree so she's going to look into that.

Gloria, a middle-class African American mother who works as an administrator in the city school district, is pleased that her daughter has done well in college and will graduate soon. Her daughter wants to be a secondary school teacher. As in the case of Anne and her husband, Gloria and her husband have told their daughter that she is "on her own" financially. Gloria said she will use her connections in the school district to help her daughter get a job:

> I'm going to help my daughter get a good teaching job. I know the woman who handles the apprentice teachers. It's hard to get the kind of job my daughter wants, but I've been working for the school district since my kids were little, so everyone knows them and they know how good they are, that they have done well in school and college. People will help my daughter get a job.

Elise is a white mother whose daughter, Allison, graduated from college a year ago. Elise's comments reflect the decisions some parents continue to face about how much financial support to give to their young adult children. Elise reported that she and her husband have provided modest financial support for Allison for the past year because her daughter's salary at a nonprofit organization is low, but they recently told her that at the end of the year, she should start supporting herself. However, Allison recently asked them for a loan. They are not sure how to handle her request:

> Allison recently asked for a loan of money to help buy a car. Her line was that with a car, she could live in a cheaper apartment a little further out of the town she lives in now and she would be nearer her job and have a

shorter commute. She said she would pay the loan back. The problem is, I didn't say no right away. So now we've been thinking what to do.

Elise and her husband decided to give Allison the money, but they will take the funds Allison wants out of a savings account they had established for her. They were hoping this savings account would grow and be valuable to Allison at a later point in her life. Elise said, "We know her salary is low, so we told her she can have that money, which means she won't have it in the future. She does say she'll pay it back, but I'm not sure, I think maybe she loaned some money to her roommate and probably her roommate can't pay it back." Elise and her husband are hoping this incident won't lead to a pattern where Allison will ask for money on an ongoing basis:

After this incident, my husband Rick and I have been thinking ahead about where we are going to draw the line if Allison asks for more money. She's got to figure out how to make it on her own. But if something unexpected comes up and she's being responsible and doing the best she can, well, then we'll see. We'll have to play it by ear.

As Elise's comment indicates, in supporting young adults, it's not always clear where to "draw the line" and when it is time for parents to tell their children they will no longer provide financial support.

Working-Class Mothers

The working-class mothers I interviewed are concerned that their young adults have jobs or a plan that will enable them to become financially independent as soon as they are able. Stella, an African American mother, is very pleased that her daughter, who has just finished college, has been accepted into a master's degree program at the university she attended. She is studying to be a social worker and will live at home while she is in the program. Another African American mother is happy that her 22-year-old daughter is in the army. According to her, "My daughter loves it; it was a good choice. I've always told my kids, when you graduate high school, you've got to decide what you want to do, I'm happy." Jane, a white mother with three children (ages 21, 17, and 13), is pleased that her 21-year-old son is an electrician. He has lived at home since finishing his apprenticeship and training but is independent. As she said:

> He's living at home now until he figures out where he wants to live next,
> but he's financially independent. He doesn't pay for rent or food, I wouldn't
> know how to figure that out. But he's independent, I feel good about that.

Other working-class mothers are worried, however. They reported that some of their young adults, primarily their sons, are adrift and without a clear path forward toward regular employment, and they are not sure what they can do to help. Alma, a white working-class mother, said her son 23-year-old son, Sam, doesn't have a direction in his life. "Sam's a wanderer. He just gets up and goes wherever he wants to go, he doesn't know what he wants to do yet, he's been doing odd jobs for people." Alma said, "Sometimes I push him kind of hard to get his act together. I listen to him too, I try to encourage him." While she was clearly worried and sounded anxious as she spoke, Alma is working to assure herself that Sam will find a way forward. She said, "I did the same thing, I was a wanderer, so I think he's alright. I know he can handle himself, he'll settle down sooner or later." Then she joked, "I don't know what I want to do yet either. I still think I'm 22 years old!" With only a high school diploma and without goals in mind, however, Sam's chances of securing an adequately paying job are uncertain.

Josephine, a white mother, stated that she is very concerned about her 24-year-old son and whether or not he will "make it." She has tried to figure out how to help him. She said, "I try to tell him to set goals, but he's very hard-headed. He has to do everything his way, like his father." Josephine is worried about whether her son can really hold down a job:

> He works at jobs but then gets mad at his boss, he quits, then he gets de-
> pressed and he gets really down on himself. Then he has to find a job again.
> I got my brother to take him for a year to see if he could do something with
> him, but he said that my son wouldn't stick to things. My brother does try to
> find work for him if he doesn't have a job. My son is into home repairs and
> my brother will call him up and tell him to come help him paint.

Josephine tries to keep in touch with her son. She said, "We're still close, but not as close as we used to be. If I don't hear from him in a while, I know something is wrong and I worry. Then I call him. He can't keep a job, he gets bored, he's not a steady worker." In concluding, Josephine said, "My real fear is that he may not make it. I think he doesn't know how to make it. He went to a community college for a while and dropped out."

As I described in Chapter 3, three working-class mothers in my sample, all African American, reported very negative outcomes for their young adult children. Tragically, one mother had a son and a daughter who both died of AIDS, which they contracted while they were using drugs. Two mothers had teens who were in prison, one for selling drugs and one for robbery.[36] In the general population of the US, one in three of the 265,600 children under 18 who were arrested in 2021 were Black children, although Black children constitute only 15 percent of the nation's youth population. Two-thirds (67 percent) of children in the juvenile justice system are children of color.[37]

In popular media, African American mothers, particularly if they are single parents, are often blamed for the failures of their children. They are believed to have not given enough time or love to promote their children's success. Researchers have differing views of what contributes to the more negative outcomes African American children, particularly boys in low-income families can experience. Some find that they are experiencing "family disadvantage"; that is, they are not receiving enough parental "inputs," particularly parental attention from their mothers, many of whom are single. However, other researchers focus on the impact of living in resource-deprived environments and argue that when African American children live in low-poverty neighborhoods that have low levels of racial bias and high rates of father presence, they experience better outcomes. However, less than 5 percent of Black children grow up in such neighborhoods compared with 63 percent of white children.[38]

Of course, the actions of individual parents exert a powerful influence over their teens and young adult children. However, the accounts of mothers demonstrate that we must give much more attention to the role environments and resources play in mothers' ability to see that their teens and young adults remain safe and receive the kind of secondary and postsecondary education and training they need to find a place in a fast-changing economy.

---

[36] See Chapter 3, note 6 for reports of serious trouble from my sample.

[37] Children's Defense Fund, "The State of America's Children 2023–Youth Justice" (Washington, DC: Children's Defense Fund, 2023).

[38] Only 4.2 percent of African American children grow up in Census tracts with a poverty rate below 10 percent where half of their fathers are present compared with 62.5 percent of white children who grow up in low-poverty areas with more than half of their fathers present. Chetty et al., "Race and Economic Opportunity in the United States."

For the mothers I interviewed, the ability to live in safe neighborhoods and find good schools for their teens is critical to raising their teens and young adults.

Based on their access to education, training, and financial support from parents, as young adults move into their twenties, they are on different tracks that provide different paths forward. The considerable advantages of some, particularly upper-middle-class young adults, have continued to build on each other and provide opportunities. After finishing college, many go to graduate school or secure well-paying jobs that enable them to pay back college debt if they have taken out loans. Higher percentages of middle- and working-class young adults who graduate from college are left with debt and face more challenges gaining financial stability while paying off college loans.[39] Those without a college degree face even more limited choices. At this point in the lives of young adults, it becomes much more difficult for them to change the trajectories of their lives.

Reflecting on Motherhood at This Point in Their Lives

As their young adult children proceed through their twenties, some mothers can experience happiness, pride, and a sense of personal accomplishment. One white working-class mother expressed relief. "Now that my two sons have graduated from college," she said, "I feel like a weight has been lifted off my soldiers. Of course you never know, bad things can happen but they both have decent jobs now and seem happy."

When they feel their young adult children are doing well, mothers expressed happiness and pride. As one mother said, "I'm glad I'm a parent. It's been one of the happiest things in my life. I'm very proud of my kids." One white working-class mother, whose son had just successfully completed a training program in carpentry and gotten a job he was hoping for, said, "Parenting can be so rewarding, especially when you see them independent and doing the right thing. It can be a long slog, but it makes you really happy."

---

[39] According to Joan Mazelis and Ariel Kuperberg, 62 percent of students graduating from four-year public or private nonprofit colleges in the US had average student debt of $28,950 in 2019, a 25 percent increase since 2008. Mazelis and Kuperberg have found that getting loans for college from parents and living with parents during college is very beneficial financially, but can extend the period of dependency of young adults by increasing their obligations to their family as they transition to adulthood. J. Mazelis and A. Kuperberg, "Student Loan Debt, Family Support, and Reciprocity in the Transition to Adulthood," *Emerging Adulthood* 10(6) (2022): 1511–1528.

As a white middle-class mother who was quoted in Chapter 1 and whose daughter has finished college and been accepted into a graduate nursing program said:

> We are very proud of our daughter. I could explode sometimes because she's just a really neat kid. She's a really neat kid. And now she's graduating from college. She did so well, I know she will succeed in the future.

Georgia, a middle-class African American mother, is very happy because her son has gotten a job in the field he prepared for. She said:

> I try to enjoy their growing up, their coming to maturity. I am so happy, my son has just been offered a job in accounting, he got his BS in accounting and he got an accounting job, I think he's going to do well.

Some mothers are happy because they believe they had a hand in the growth of their teens, and they get a feeling of accomplishment about things their teens and young adults have achieved. One white upper-middle-class mother expressed pride in her daughter's accomplishments; her daughter had just been hired for her first teaching job and become engaged to marry her college boyfriend. She said, "There are rewards when you see your child is successful. It makes you happy. You feel like you did something positive in your life." As another mother phrased it, "It's rewarding because you have a role in shaping their lives." Another mother felt she has contributed to seeing her children "blossom and grow":

> I like seeing the kids become more individuals, seeing their interests, their relationships, seeing them enjoy life—and feeling I've been able to contribute to that—to see them blossom and grow and take responsibility for their actions, that's a great feeling.

Jane, a white working-class mother, feels a sense of pride in herself because, she said, "My kids take responsibility for themselves. They got into community college and they are paying their way." She continued:

> I feel I did a good job being a mother, I don't feel guilty about anything. I see other parents—sometimes their kids are going around with a bad group, or gangs—the kids get pressured into gangs.

Mothers are also proud when their children turn out to be nice people. As one upper-middle-class white mother said, "I like my children. You always love your children, but that doesn't necessarily mean they know how to be nice people." She added:

> If your kids are really nice to somebody you feel like—that's great, I did something right. So being a parent in that way I think is very rewarding. To see the good things that can happen.

One working-class African American mother said:

> I'm proud of my children, I am proud of them at the point that they are at now, not only because of their accomplishments, but I'm proud of them as the individuals they turned out to be. Because they are good and they are decent. You know what I mean? They treat people pretty well and they're nice.

Mothers can also find satisfaction in their changed role. They can talk to their older children on more of an adult level and less in the role of "teacher" or disciplinarian. Some said they can become friends, a role which, as described in Chapter 2, they felt they should hesitate about adopting when their children were teens. One white working-class mother with four children (ages 22, 29, 13, and 9) said she liked moving out of the role of disciplinarian:

> We're very close to the older two—and I think that we have more of an adult relationship now because I don't have to be a disciplinarian anymore. I am still their mother, but now I am their girlfriend too.

She contrasts this time with an earlier point in their lives. "When they are younger," she said, "when it's like somebody has to be the bad guy, you can't be friends. You have to make decisions they don't like and they're going to be mad at you. But now I don't have to be a disciplinarian and I can let my guard down and just be more, you know, friends. Talk about what we're up to, gossip about people, you know." Another mother spoke about moving out of the role of "teacher":

> I like the challenge of parenting, I like the idea of seeing a child grow into an adult, it's fascinating. And then being able to converse with them on an

adult level. I like that they're not little children anymore, I like not being the teacher anymore. They might have temporary needs but it's different. I do like it, I like the teenagers' older years as opposed to the younger ones.

A white middle-class mother also reported being happy that her two young adults (a daughter aged 24 and a son aged 22), but especially her 24-year-old daughter, are friends:

I liked them when they were younger, teaching them things and doing things with them and watching them grow. What I like now is that I like that they're friends, especially my daughter, and I feel like we're really good friends. We can talk about anything. We like being together and doing things together.

There are mothers who feel they have less connection to their sons, as some also felt when their sons were teens. This same mother, for example, said it's a little different with her son: "I wouldn't say exactly that we're friends. He doesn't confide as much or anything but for important things," she said, "he'll call me up and ask me about this and that. I like that, I hope it stays that way."

Mothers also experience satisfaction when their young adults acknowledge how their mothers have helped them. As one white mother said, she is very happy when her teens "give back, when I'm not just the one giving, giving, giving." Gertrude, a working-class African American mother who is the mother of five children, had made extensive efforts to see that one of her sons, who is now 21 years old, would stay in high school and graduate. Gertrude provided positive encouragement to him, insisted he come to teacher conferences with her, and found someone in her church who could help him with his math homework. According to Gertrude, "My son thanked me. That felt really good. He could have gone a different way. He was thinking of dropping out of school."

An African American working-class mother who raised her children as a single parent said that her young adult children (ages 22, 23, and 25) "gave back" and invited her to go on a vacation with them. It moved her deeply:

When my kids give back it's wonderful. We just came home from vacation. They wanted me to go on vacation with them, that was so great. It made me cry when they told me, "Mom, we want you to go on vacation with us."

I said, "Really, you do? You want me to go on vacation with you?" We went to [a beach resort]. Just the four of us for almost a week, it was wonderful. And it was my birthday. They also gave me beautiful cards, they wrote in them, it made me cry that they had so many good memories despite the tough times.

This mother said that she was especially moved because her children "understood how hard I worked for them with me being a single parent."

When mothers have warm relationships with their young adults, it can be hard when they go away to college. As one said, "When we took him to college in [another state], I tried to hide how I was shedding tears. I wanted it to be a happy occasion for him, but I knew I was going to miss him so much. It had gotten to be so nice to have my son around after all those early teen years which were sometimes hard. And then they leave." A white upper-middle-class mother reported, "When my husband and I dropped our daughter off at college in another state, we put on our smiley faces and said a warm and wonderful good-bye. Then we got in the car and cried. But we've adjusted and we're happy for her."

As one African American working-class mother described it, if young adult children move away to a place at some distance from home after college, they can miss them a great deal:

I'm happy about how they've turned out, but I felt terrible when my son, my last child, left after college in our city. He got a job in another city. Terrible, like my heart was pulled out. I really like it better living with kids. I'd prefer it that way, I mean, it's okay now, but I like that better.

One white upper-middle-class mother said her house seems a bit empty now that her daughter has graduated from college and gone to another city where she has gotten a job. "She's such a good kid," she said, "she has her head in the right place, you know? And she's a joy, she really is. I mean, when she's not around, it's a little lonely, she's so full of energy and does lots of neat things." A middle-class African American mother said she was "melancholy" because her children are finishing college and will be moving to other places:

The hardest thing for me has been just watching them grow and leave home. That's been the hardest thing. Them leaving home and me not knowing how they were going to make out in another state, that's been the hardest. They are okay, but I miss them. It's over so quickly, it makes you a little melancholy.

Letting Go and Adjusting Expectations: Dealing with Disappointment and Regrets

Mothers whose young adult children are struggling to find work or a direction in their life can experience disappointment and worry. Some feel things are out of their hands now, that they have much less control over what happens to their young adults. Some have to let go of their expectations. If their young adults have gotten in trouble with the law or experienced drug or alcohol problems, they are particularly worried, as are those whose young adults have begun to experience mental illness. Some mothers have to deal with disappointment about important identity and lifestyle choices their teens have made that will shape their lives going forward.

Dorothy, a white working-class mother, has wrestled with the fact that her daughter has come out as a lesbian. Dorothy is a Christian who believes that homosexuality is wrong. She has struggled to accept her daughter's new identity given that she is not in control of her daughter's life anymore. She said:

> I think we want our kids to be a certain way. I've learned that you want them to be what you want them to be. When you come to that point that you are not in control of their life, and you see they are individuals, they are going to make their own choices and you've got to learn to accept it whether you like it or not.

Dorothy said that at first, she had a hard time accepting that her daughter was a lesbian. "But then," she said, "after I got over, like, the initial shock, it was, well, a slow process of learning. It's a slow process, it's not something like—whack—hits you all in one day. You learn, you know that they're not going to do what you thought." Dorothy then chuckled, adding, "I do have to say I like my daughter's partner, we like to play the same card games. That can be fun."

Bernadette, a middle-class African American mother, said she has also struggled with her daughter's lesbian identity.

It's been hard to accept my daughter's lifestyle, but it's her life. She has to live her own life so, you know, she's not shut out. I mean it's not that we're not, you know, she was here to visit on Sunday—her and her partner and her partner's little girl. It's not something that I shut her out for, you know, I guess because I love her. But it's not easy.

Bernadette said one thing has been particularly hard for her: "My grand-daughter knowing there were two mommies sleeping together, she probably figured it out. That's kind of got me a little uptight." Bernadette concluded with a comment that at this stage of her daughter's life, she was in a different position where she couldn't control major choices anymore. Like Dorothy, Bernadette said, "What can I do? You know I can't do anything about it, I have to accept that it's her life."

Some mothers and fathers face young adults who will need assistance for a long time and who may never achieve financial independence. These parents may face a lot of work trying to find professional and social support for their young adult and adult children on a long-term basis, support that can be expensive and hard to come by. The mother who reported that her son had to drop out of college because he had been diagnosed with depression is wondering how long it will take for him to get better and whether he will be able to return to college. Because there have been others in her family of origin who have suffered from mental illness, she knows it could take a long time to get the right medication for her son. She really hopes her son will be able to return to college at some point and gain skills that will enable him to do productive work.

A few mothers expressed regrets about how their actions may have caused harm to their children. As described in a previous chapter, one white working-class mother reported that she had suffered from depression when her daughter was in high school, and she wasn't able to spend as much time with her as she wished. It has taken her time to rebuild a meaningful relationship with her daughter. She is feeling reassured now that her daughter is a young adult, she said, "We are getting closer." Several divorced mothers worried about the long-term impact of a difficult divorce on their children. Cecilia, a white working-class mother with two daughters in college, said her ex-husband was very controlling. She regrets that her daughter saw the conflicts between her and her husband before they divorced. As she noted:

I regret that I think that sometimes my second daughter was in the middle between me and my husband. I tried really hard for that not to happen, but I think it did a few times. My husband would also tell her certain things, I don't know if he was trying to turn her against me. I tried really hard not to badmouth him. My older son won't spend the day with him.

Finally, mothers whose young adults have had serious trouble experience deep disappointment and worry. The two mothers who have sons in prison are holding out hope that their sons will work to obtain a GED (a high school equivalency degree) in prison and find a direction for their lives after they complete their prison sentences. But they worry.

While most mothers said they feel very happy if they believe their young adults are finding a path forward, it is also the case that as their children move further into young adulthood, there are no guarantees of success for any group of young adults. In the current era of economic insecurity, parents, whatever their social class, continue to worry. Emerging adulthood extends for a longer period of time, and it takes more time to secure an adequately paying job or to establish a career. Further, in recent decades, the percentage of children who grow up to earn more than their parents has been falling.[40] Working-class parents particularly worry about whether their young adults will find jobs that provide an adequate standard of living. Like all parents, African American parents worry about jobs and economic security for their young adults, and they also live with fear that given the widespread racism in the United States, their sons and daughters could face not only unfair treatment but harm, including from the police.

Mothers also find themselves thinking about how their children's lives will be in the future. Will they be happy? Will they find a good partner? Will they be safe, or will they experience health problems, or a run-in with the law? Kimberly, a working-class African-American mother with a 17-year-old son and a 23-year-old daughter said, "you always worry." She spoke confidently about her daughter's future: "My daughter has a good foundation now, she's motivated, she's going to do well." At the same time, pausing for a moment, she said:

---

[40] Ninety-two percent of young adults who were born in 1940 earned more than their parents, compared to 50 percent of young adults who were born in the 1980s. R. Chetty and N. Hendren, "Ensuring the American Dream," *Finance and Development* (Washington, DC: International Monetary Fund, 2022).

When things are going well with your kids, you are happy. But when you're 90 and they're 50, you still worry, you always have the fear that something could happen to them no matter what their age. You pray, you never know. Being a mother is the hardest job.

Finishing her thoughts, she concluded by saying, "Being a mother is also one of the best things in life, having children you love and children who love you."

Conclusion

In the past, young adults were expected to become independent at age 18, to begin supporting themselves and preparing to start a family. In the current era, however, while young adults become more independent in their social lives at age 18, most face an extended period of financial dependency. Increasing levels of education are required to enter the labor force and achieve an adequate standard of living. As a result, young adulthood has become a critical time for obtaining educational credentials. Parents provide a lot of assistance to their young adults to help them gain these credentials. Many parents support their young adults financially as they can. Mothers I interviewed also spoke of providing emotional support, advice, and assistance in dealing with trouble as it arises during this time. This work is often invisible and underappreciated but can be critical in helping their young adult children succeed.

Upper-middle-class mothers provide academic and emotional support for their college students. Most provide financial support. When their college students graduate, they are able to support them financially for a longer period of time, sometimes into their twenties and beyond, which enables them to go on to further postgraduate training if they choose. Middle- and working-class mothers support their college students financially as they can, but they worry about paying for college. They urge them to find a career path and start paying more of their own expenses earlier than upper-middle-class parents do. They negotiate with their young adult children about when they should start contributing to college costs or to family expenses if they are living at home. Working-class parents whose young adults do not go to college or gain some type of training or certification worry about their children's future. These young adults are at a serious disadvantage in finding a place in the labor force and achieving financial independence.

In supporting their children through young adulthood, those with resources are able to transfer their privilege. Inequality in education and opportunities accumulate throughout childhood and young adulthood. Those who graduate from college are on a track that enables them to gain skills and the potential to move forward. Those who don't go to college find themselves in real-life situations earlier, needing to earn income to support themselves. Some appear at a standstill, unable to find training or jobs that will help them find a path toward achieving an adequate standard of living. In the face of persistent racism, African American adults continue to face disadvantages in receiving fair treatment at work and advancing in their careers.

Although parents of all backgrounds never stop worrying, for those whose young adult children are doing well and are on a path forward, there are untold rewards—happiness, a feeling of accomplishment, and a sense of pride. Some mothers feel pleased and happy that they have helped their teens grow into young adulthood. While they understand that success for their young adult children is not guaranteed, they believe their children are on track to have steady work or careers, and hopefully happy family lives. Their relationships with their young adult children have become more equal, and they are happy to move out of the role of disciplinarian and into a role that can be more like that of a friend. As one mother quoted earlier said, "Now it's like we're at a play. Our older kids are on the stage and we are in the audience. As long as things are going well, we can step back a little and enjoy the play."

For those whose young adult children are struggling, who have not found adequately paying jobs or a direction in their lives, there is ongoing worry. These mothers live with uncertainty about what kind of future their young adults will have. It is also the case that as their children move further into young adulthood, there are no guarantees for any group of young adults. As Kimberly, the mother quoted above said, "When you're 90 and they're 50, you still worry, no matter what their age." However when their children are doing well, parents can experience the great pleasure that comes from seeing the children they love achieve some happiness in their personal and family lives and success at the work and professions they have chosen.

6

Conclusion

As I wrote in the preface to this book, I have long wanted to understand more about the day-to-day work of parenting and its challenges. Parenting is central to the lives of mothers and fathers; it is a key feature of their identities as well as being all-consuming work. It provides tremendous rewards. When children, teens, and young adults do well, it is a source of enormous pride and happiness for parents. As one mother said, ""Being a mother is also one of the best things in life, having children you love and children who love you." Parenting is also one of the most important tasks of any society. Mothers and fathers and other caregivers are pivotal figures in raising a new generation. Yet popular narratives of parenting fail to reflect the challenges parents face in raising children, teens, and young adults. Current popular understandings of parenting are based on models that are limiting, that assume that parenting is primarily the job of mothers and that their actions are key in determining their children's success or failure. If children have difficulties, mothers are said to have failed in their responsibilities.

These individualist models assume a degree of control parents do not have. They disregard many of the challenges of raising children, who are intimately involved in the parenting process. They typically don't give sufficient attention to the need for resources. In the absence of a more accurate understanding of what it takes to raise children, teens, and young adults, popular narratives often blame mothers. Some critics fault parents, particularly mothers, for not doing enough, and others for "helicopter parenting," or trying to micromanage the affairs of their children.

To understand more about what it takes to raise children to young adulthood, it is essential to listen to parents. It is through listening to mothers and fathers that we can understand what is actually required to raise children, teens, and young adults. In this book I have focused on mothers and the work they do to manage their children's transition from late childhood to young adulthood. This is a critical time when teens and young adults must navigate the biological, personal, intellectual, and social changes of adolescence and gain the educational credentials and skills that are essential for moving

Letting Go. Demie Kurz, Oxford University Press. © Oxford University Press 2024.
DOI: 10.1093/9780190222482.003.0006

into adulthood. Teens and young adults achieve important milestones at this time. They graduate from high school and attend college or a post–high school training program.

Parents have tremendous responsibilities for seeing that their teens and young adults move successfully on to adulthood. They work to keep teens safe at a time that is viewed as posing risks. They work to ensure that their teens successfully complete secondary school and move on to college or further training at a time when increasing levels of education are required to secure an adequate standard of living. When their teens successfully move on to young adulthood, they feel a sense of accomplishment. Many are proud of their children.

At the same time, mothers and fathers worry about what can happen to their teens and young adults. Some teens get into trouble. They can get into more minor trouble, such as being caught drinking or smoking marijuana in parks, or receiving a citation for breaking city or town curfews. A small number get into more serious trouble: they are suspended or even expelled from school, and they experience car accidents, sexual assault, serious mental health problems, even suicide.

To gain more understanding of the challenges of parenting, I have focused on a task mothers identify as one of the most demanding: letting go, managing teens' passage from early adolescence to young adulthood. Mothers' accounts of managing this transition and letting go provide a valuable understanding of parenting at this critical stage in children's lives as well as a greater understanding of the parenting process more generally. They extend our understanding beyond common views of parenting as a top-down process in which mothers and fathers impart knowledge to their children and teens, who then absorb what they are taught. In this view, it is believed that if children are properly raised, they will develop into successful adults.

As they guide teens through the challenges of adolescence and young adulthood and see that they move on successfully to adulthood, mothers are expected to remain in control. At the same time, while monitoring, supervising, and guiding teens and young adults through this process, parents must engage in letting go: promoting their autonomy, as mothers say, giving kids their freedom. A key task of adolescents and young adults is to develop more autonomy, to learn to make good decisions, take more responsibility for their lives, and begin to plan for their futures. As part of this process, teens engage in new activities in person and online, go new places without adult supervision, and spend less time with their parents and more time with friends.

Letting go and promoting teens' autonomy is a challenging, uncertain process. As they engage in letting go, mothers are continually renegotiating control with their teens and young adults, deciding who has the right to make decisions about their teens' lives- their participation in activities, the effort they should put into their schoolwork, where they can go without adult supervision, their use of cell phones and social media. The process of renegotiating authority and control between parents and children occurs at all ages, but it can be particularly challenging at adolescence, when teenage children make new demands, argue more strenuously for their views, and become more resistant to parents' suggestions. Teens may not tell their parents everything they would like to know. They spend more time away from home and it becomes more difficult to monitor their activities, which are often in environments mothers aren't familiar with.

As they engage in renegotiating control and letting go, mothers face challenging decisions about when to intervene in teens' lives, when to restrict their freedoms, and when to allow teens to do what they want. We see these challenges in the three arenas parents identify as critical to their parenting that I have described in this book: keeping their teens safe, seeing that they complete their secondary education and move on to college or further training, and finding a successful path forward in young adulthood. In monitoring teens' safety, mothers face the challenge of deciding what new freedoms to grant their teens without, as some said, policing them all the time. They negotiate new agreements about where teens can and cannot go, what events they can attend, their curfews, and the time they can spend on social media. These negotiations can be challenging. Parents can face difficult decisions at a time when teens form their own ideas about safety, they share less about their activities, they may not listen when parents discuss safety, and they may just do things on their own.

Promoting teens' success in school, seeing that they successfully complete high school and move on to college or postsecondary training, presents a different set of challenges in letting go. Teens' successful completion of secondary school is critical for continuing along the path to young adulthood. Mothers are expected and expect themselves to ensure that their teens complete their schoolwork and take responsibility for their school performance. They assist with schoolwork as needed, provide encouragement, and monitor their teens' progress in school. When students like school and are highly motivated, letting go takes place relatively smoothly as teens take more responsibility for their assignments on their own.

However, while some teens like school and do well, others are not engaged in their schoolwork, which becomes increasingly challenging in junior high and high school. To motivate them, mothers encourage them, push them to do better, and negotiate with them over how much time they need to spend on schoolwork. Pressuring teens to become motivated can be challenging. As one mother said, "You can lead a horse to water, but you can't make him drink." As another mother whose son was not completing his schoolwork said, "I can't duct tape my son to his desk." Some mothers stop pushing their teens. They let go and decide their teens just have to fail a class or classes when they are not applying themselves, hoping that this experience will motivate them to take more responsibility for their education. Mothers also support their teens and young adults who are experiencing stress in their schoolwork at a time when the pressure to get good grades to be accepted at college increases and schoolwork in junior high and high school becomes more difficult.

When their older teens turn 18 and enter the period known as "young adulthood," mothers and fathers face new decisions about letting go, including how long to support their young adults financially and when their young adults should take more responsibility for supporting themselves. Although young adults gain new legal rights and social freedoms when they turn 18, in the current era, young adulthood is a time when many young people remain highly dependent on their parents. A college degree is necessary to achieve an adequate standard of living, but attending college is costly. Many parents provide financial support as they can. Parents must decide how long to support their young adult children and when to let go and push them to be more independent, to begin earning more money on their own, or in some cases, to support themselves. For some parents, letting go can take a different form. Their young adults face various conditions or disabilities that mean they may never achieve financial independence and will need assistance of some kind from their parents for a long time.

All mothers share common experiences as they engage in promoting their teens' autonomy and letting go. At the same time, mothers' support for their teens and young adults is shaped and constrained by their positions in hierarchies based on their social class, race, and gender. As they renegotiate control and engage in letting go, mothers rely on resources to promote their teens' success. Parents' actions are, of course, critical in raising children, but parents cannot keep teens safe and see that they successfully complete their secondary school education on their own. Parents require good schools to help their teens gain the credentials they need to attend college or enter a training program that will prepare them for a good job. They need safe neighborhoods to help keep their teenage children out of trouble and promote their safe passage through adolescence. In the US there are great disparities in parents' ability to access these resources based on their social class and race. Families with resources have tremendous advantages. Lower-income families face underresourced schools and neighborhoods, which puts them at a major disadvantage in promoting their teens' success. African American mothers and fathers worry that their sons and daughters could face not only unfair treatment, but harm at the hands of the police.

As mothers describe it, parenting is all-consuming and continually challenging. And as Kimberly, a working-class African American mother with a 16-year-old son and a 20-year-old daughter, who was quoted in the previous chapter, said "You always worry":

> When things are well with your kids, you are happy. But when you're 90 and they're 50, you still worry, you always have the fear that something could happen to them no matter what their age. You pray, you never know. Being a mother is the hardest job. It's also one of the best things in life, having children you love and children who love you.

Carla, a white upper-middle-class mother of 15-year-old twin boys who was quoted in Chapter 2, spoke of parenting as a humbling experience: "You can't control as many things, you are not the be-all and end-all," she said. "It's a humbling thing to be a parent. Teens can be obnoxious. It changes you." She continued:

> You become vulnerable in a new way that gives you depth. It can make you a better person. I guess if you were already fairly healthy, it can make you healthier. And I guess if you were already having trouble, it could really put you over the edge! [Laughing]

While parenting presents major challenges for both mothers and fathers, it is also the case that parenting is one of the most meaningful aspects of the lives of those who are raising children. Mothers experience times of great connection and joy. Most have deep feelings of love for their children.

Mothers described the pride they felt when their children were doing well or had been successful at school, in sports or the arts, or in their personal growth- taking responsibility for things, helping others. One white working-class mother, who was quoted earlier in this book, reported that her daughter has always done well in school:

> When she was in third grade, her teacher recommended we have her tested for a mentally gifted program and she got in. She got involved in student council in grade school and went to a weekend workshop for school leaders and ever since then, she's just like, she's always been involved in school, she's a leader, we are so proud of her.

The Value of Understanding Letting Go and the Parenting Process

An examination of parenting adolescents and young adults and letting go provides valuable insights for researchers, parents, and social policymakers in understanding the challenges of raising teens and young adults. Mothers' accounts can also help develop new narratives and models of parenting. They illustrate key features of parenting that need to be more widely understood:

- Parenting is not simply a top-down process; it is a process that is negotiated between parents and their children, teens, and young adults who are integral to the parenting process.
- Letting go is a key feature of parenting. Parents must renegotiate control and engage in letting go in order to promote the autonomy of their children and teens.
- Parenting is not a static process but is an ongoing one, a process of parenting as you go that is continually changing as parents and their children, teens, and young adults renegotiate their roles and responsibilities.
- Parenting is characterized by uncertainty. Parents can't guarantee that things will turn out according to their plans. Some children and teens stay safe, become highly motivated, and achieve success in school. Others struggle, and some get into trouble.
- Parenting requires resources. They are an essential part of the parenting process and provide those who have them with many advantages in promoting the success of their children.

The accounts of mothers presented here demonstrate how researchers can expand our understanding of parenting by including the role of children and teens in their models of the parenting process. Sociologists and psychologists have studied parenting extensively. Their research has greatly increased our understanding of the impact of parenting styles and logics on outcomes for children and teens and other aspects of parenting. At the same time, it often assumes a process of linear control, a top-down process in which parents are in charge. We do not see the integral role of children in the parenting process and the ongoing negotiations at the heart of parenting.

Viewing parenting through the lens of its negotiated character can assist in the development of expanded models of parenting. Using negotiated models of parenting, for example, researchers can increase our knowledge of important issues of control. Mothers' accounts provide insight into what parents actually control, their options for maintaining control, and in what circumstances mothers and fathers do and do not have control over their children. Along with issues of control, researchers can further our understanding of the critical role resources play in the parenting process and the impact of parents' social class, race, and gender on their ability to promote the success of their teens and young adults.

A clearer understanding of parenting can also be valuable to parents. When children don't do well, we ask where their parenting went wrong and sometimes blame parents for their children's problems. Parents, in turn, can blame themselves when their children, teens, or young adults face difficulties. It is important for them to know that the parenting process is by nature uncertain, and that being unsure about their parenting is not necessarily due to a failure on their part. Finding a balance between maintaining control while letting go is challenging. As parents say, there is no guidebook, and things often come up suddenly. Given the uncertainty of parenting, mothers and fathers can also benefit from a greater appreciation of the critical role resources play in their ability to promote the safety and success of their teens and young adults and perhaps become motivated to demand more resources from local and state governments.

Mothers' accounts of the work of parenting also point to the urgent need for social policies that support families. In the United States, parenting is viewed as the private responsibility of individual families and social services and public institutions are often underfunded, creating serious disparities in resources parents can access.

The resulting inequality in the resources available to parents not only makes the lives of mothers and fathers more difficult; it also has an enormous impact on the trajectory of children's lives. Based on their families' resources, teens end up on different paths as they enter young adulthood and beyond. In my sample, those from upper-middle-class families have choices. Although some may have college debt, a number of them are going to graduate school and are likely to end up in lucrative professions and careers. Young adults from middle-class families have been able to attend college and most will have employment opportunities, although they, and in some cases their parents, will have to pay back college loans. Young adults from working-class families who have college degrees or some type of postsecondary training have the possibility of finding work that provides for an adequate standard of living although many will also have to pay back money they borrowed to finance their education and training.

Those without these credentials face a great deal of uncertainty in their future. As noted above, young men who have not attended college or received postsecondary training face higher rates of unemployment. Some working-class mothers in my sample whose young adults are not attending college or in a training program reported that their sons can't find jobs that enable them to obtain an adequate standard of living. African American men, who face the highest rates of arrest and imprisonment, are at particular risk.[1]

In order to support mothers and fathers and promote the success of children, teens, and young adults, we need major investments in infrastructure and family-friendly social policies:

(1) Increased investment in infrastructure including:
   - Resources for neighborhoods-- affordable housing, parks, and recreational activities that provide safety and enrichment for all children and youth
   - A public education system that provides equal funding and resources for all schools
   - Public subsidies for college attendance and debt relief for college students
   - A greater number of institutions for training young adults who don't attend college so they can gain the skills needed to find work and develop a path toward ongoing participation in the workforce

[1] R. Chetty et al., "Race and Economic Opportunity in the United States: An Intergenerational Perspective," *Quarterly Journal of Economics* 135(2) (2020): 711–783; A. Case and A. Deaton, "The Great Divide: Education, Despair, and Death," *Annual Review of Economics* 14 (2022): 1–21.

- Criminal justice reforms that end the profiling and harsher sentencing of Black and minority youth
(2) Flexible work-family policies to assist mothers and fathers as they raise teens, not just young children.

Building public support for social policies that promote the well-being of children and families is challenging. To move beyond the deep-seated culture of individualism in the United States which views raising children as a private family responsibility—typically the responsibility of mothers—we need public narratives that recognize the value of this work as a public good. Raising children has enormous social value. Our society requires educated workers who can maintain and increase the productivity of our economy, workers who will also pay the taxes that fund Social Security and guarantee that retirees can receive the benefits they have earned. Supporting mothers and fathers in the work of parenting should be one of our society's highest priorities. Investing in the safety and education of children, teens, and young adults would not only take some of the burden off of mothers and fathers as they work to promote the success of their children and guide them safely through to young adulthood—it would benefit everyone.

Appendix

To provide a better understanding of the work of parenting adolescents and young adults and the work of parenting more generally, I interviewed a diverse group of mothers. I drew respondents from several samples, which are described below. I interviewed white and African American mothers from different social class groups who live in the wider metropolitan area of a large northeastern city. While the mothers I interviewed cannot be considered representative of all white and African American mothers from the city or the suburbs where they live, or white and African American mothers more generally, their accounts provide a way to understand critical aspects of parenting teens and young adults and how their parenting is shaped and constrained by racial and class hierarchies.

Because of other career and life responsibilities, my work on this book extended longer than I anticipated. As a result, I interviewed mothers in two stages. At each stage, I asked mothers identical questions about how they were coping with the changes occurring in their relationships with their teens and young adults, and the new demands they faced in letting go and promoting their autonomy. In the interviews in stage 2, I added additional questions about technology and social media to understand their impact on the relationships between mothers, teens, and young adults. The interviews generally lasted for an hour and a half to two hours and were taped and transcribed.

As I describe below, I interviewed a total of 118 mothers. In stage 1, I interviewed 88 mothers who had teens and young adults ages 13 to 21, and in stage 2, I interviewed 30 mothers who had teens and young adults ages 13 to 21. Twenty-one percent of the sample (20 of the mothers in stage 1 and five of the mothers in stage 2) also had a child who was a young adult between the ages of 22 and 25. While I do not have anything like a representative group of mothers of 22- to 25-year-olds, as I describe in Chapter 5, these interviews provided valuable information about issues and challenges in parenting young adults.

Designation of Social Classes

Social scientists have long debated how best to conceptualize social class. For this book, I designated three different social class groups—upper-, middle-, and working-class—which were based on mothers' level of education, their occupation, and the median income of homes in their neighborhood (as defined by their zip code):

- Mothers' neighborhoods provided indicators of the conditions in which they were raising their teens, including a neighborhood's safety and the quality of its schools. Neighborhoods were also an indicator of the economic resources available to mothers.
- Occupation was also important as an indicator of mothers' economic resources as well as their social and cultural capital.
- Education level was an important indicator of mothers' social and cultural capital, including access to knowledge of what opportunities are available for their teens and young adult children and how to advocate for them in schools and other institutions.

Researchers frequently use mothers' income as an indicator of social class, but I did not do that because the data were incomplete. Some mothers were homemakers relying on their husbands' income, some were in transition between jobs and temporarily unemployed. Some were cutting back hours at work to spend more time with their teenage children.

In my study, to be considered upper-middle-class, mothers must have at least one of the following:

- Some postgraduate education—typically a masters, PhD, MD, or law degree
- An upper-middle-class occupation (work in professions with some autonomy, including medicine, law, psychology, and high-level administration)
- A home in a neighborhood (as defined by zip code) where the median value of houses was $500,000 (all figures are in 2020 values)

To be considered middle-class, mothers must have:

- A college degree or an associate's degree
- An occupation requiring an associate's or college degree (secondary school teacher, RN nurse, accountant)
- A home in a neighborhood (as defined by zip code) where the median value of houses was $270,000

To be considered working-class, mothers must have:

- A high school diploma
- An occupation not requiring a college degree (secretary/administrative assistant, assistant in a nursing home or other healthcare facility, day care worker, home health aide)
- Home in a neighborhood (as defined by zip code) where the median value of houses was $160,000

My sample did not include mothers at the lowest income levels.

The Samples

Stage 1: 2011–2014, 88 Mothers

Middle-class and working-class respondents were drawn randomly from the following three samples, two from the large northeastern city and one from a surrounding suburb:

- A sample drawn randomly from citywide school records that included upper-middle-class, middle-class, and working-class mothers.
- A sample drawn randomly from the city's census tracts that were chosen to represent primarily working-class households but also included some lower-middle-class households.
- A sample drawn randomly from the enrollment lists of the junior high and high school of a white middle-class suburban neighborhood not far from the large central city.

The sample of upper-middle-class mothers was a snowball sample drawn as follows:

- I sought out mothers to interview who were not known to each other and who lived in different neighborhoods (city and suburban) and worked in different professions and occupations. I asked each of them for the names of several mothers whose backgrounds were similar to theirs, whom they thought I could interview. Those I contacted through this process all agreed to be interviewed. Using snowball sampling, I also interviewed several lesbian mothers and a few mothers whose teens have disabilities.

Stage 2: 2021–2023, 30 Mothers

In stage 2, I interviewed 30 mothers. Using snowball sampling, I selected interviewees from upper-middle-class, middle-class, and working-class neighborhoods. As in the case of the upper-middle-class mothers in stage 1, I sought out mothers who were not known to each other and who lived in different city and suburban neighborhoods and worked in different professions and occupations. I then asked each of them for the names of several people whom they thought I could interview. Those I contacted through this process agreed to be interviewed.

Sample Characteristics

A. Social Class

Class Membership in Stage 1 and Stage 2 samples:

- Stage 1 sample: Of the 88 mothers, 29 were upper-middle-class, 29 were middle-class, and 30 were working-class.
- Stage 2 sample: Of the 30 mothers, 11 were upper-middle-class, 10 were middle-class, and 9 were working-class.

B. Racial Background

1) Stage 1 Sample: 88 Mothers
The majority of mothers, 65 percent (57 mothers), are white, while 35 percent (31 mothers) are African American. There are more white than African American mothers in the upper-middle- and middle-class sample, and more African American mothers in the working-class sample. In the suburban town where the of middle-class interviewees live, the majority of residents are white.

2) The Stage 2 Sample: 30 Mothers
22 mothers are white, 8 mothers are African American.

Table A.1 Stage 1 Sample: Mothers' Social Class and Race

	White	African American	Total
Upper-Middle- Class	24 (80%)	6 (20%)	30 (100%)
Middle-Class	23 (79%)	6 (21%)	29 (100%)
Working-Class	10 (34%)	19 (66%)	29 (100%)
Total	57 (65%)	31 (35%)	88 (65% white, 35% AA)

Table A.2 Stage 2 Sample: Mothers' Social Class and Race

	White	African American	Total
Upper-Middle- Class	8 (73%)	3 (27%)	11 (100%)
Middle-Class	7 (70%)	3 (20%)	10 (100%)
Working-Class	7 (78%)	2 (22%)	9 (100%)
Total	22 (73%)	8 (27%)	30 (65% white, 35% AA)

C. Marital Status

1) Stage 1 Sample: 88 Mothers

The majority of white mothers, 78 percent (46 mothers), are married, while only 41 percent of African American mothers (12 mothers) are married. A small number of mothers have live-in partners who assist with parenting. Counting these partners, 19 percent of white mothers and 45 percent of African American mothers are parenting as single mothers.

2) Stage 2 Sample

The majority of white mothers, 81 percent of the 22 mothers (18 mothers), are married; 2 have partners, 2 are single. Half of the 4 African American mothers are married or live with a partner, 2 are single.

Table A.3 Stage 1 Sample: Marital Status by Race

	Married	With Partner	Single	Total
White	46 (78%)	2 (3%)	11 (19%)	59 (67%)
African American	12 (41%)	4 (14%)	13 (45%)	29 (33%)
Total	58 (66%)	6 (7%)	24 (27%)	88 (100%)

Table A.4 Stage 2: Marital Status by Race

	Married	With Partner	Single	Total
White	18 (81%)	2 (9%)	2 (9%)	22 (73%)
African American	4 (50%)	2 (25%)	2 (25%)	8 (27%)
Total	22 (73%)	4 (13%)	4 (13%)	30 (100%)

Limitations of This Study

It goes without saying that this book doesn't tell the complete story of raising teens and young adults. I have written about only one aspect of the highly demanding, multifaceted, nonstop work of parenting—the work of promoting teens' autonomy and letting go, of how mothers renegotiate power and control with their teens as they transition from childhood to young adulthood. I don't show the extensive work mothers do to support their teens on a day-to-day basis such as seeing that they have school supplies, driving teens to school events and extracurricular activities, supporting their participation in sports. I describe some of the emotion work mothers do on behalf of their teens, but I don't analyze the psychological dynamics between parents and teens.

There are also many differences between mothers I have not addressed. Mothers have different personalities, which can make the task of raising teens through adolescence and beyond easier or more difficult for them and their children. Some are more anxious, some are more strict, some are more easy-going. As I have described, my sample is somewhat representative on the basis of social class and race, but it is limited to one geographical area and doesn't include mothers of diverse ethnicities or religious backgrounds, very poor mothers, mothers who are imprisoned, or those whose children are in foster care. However, the diversity of the mothers I interviewed, as well as their detailed accounts, do provide valuable information about the work involved in parenting teens and young adults, and on parenting more generally.

Ideally, a study like this would also include the perspectives of fathers, teens, and young adults, but I found it was not possible to do justice to their roles while also writing in-depth about the work of mothers. However, to gain some understanding of their views, using a snowball sample, I interviewed a small number of both: 15 fathers and 20 young adults. I also conducted four focus groups, two with junior high students and two with high school students. Fathers shared many of the views of mothers I have outlined here, and they said they faced similar challenges in parenting and managing the process of letting go. Most of them said they leave the majority of parenting to mothers. In their accounts, the young people in junior high, high school, and college with whom I spoke were very concerned with issues of autonomy, which they often framed in terms of how much freedom they had and how strict their parents were. They described how they negotiated with mothers to get things they wanted and described concealing things from their parents that they believed their parents would disapprove of. Most of them also spoke of happy times they had with their parents, particularly on family vacations.

Doing Interviews

When contacted about being interviewed, almost all mothers agreed to the interview. Mothers are identified by a first name that is different from their own. I did the majority of the interviews with mothers in their homes. When introducing myself to interviewees, I stated, "I'm very interested in the nature of parenting, which is one of the most important tasks of any society, but I don't think it's well enough understood. Parents are often told what to do without an adequate understanding of what it takes to raise teens and young adults." Because an issue in the interviewing process is whether respondents give socially desirable responses (presenting themselves in a more positive light than they might to a close confidant), I wondered if mothers would feel comfortable sharing their parenting challenges with me. When I introduced myself, I explained my study—what it was about and how I was carrying it out. I also said that as a mother myself, I had found adolescence and young adulthood to be challenging periods of parenting. I said this not only by way of introducing myself but because, as I write in this book, many mothers feel judged and judge themselves, believing that they are not doing a good enough job. I felt that by saying that I had faced challenges, people would hopefully understand that I would not be judging them.

Mothers spoke easily about parenting, and openly offered descriptions of challenges they faced. In fact, I found that with most interviewees, I had to explicitly ask if there were things they found pleasurable about parenting or being with their teen or young adult. As I have written, they did report pleasurable times with their teen and young adult children. One reason mothers may feel fairly comfortable talking about the difficult aspects of parenting adolescents is because it is widely viewed as a challenging time and teens are often seen as demanding and "rebellious," making it more socially acceptable to talk about difficulties in parenting teens. It is of course the case that mothers may not have told me things about their parenting because they wanted to keep them private or were embarrassed about them.

To try and accurately capture as much of the experience of African American mothers as possible, I explicitly asked them whether they felt that they or their teens had had different experiences based on their race, including whether they had experienced discrimination or other forms of racism. All African American mothers described some aspect of their parenting that was impacted by the fact that they were African American, particularly their fear that their teens or young adults would experience police harassment or violence. Some also described their efforts to educate their teens about the rich heritage and culture of African Americans. However, it is certainly the case that African American mothers may not have shared as much with me, a white woman who has not experienced racism, as they would have with an African American interviewer.

Interview Topics

- Changes mothers experienced in their relationships with their teens during adolescence
- The nature of parenting work—the major tasks, the major challenges—both the interpersonal work with teens and the work to obtain resources
- Mothers' work managing teens' safety and their education, and their work to support their older teens as they become young adults

- Specific challenges African American mothers face raising children in a society where there is ongoing discrimination and where they fear police violence towards their teens and young adults
- Issues in renegotiating authority and control
- Help secured from others, if any—from another parent, relatives, friends, or professional experts
- Access to resources

Fathers

I interviewed 15 fathers to gain some insight into their perspectives on parenting teens and young adults. Three fathers were married to or partners of mothers I interviewed from random samples. The remaining fathers were chosen through a snowball sample. One is a single father who was also gay; the rest of the fathers were married. Three of the fathers are working-class, five are middle-class, and eight are upper-middle-class. As it was with my sampling of mothers, I sought out a few fathers who were not known to each other and who lived in different neighborhoods and were in different professions and occupations. I then asked each of them for the names of several fathers whom they thought I could interview. Those I contacted through this process agreed to be interviewed. It was certainly valuable to hear fathers' perspectives but given the scope of my project I was not able to interview enough to incorporate their perspectives into the book.

Teens and Young Adults

To gain some insight into the perspectives of teens and young adults, I conducted five focus groups of 10 to 15 students each:

- One focus group with 14 students at a public junior high school, and one with high school students at a private school. Both schools had some racial/ethnic diversity.
- Three focus groups of 10 to 15 students from a private university (ages 18 to 22).

It was valuable to hear the perspectives of teens and young adults, but as in the case of fathers, my project didn't enable me to interview enough to incorporate their experiences into my analysis.

Bibliography

Abel, J. R., and R. Deitz (2019). "Despite Rising Costs, College Is Still a Good Investment." Liberty Street Economics. New York: Federal Reserve Bank of New York.

Agillias, K. (2017). *Family Estrangement: A Matter of Perspective.* New York: Routledge.

Allegretto, S., E. García, and E. Weiss (2022). "Public Education Funding in the U.S. Needs an Overhaul." Washington, DC: Economic Policy Institute, July 12.

Allen, Q., and K. White-Smith (2018). "'That's Why I Say Stay in School': Black Mothers' Parental Involvement, Cultural Wealth, and Exclusion in Their Son's Schooling." *Urban Education* 53(3): 409–435.

Anderson, E. (1999). *Code of the Street: Decency, Violence, and the Moral Life of the Inner City.* New York: Norton.

Anderson, M. (2016). "Parents, Teens, and Digital Monitoring." Washington, DC: Pew Research Center.

Anderson, M., M. Faverio, and J. Gottfried (2023). "Teens, Social Media and Technology 2023: YouTube, TikTok, Snapchat and Instagram Remain the Most Widely Used Online Platforms Among U.S. Teens." Washington, DC: Pew Research Center.

Anderson, M., M. Favario, and E. Park (2024, March 12). "How Teens and Parents Approach Screen Time." Washington, DC: Pew Research Center.

Anderson, M., and Jiang, J. (2018). "Teens, Social Media & Technology, 2018." Washington, DC: Pew Research Center.

Anderson, M., E. A. Vogels, A. Perrin, and L. Raine (2022). "Connection, Creativity, and Drama: Teen Life on Social Media in 2022." Washington, DC: Pew Research Center.

Arnett, J. J. (2015). *Emerging Adulthood: The Winding Road from the Late Teens Through the Twenties.* New York: Oxford University Press.

Autor, D., D. Figlio, K. Karbownik, J. Roth, and M. Wasserman (2019). "Family Disadvantage and the Gender Gap in Behavioral and Educational Outcomes." *American Economic Journal: Applied Economics* 11(3): 338–381.

Baker, B., M. Di Carlo, and M. Weber (2024). "Is School Funding Fair?" Albert Shanker Institute, University of Miami School of Education and Human Development, and Rutgers Graduate School of Education.

Barroso, A., K. Parker, and R. Fry (2019). "Majority of Americans Say Parents are Doing Too Much for Their Young Adult Children." Washington, DC: Pew Research Center.

Baumgartner, F., D. Epp, and K. Shoub (2018). *Suspect Citizens: What 20 Million Traffic Stops Tell Us About Policing and Race.* New York: Cambridge University Press.

Best, A. L. (2006). "Freedom, Constraint, and Family Responsibility: Teens and Parents Collaboratively Negotiate Around the Car, Class, Gender, and Culture." *Journal of Family Issues* 27(1): 55–84.

Bi, X., Y. Yang, L. Hailei, M. Wang, W. Zhang, and K. Deater-Dexter (2018). "Parenting Styles and Parent–Adolescent Relationships: The Mediating Roles of Behavioral Autonomy and Parental Authority." *Frontiers in Psychology* 9: 2187. https://doi.org/10.3389/fpsyg.2018.02187.

Bitsko, R. H., A. H. Claussen, J. Lichstein, L. I. Black, S. E. Jones, M. L. Danielson, J. M. Hoenig, S. P. Davis Jack, D. J. Brody, S. Gyawali, M. J. Maenner, M. Warner, K. M. Holland, R. Perou, A. E. Crosby, S. J. Blumberg, S. Avenevoli, J. W. Kaminski, and R.M. Ghandour (2022). "Mental Health Surveillance Among Children—United States, 2013–2019." *Morbidity and Mortality Weekly Report* Supplements 71(2): 1–42.

Bouchrika, I. (2024). "List of College Acceptance Rates in 2024." April 17, research.com.

Bowdler, J., and B. Harris (2022). "Racial Inequality in the United States." Washington, DC: US Department of the Treasury.

Bowen Matthew, D. B., and R. V. Reeves (2017). "Trump Won White Voters, But Serious Inequities Remain for Black Americans." *Social Mobility Memos.* Washington, DC: Brookings Institution.

Braga, D., and K. Parker (2022). "Most K-12 Parents Say First Year of Pandemic Had a Negative Effect on their Children's Education." Washington, DC: Pew Research Center.

Breehl, L., and O. Caban (2023). "Physiology, Puberty." 2023 Mar 27. In: StatPearls [Internet]. Treasure Island (FL): StatPearls Publishing; 2024 Jan–. PMID: 30521248.

Bronson, J., and E. A. Carson (2019). "Prisoners in 2017 (NJC 252156)." Washington, DC: Bureau of Justice Statistics. https://www.bjs.gov/content/pub/pdf/p17.pdf.

Bureau of Labor Statistics (2022). "American Time Use Survey—2021 Results." Washington, DC: US Department of Labor.

Calarco, J. M. (2024). Holding It Together: How Women Became America's Safety Net. New York: Penguin Random House.

Calarco, J. M. (2018). *Negotiating Opportunities: How the Middle Class Secures Advantages in School.* New York: Oxford University Press.

Campione-Barr, N., and J. G. Smetana. (2018). "Families with Adolescents." In *APA Handbook of Contemporary Family Psychology: Foundations, Methods, and Changing Forms,* Vol. 1, ed. B. H. Fiese, M. Celano, K. Deater-Deckard, E. N. Jouriles, and M. A. Whisman. Washington, DC: American Psychological Association.

Cantor, D., H. Lee, B. Fisher, C. Bruce, S. Chibnall, G. Thomas, and R. Townsend. (2020, January 17). "Report on the AAU Campus Climate Survey on Sexual Assault and Misconduct." Rockville, MD: Westat.

Carnevale, A. P., J. Strohl, N. Ridley, and A. Gulish. (2018). "Three Educational Pathways to Good Jobs: High School, Middle Skills, and Bachelor's Degree." Washington, DC: Georgetown University Center on Education and the Workforce.

Case, A., and W. A. Deaton (2022). "The Great Divide: Education, Despair, and Death." *Annual Review of Economics* 14: 1–21.

Cazenave, N. A. (2018). *Killing Black Americans: Police and Vigilante Violence as a Racial Control Mechanism.* New York: Routledge.

Centers for Disease Control and Prevention (2023). "Preventing Youth Violence." Atlanta: Centers for Disease Control and Prevention.

Centers for Disease Control and Prevention (2021). "Reproductive Health: About Teen Pregnancy." Atlanta: Centers for Disease Control and Prevention.

Centers for Disease Control and Prevention (2022). "Teen Drivers: Get the Facts." Atlanta: Centers for Disease Control and Prevention.

Centers for Disease Control and Prevention. (2020). "Youth Risk Behavior Surveillance System (YRBSS) Overview." Atlanta: Centers for Disease Control and Prevention.

Centers for Disease Control and Prevention (2020). "Youth Risk Behavior Survey: Data Summary and Trends Report: 2009–2019." Atlanta: Centers for Disease Control and Prevention.

Centers for Disease Control and Prevention. (2023). "Youth Risk Behavior Survey 2011–2021: Data Summary and Trends Report." Atlanta: Centers for Disease Control and Prevention.

Chan, H-Y., B. B. Brown, and H. von Bank, (2015). "Adolescent Disclosure of Information About Peers: The Mediating Role of Perceptions of Parents' Right to Know." *Journal of Youth and Adolescence* 44: 1048–1065.

Chetty, R., D. J. Deming, and J. Friedman (2023). "Diversifying Society's Leaders? The Determinants and Consequences of Admission to Highly Selective Private Colleges." Working Paper 31492. Cambridge, MA: National Bureau of Economic Research.

Chetty, R., D. Grusky, M. Hell, N. Hendren, R. Manduca, and J. Narang (2017). "The Fading American Dream: Trends in Absolute Income Mobility Since 1940." *Science* 356(6336) (2017): 398–406.

Chetty, R., and N. Hendren (2022). "Ensuring the American Dream." *Finance and Development.* Washington, DC: International Monetary Fund.

Chetty, R.. N. Hendren, M. R. Jones, and S. R. Porter, S. R. (2020). "Race and Economic Opportunity in the United States: An Intergenerational Perspective." *Quarterly Journal of Economics* 135(2): 711–783.

Children's Defense Fund (2017). "Protect Children Not Guns: Fact Sheet 2017." Washington, DC: Children's Defense Fund.

Children's Defense Fund (2022). "The State of America's Children 2021: Gun Violence." Washington, DC: Children's Defense Fund.

Children's Defense Fund (2023). "The State of America's Children 2023: Youth Justice." Washington, DC: Children's Defense Fund.

Cochrane, E., A. Harmon, A. Hartocollis, and A. Betts (2023, July 31). "The Legacy Dilemma: What to Do About Privileges for the Privileged?" *New York Times.*

Cohen, J. W., and R. A. Brooks (2014). *Confronting School Bullying: Kids, Culture, and the Making of a Social Problem.* Boulder, CO: Lynne Rienner.

College Board Communications (2023, March 17). "Education Pays 2023 Presents Data on the Benefits of Education for Individuals and Society." https://allaccess.collegeboard.org/education-pays-2023-presents-data-benefits-education-individuals-and-society.

Collins, P. H. (2022). *Black Feminist Thought 30th Anniversary Edition: Knowledge, Consciousness, and the Politics of Empowerment.* New York: Routledge.

Collins, W. A., and L. Steinberg (2006). "Adolescent Development in Interpersonal Context." In *Handbook of Child Psychology: Social, Emotional, and Personality Development* Vol. 3, ed. N. Eisenberg, 1003–1067. New York: Wiley.

Connor, J. O., and D. C. Pope (2013). "Not Just Robo-Students: Why Full Engagement Matters and How Schools Can Promote It." *Journal of Youth and Adolescence* 42: 1426–1442.

Craft, Sandra (2021, December 18). "Community College Statistics." ThinkImpact. https://www.thinkimpact.com/community-college-statistics/.

Davis, K. (1940). "The Sociology of Parent-Youth Conflict." *American Sociological Review* 5(4): 523–535.

De Goede, I. H. A., S. Branje, and W. H. J. Meeus (2009). "Developmental Changes in Adolescents' Perceptions of Relationships with Their Parents." *Journal of Youth and Adolescence* 38(1): 75–88.

Deaton, A., and A. Case (2020). *Deaths of Despair and the Future of Capitalism.* Princeton, NJ: Princeton University Press.

Deloitte Access Economics. (2020, June). *The Social and Economic Cost of Eating Disorders in the United States of America: A Report for the Strategic Training Initiative for the Prevention of Eating Disorders and the Academy for Eating Disorders.* Harvard T. H. Tan School of Public Health, Harvard University. https://www.hsph.harvard.edu/striped/report-economic-costs-of-eating-disorders/.

Del Toro, J. D., and M. Wang (2022). "The Roles of Suspensions for Minor Infractions and School Climate in Predicting Academic Performance Among Adolescents." *American Psychologist,* 77(2): 173–185.

DeVault, M. L. (1991). *Feeding the Family: The Social Organization of Caring as Gendered Work.* Chicago: University of Chicago Press.

Dow, D. M. (2016). "The Deadly Challenges of Raising African American Boys: Navigating the Controlling Image of the 'Thug'." *Gender & Society* 30(2): 161–188.

Duell, N., and L. Steinberg (2019). "Positive Risk Taking in Adolescence." *Child Development Perspectives* 13(1): 48–52.

Duffy, M. E., J. M. Twenge, and T. E. Joiner (2019). "Trends in Mood and Anxiety Symptoms and Suicide-Related Outcomes Among US Undergraduates, 2007–2018: Evidence from Two National Surveys." *Journal of Adolescent Health* 65: 590–598.

Elliott, S. (2012). *Not My Kid: What Parents Believe About the Sex Lives of Their Teenagers.* New York: New York University Press.

Elliott, S., and S. Bowen (2018). "Defending Motherhood: Morality, Responsibility and Double Binds in Feeding Children." *Journal of Marriage and Family* 80: 499–520.

Fabina, J., E. L. Hernandez, and K. McElrath (2023, June 8). "School Enrollment in the United States: 2021." American Community Survey Reports. Washington, DC: US Census Bureau, June 8, 2023.

Federal Interagency Forum on Child and Family Statistics (2023). *America's Children: Key National Indicators of Well-Being, 2023.* Washington, DC: US Government Printing Office.

Feldman, S. S., and T. Quatman (1988). "Factors Influencing Age Expectations for Adolescent Autonomy: A Study of Early Adolescents and Parents." *Journal of Early Adolescence* 8(4): 325–343.

Filardo, M., J. M. Vincent, and K. Sullivan (2019). "How Crumbling School Facilities Perpetuate Inequality." *Phi Delta Kappan* 100(8): 27–31.

Finkenauer, C., R. Engels, and W. Meeus (2002). "Keeping Secrets from Parents: Advantages and Disadvantages of Secrecy in Adolescence." *Journal of Youth and Adolescence* 31(2): 123–136.

Fletcher, K. L, E. E. Pierson, K. L. Neumeister, and H. Finch (2020). "Overparenting and Perfectionistic Concerns Predict Academic Entitlement in Young Adults." *Journal of Child and Family Studies* 29: 348–357.

Folbre, N., ed. (2012). *For Love and Money: Care Provision in the U.S.* New York: Russell Sage Foundation.

Fry, R., C. Aragão, K. Hurst, and K. Parker (2023, April 13). "In a Growing Share of U.S. Marriages, Husbands and Wives Earn About the Same." Washington, DC: Pew Research Center.

Furstenberg, F. F. (2020). "On a New Schedule: Transitions to Adulthood and Family Change." *The Future of Children* 20(1): 67–87.

Furstenberg, F. F., Jacquelynne E., Glen H. Elder, G. H. Jr., and A. Sameroff. (1999). *Managing to Make It: Urban Families and Adolescent Success.* Chicago: University of Chicago Press.

Gebeloff, D., B. Marsh, A. McCann, and A. Sun (2022, December 14). "Childhood's Greatest Danger: The Data on Kids and Gun Violence." New York Times Magazine.

Gelles-Watnick, R. (2022). "Explicit Content, Time-Wasting Are Key Social Media Worries for Parents of US Teens." Washington, DC: Pew Research Center.

Gillen-O'Neel, C., and A. Fuligni (2013). "A Longitudinal Study of School Belonging and Academic Motivation Across High School." *Child Development* 84: 678–692.

Gingo, M., A. D. Roded, and E. Turiel (2017). "Authority, Autonomy, and Deception: Evaluating the Legitimacy of Parental Authority and Adolescent Deceit." *Journal of Research on Adolescence* 27: 862–877.

Glaser, J. (2015). *Suspect Race: Causes and Consequences of Racial Profiling.* New York: Oxford University Press.

Glassner, B. (2018). *The Culture of Fear: Why Americans Are Afraid of the Wrong Things.* New York: Basic Books.

Goffman, E. (1969). *Strategic Interaction.* Philadelphia: University of Pennsylvania Press.

Gubbels, J., C. E. van der Put, and M. Assink, M. (2019). "Risk Factors for School Absenteeism and Dropout: A Meta-Analytic Review." *Journal of Youth and Adolescence* 48(9): 1637–1667.

Gun Violence Archive (2023). Washington, DC: Gun Violence Archive. https://www.gunviolencearchive.org/.

Hahn, A., and J. Tarver (2024). "2024 Student Loan Debt Statistics: Average Student Loan Debt." *Forbes Advisor.* New York: Forbes. April 18.

Haidt, J. (2024). *The Anxious Generation: How the Great Rewiring of Childhood Is Causing an Epidemic of Mental Illness.* New York: Penguin Press.

Hamilton, L. T. (2016). *Parenting to a Degree: How Family Matters for College Women's Success.* Chicago: University of Chicago Press.

Hamilton, L., J. Roksa, and J. Nielsen (2018). "Providing a 'Leg Up': Parental Involvement and Opportunity Hoarding in College." *Sociology of Education* 91(2): 111–131.

Hanson, M. (2023). "College Dropout Rate." Education Data Initiative. https://educationdata. org/college-dropout-rates.

Hanson, M. (2024). "College Enrollment & Student Demographic Statistics." Education Data Initiative.

Harris, A. J. (2014). "Understanding the World of Digital Youth." In *Adolescent Sexual Behavior in the Digital Age*, ed. F. Saleh, A. Grudzinkas, and A. Judge, 24–42. New York: Oxford University Press.

Harris, L. E., and J. A. Jacobs (2023). "Emerging Ideas. Digital Parenting Advice: Online Guidance Regarding Children's Use of the Internet and Social Media." *Family Relations* 72 (5): 2551–2568.

Harter, S. (2011). "Self-Development During Adolescence." In *Encyclopedia of Adolescence*, ed. B. B. Brown and M. J. Prinstein, 307–315. New York: Academic Press.

Hatfield, J. (2023, May 3). "Young Adults in the U.S. Are Less Likely Than Those in Most of Europe to Live in Their Parents' Home." Washington, DC: Pew Research Center.

Hibbs, B. J., and A. Rostain (2019). *The Stressed Years of Their Lives: Helping Your Kid Survive and Thrive During Their College Years.* New York: St. Martin's Press.

Hine, Thomas (1999). *The Rise and Fall of the American Teenager.* New York: Perennial.

Hofferth, S. L., S. M. Flood, and M. Sobek (2017). "American Time Use Survey Data Extract Builder: Version 2.6." College Park and Minneapolis: University of Maryland and University of Minnesota.

Horowitz, J. M., and N. Graf (2019). "Most U.S. Teens See Anxiety and Depression as a Major Problem Among Their Peers." Washington, DC: Pew Research Center.

Howarth, R., and W. Barkley-Denney (2019). "New Stats on For-Profit Colleges by State Show Continued Poor Outcomes and Disproportionate Impacts." Durham, NC: Center for Responsible Lending.

Hulbert, A. (2004). *Raising America: Experts, Parents, and a Century of Advice About Children.* New York: Vintage Books.

Inside Higher Ed (2024, February 28). "The 2018 Survey of College and University Admissions Directors: A Study by Inside Higher Ed and Gallup." https://www.insidehighered.com/ news/survey/2018-surveys-admissions-leaders-pressure-grows.

Institute of Education Sciences (2020). "Degrees Conferred by Postsecondary Institutions, by Level of Degree and Sex of Student: Selected Years, 1869–70 through 2029–30," Digest of Education Statistics Table 318.10. Washington, DC: US Department of Education.

Institute for Social Research. *Monitoring the Future Monograph Series.* Ann Arbor: Institute for Social Research, University of Michigan.

Irwin, V., K. Wang, T. Tezil, J. Zhang, A. Filbey, J. Jung, F. Bullock Mann, R. Dilig, and S. Parker (2023). *Report on the Condition of Education 2023.* NCES 2023-144. Washington, DC: National Center for Education Statistics.

Jager, J., C. X. Yuen, D. L. Putnick, C. Hendricks, and M. H. Bornstein. (2015). "Adolescent-Peer Relationships, Separation and Detachment from Parents, and Internalizing and Externalizing Behaviors: Linkages and Interactions." *Journal of Early Adolescence* 35(4): 511–537.

Jäggi, L. (2016). "The Relationship Between Trauma, Arrest, and Incarceration History Among Black Americans: Findings from the National Survey of American Life." *Society and Mental Health* 6(3): 187–206.

Jee, E., J. Misra, and M. Murray-Close (2019). "Motherhood Penalties in the U.S., 1986–2014." *Journal of Marriage and Family* 81(2): 434–449.

Jiang, J. J. (2018). "How Teens and Parents Navigate Screen Time and Device Distractions." Washington, DC: Pew Research Center.

Johnson, J., and J. Rochkind (2020). "With Their Whole Lives Ahead of Them: Myths and Realities About Why So Many Students Fail to Finish College." Public Agenda. Prepared with support from the Bill and Melinda Gates Foundation.

Jones, T. (2022). "10 Easy Ways Kids Can Bypass Internet Filters: Parent Should Know." FamliSafe. https://famisafe.wondershare.com/internet-filter/get-around-internet-filters.html.

Kochhar, R., and M. Moslimani (2023, December). "Wealth Surged in the Pandemic, but Debt Endures for Poorer Black and Hispanic Families." Washington, DC: Pew Research Center.

Kuhfeld, M., J. Soland, K. Lewis, and M. Morton (2022). "The Pandemic Has Had Devastating Impacts on Learning. What Will It Take To Help Students Catch Up?" Washington, DC: Brookings Institution.

Lareau, A. (2021). *Listening to People: A Practical Guide to Interviewing, Participant Observation, Data Analysis, and Writing It All Up.* Chicago: University of Chicago Press.

Lareau, A. (2011). *Unequal Childhoods: Class, Race, and Family Life Second Edition With an Update a Decade Later.* Berkeley: University of California Press.

Lareau, A., and A. Cox (2011). "Social Class and the Transition to Adulthood: Differences in Parents' Interactions with Institutions." In *Social Class and Changing Families in an Unequal America*, ed. M. Carlson and P. England, 134–164. Stanford, CA: Stanford University Press.

Larson, R., and M. H. Richards (1994). *Divergent Realities: The Emotional Lives of Mothers, Fathers, and Adolescents.* New York: BasicBooks.

Leachman, M., K. Masterson, and E. Figueroa (2017). "A Punishing Decade for School Funding." Washington, DC: Center on Budget and Policy Priorities.

Lewis, A. E., and J. B. Diamond (2015). *Despite the Best Intentions: How Racial Inequality Thrives in Good Schools.* New York: Oxford University Press.

Little, B. (2020). "The Role of Peers in Personality Development." In *Encyclopedia of Personality and Individual Differences*, ed. V. Zeigler-Hill and T. K. Shackelford, 4499–4504. Cham: Springer.

Lloyd, C. M., J. Alvira-Hammond, J. Carlson, and D. Logan (2021, March 5). "Family, Economic, and Geographic Characteristics of Black Families with Children." Child Trends. https://www.childtrends.org/publications/family-economic-and-geographic-characteristics-of-black-families-with-children.

Lundberg, S. (2020). "Educational Gender Gaps." *Southern Economic Journal* 7: 416–439.

Malkus, N. (2024, January 31). "Long COVID for Public Schools: Chronic Absenteeism Before and After the Pandemic." Washington, DC: American Enterprise Institute.

Marbell-Pierre, K. N., W. Grolnick, A. L. Stewart, and J. N. Raftery-Helmer (2019). "Parental Autonomy Support in Two Cultures: The Moderating Effects of Adolescents' Self-Construals " *Child Development* 90(3): 825–845.

Marrero, L. (2019, February 1). "Why School Counselors Matter." Washington, DC: The Education Trust.

Mayo Clinic Staff (2023, August 23). "Teens and Social Media Use: What's the Impact?" Mayo Clinic. https://www.mayoclinic.org/healthy-lifestyle/tween-and-teen-health/in-depth/teens-and-social-media-use/art-20474437.

Mazelis, J., and A. Kuperberg (2022). "Student Loan Debt, Family Support, and Reciprocity in the Transition to Adulthood." *Emerging Adulthood* 10(6): 1511–1528.

McKinney, C., M. Morse, and J. Pastuszak. (2016). "Effective and Ineffective Parenting: Associations with Psychological Adjustments in Emerging Adults." *Journal of Family Issues* 37(9): 1203–1225.

Meier, A., K. Musick, J. Fischer, and S. Flood (2016). "Mothers' and Fathers' Well-Being in Parenting Across the Arch of Child Development." *Marriage and Family* 80(4): 992–1004.

BIBLIOGRAPHY 241

Michelmore, K., and P. Rich (2022). "Contextual Origins of Black-White Educational Disparities in the 21st Century: Evaluating Long-Term Disadvantage Across Three Domains." *Social Forces* 101: 1–30.

Michelmore, T. T. (2008). "Family Capital and the Invisible Transfer of Privilege: Intergenerational Support and Social Class in Early Adulthood." *New Directions for Child and Adolescent Development* 119: 11–24.

Miech, R. A., L. D. Johnston, M. E. Patrick, P. M. O'Malley, J. G. Bachman, and J. E. Schulenberg (2023). "Monitoring the Future National Survey Results on Drug Use, 1975–2022: Secondary School Students." Ann Arbor: Institute for Social Research, University of Michigan.

Mills, K. L., F. Lalonde, L. S. Clasen, J. N. Giedd, and S-J. Blakemore (2014). "Developmental Changes in the Structure of the Social Brain in Late Childhood and Adolescence." *Social Cognitive Affective Neuroscience* 9(1): 123–131.

Minkin, R., K. Parker, J. Horowitz, and C. Aragão (2024, January). "Parents, Young Adult Children and the Transition to Adulthood." Washington, DC: Pew Research Center.

Moellera, J., M. A. Brackett, Z. Ivcevic, and A. E. White (2020). "High School Students' Feelings: Discoveries from a Large National Survey and an Experience Sampling Study." *Learning and Instruction* 66, 101301: 1–15.

Moody, J. (2019, April 4). "What to Look For When Hiring a College Consultant." *U.S. News and World Report.* https://www.usnews.com/education/best-colleges/articles/2019-04-04/what-to-look-for-when-hiring-a-college-consultant.

Morgan, I., and A. (2018). "Funding Gaps: An Analysis of School Funding Equity across the US and within Each State." Washington, DC: The Education Trust. https://edtrust.org/resource/funding-gaps-2018/.

Napolitano, L. (2015). " 'I'm Not Going to Leave Her High and Dry': Young Adult Support to Parents During the Transition to Adulthood." *Sociological Quarterly* 56(2): 329–354.

National Center for Education Statistics (2020). "College Enrollment & Student Demographic Statistics, US Integrated Postsecondary Education Data System (IPEDS) 12-month Enrollment Component, 2018–19 Provisional Data. Washington, DC: US Department of Education

National Center for Education Statistics (2023). "Immediate College Enrollment Rate. Condition of Education." US Department of Education, Institute of Education Sciences. https://nces.ed.gov/programs/coe/indicator/cpb/college-enrollment-rate.

National Center for Education Statistics (2019). "The Nation's Report Card: Results from the 2019 Mathematics and Reading Assessments: National Assessment of Educational Progress (NAEP), 1990–2019 Mathematics and Reading Assessments." Washington, DC: US Department of Education, Institute of Education Sciences.

National Center for Injury Prevention and Control (2022). "Fast Facts: Preventing Sexual Violence." Atlanta: Centers for Disease Control and Prevention.

Nelson, M. K. (2019). "Helicopter Parents: A New Moral Panic?" In *Contemporary Parenting and Parenthood: From Headlines to New Research*, ed. M. Janning, 3–30. Santa Barbara, CA: Praeger.

Nelson, M. K. (2010). *Parenting Out of Control: Anxious Parents in Uncertain Times.* New York: New York University Press.

Nichols, A. H., and Anthony, M. Jr. (2020). "Graduation Rates Don't Tell the Full Story: Racial Gaps in College Success Are Larger Than We Think." Washington, DC: The Education Trust.

Office of the Surgeon General (2023). "Social Media and Youth Mental Health: The U.S. Surgeon General's Advisor." Washington, DC, Office of the Surgeon General

Organization for Economic Cooperation and Development. (2015). "The ABC of Gender Equality in Education: Aptitude, Behaviour, Confidence." Paris: OECD Publishing.

Organization for Economic Cooperation and Development (2017). *PISA 2015 Results (Volume III).* Paris: OECD.

Palladino, G. (1996). *Teenagers: An American History.* New York: Basic Books, 1996.

Pascoe, M. C., S. Hetrick, and A. G. Parker (2020). "The Impact of Stress on Students in Secondary School and Higher Education." *International Journal of Adolescence and Youth* 25(1): 104–112.

Pew Research Center (2022). "Teens, Social Media and Technology 2022." Washington, DC: Pew Research Center. https://www.pewresearch.org/wp-content/uploads/sites/20/2022/08/PI_2022.08.10_Teens-and-Tech_FINAL.pdf.

Pickhardt, C. E. (2019, August 5). "Why Adolescence Can Be the Harder Half of Parenting." *Psychology Today*.

Pirius, R. (2019). "The Legislative Primer Series for Front-End Justice: Young Adults in the Justice System." Denver: National Conference of State Legislatures.

Puzzanchera, C. (2022). "Trends in Youth Arrests for Violent Crimes." Washington, DC: National Institute of Justice.

Reardon, S., E. M. Fahle, and R. C. Zarate (2019). "Gender Achievement Gaps in the U.S. School Districts." *American Educational Research Journal* 56(6): 2474–2508.

Reeves, R. V. (2017). *Dream Hoarders: How the American Upper Middle Class is Leaving Everyone Else in the Dust, Why That is a Problem, and What To Do About It*. Washington, DC: Brookings Institution Press.

Reeves, R. V. (2022). *Of Boys and Men: Why the Modern Male is Struggling, Why It Matters, and What To Do About It* Washington, DC: Brookings Institution Press.

Richtel, M. (2022). "Hundreds of Suicidal Teens Sleep in Emergency Rooms. Every Night." *New York Times*. https://www.nytimes.com/2022/05/08/health/emergency-rooms-teen-mental-health.html. May 8.

Rideout, V., A. Peebles, S. Mann, and M. B. Robb (2022). "Common Sense Census: Media Use by Tweens and Teens, 2021." San Francisco, CA: Common Sense.

Rivera, L. (2015). *Pedigree: How Elite Students Get Elite Jobs*. Princeton, NJ: Princeton University Press.

Roksa, J. (2019). "Intergenerational Exchange of Support in Low-Income Families: Understanding Resource Dilution and Increased Contribution." *Journal of Marriage and Family* 81(3): 601–615.

Sallie Mae (2020). "How America Pays for College 2020." Newark, DE: Sallie Mae and Ipsos.

Sallie Mae (2023). "How America Pays for College 2023." Newark, DE: Sallie Mae and Ipsos.

Substance Abuse and Mental Health Services Administration (SAMHSA) (2023). "Key Substance Use and Mental Health Indicators in the United States: Results from the 2022 National Survey on Drug Use and Health (HHS Publication No. PEP23-07-01-006, NSDUH Series H-58)." Rockville, MD: Substance Abuse and Mental Health Services Administration.

Substance Abuse and Mental Health Services Administration (SAMHSA) (2019). "National Survey on Drug Use and Health. Table 6.21B—Types of Illicit Drug, Tobacco Product, and Alcohol Use in Past Month among Persons Aged 18 to 22, by College Enrollment Status and Gender: Percentages, 2018 and 2019." Rockville, MD: Substance Abuse and Mental Health Services Administration.

Sampson, R. J. (2012). *Great American City: Chicago and the Enduring Neighborhood Effect*. Chicago: University of Chicago Press.

Schaeffer, K. (2023, November 7). "9 Facts About Bullying in the U.S." Washington, DC: Pew Research Center.

Schak, O., N. Wong, and A. Ana Fung (2019): 15th Annual Report. Washington, DC: The Institute for College Access and Success.

Schalet, A. T. (2011). *Not Under My Roof: Parents, Teens, and the Culture of Sex*. Chicago: University of Chicago Press.

Schulenberg, J. E. (2021, September 8). "Daily Marijuana Use Among US College Students Reaches New 40-year High." Monitoring the Future Press Release. Ann Arbor: University of Michigan. https://news.umich.edu/daily-marijuana-use-among-us-college-students-reaches-new-40-year-high/.

Seltzer, V. C. (1989). *Psychosocial Worlds of the Adolescent: Public and Private.* New York: Wiley.

Silver, B. R. (2020). *The Cost of Inclusion: How Student Conformity Leads to Inequality on College Campuses.* Chicago: University of Chicago Press.

Smetana, J. G. (2011). *Adolescents, Families, and Social Development: How Teens Construct Their Worlds.* New York: Wiley-Blackwell.

Smetana, J. G. (2017, June). "Current Research on Parenting Styles, Dimensions, and Beliefs." *Current Opinion in Psychology* 15: 19–25.

Smetana, J. G. (2015). "Goals, Goal Pursuit, and Adolescent-Parent Relationships." In *Self Regulation in Adolescence,* ed. P. Gollwitzer and G. Oettingen, 243–265. New York: Cambridge University Press.

Smetana, J. G., A. Metzger, D. C. Gettman, and N. Campione-Barr. (2006). "Disclosure and Secrecy in Adolescent–Parent Relationships." *Child Development* 77(1): 201–217.

Smetana, J., and M. Rote (2019). "Adolescent–Parent Relationships: Progress, Processes, and Prospects." *Annual Review of Developmental Psychology* 1: 41–68.

Smetana, J., M. Villalobos, M. Tasopoulos-Chan, D. C. Gettman, and N. Campione-Barr (2009). "Early and Middle Adolescents' Disclosure to Parents About Activities in Different Domains." *Journal of Adolescence* 32: 693–713.

Snyder, T. D., and S. A. Dillow (2019). "Statistics, Digest of Education Statistics, 2018 (NCES 2020-009)," Chapter 1. Washington, DC: US Department of Education.

Soenens, B., M. Vansteenkiste, and S. Van Petegem, S. (2017). *Autonomy in Adolescence: Towards Conceptual Clarity.* Studies in Adolescent Development. New York: Routledge.

Sparks, S. D. (2018). "How Many Students Are Chronically Absent in Your State? Federal Data Show Rates Rising." *Education Week.* https://www.edweek.org/leadership/how-many-students-are-chronically-absent-in-your-state-federal-data-show-rates-rising/2018/04.

Spengler, T. (2020). "Things You Can Do at 21 Years of Age, But Not at 18." Legal Beagle. https://legalbeagle.com/8649600-things-age-but-not-18.html.

Spengler, T. (2020). "What You Can Legally Do When You're 18." Legal Beagle. https://legalbea gle.com/4744720-can-legally-do-youre-18.html.

Steinberg, L. (2020). *Adolescence.* New York: McGraw-Hill Education.

Steinberg, L., G. Icenogle, E. P. Shulman, K. Breiner, J. Chein, D. Bacchini, L. Chang, N. Chaudhary, L. Di Giunta, K. A. Dodge, K. A. Fanti, J. E. Lansford, P. S. Malone, P. Oburu, C. Pastorelli, A. T. Skinner, E. Sorbring, S. Tapanya, L. M. U. Tirado, L. P. Peña Alampay, S. M. Al-Hussan, and H. M. S. Takash. (2018). "Around the World, Adolescence Is a Time of Heightened Sensation Seeking and Immature Self-Regulation." *Developmental Science* 21(2): 1–13.

Shores, K., and M. Steinberg. (2022). "Fiscal Federalism and K–12 Education Funding: Policy Lessons from Two Educational Crises." *Educational Researcher* 51(8): 551–558.

Substance Abuse and Mental Health Services Administration (SAMHSA) (2021). National Mental Health Services Survey (N-MHSS): 2020 Data on Mental Health Treatment Facilities. Rockville, MD: SAMHSA.

Swartz, T. T., M. Kim, M. Uno, J. Mortimer, and K. Bengtson O'Brien (2011). "Safety Nets and Scaffolds: Parental Support in the Transition to Adulthood." *Journal of Marriage and Family* 73(2): 414–429.

The Education Trust with Dorothyjean Cratty (2019). "School Counselors Matter." Washington, DC: The Education Trust.

The Institute for College Access and Success (2020). "Student Debt and the Class of 2019, 15th Annual Report." https://ticas.org/wp-content/uploads/2020/10/classof2019.pdf.

Torche, F. (2018). "Intergenerational Mobility at the Top of the Educational Distribution." *Sociology of Education* 91(4): 266–289.

US Department of Education (2011). "The Family Educational Rights and Privacy Act Guidance for Eligible Students US Department of Education." Washington, DC: US Department of Education.

US Government Accountability Office (2018). "K-12 Education: Discipline Disparities for Black Students, Boys, and Students with Disabilities." Washington, DC: US Government Accountability Office.

van Stee, E. G. (2022). "Parenting Young Adults Across Social Class: A Review and Synthesis." *Sociology Compass* e13021: 1–16. https://doi.org/10.1111/soc4.13021.

van Stee, E. G. (2023). "Privileged Dependence, Precarious Autonomy: Parent/Young Adult Relationships Through the Lens of COVID-19." *Journal of Marriage and Family* 85 (1): 215–232.

Vega, D., and A. M. Puff (2020). "It Takes a Village: How Counselors and Psychologists Support the College Aspirations of Students of Color." *Phi Delta Kappan* 102(4): 40–45.

Vogels, E. A. (2022). "Teens and Cyberbullying 2022." Washington, DC: Pew Research Center.

Wang, D., J. K. Choi, and J. Shin (2020). "Long-Term Neighborhood Effects on Adolescent Outcomes: Mediated Through Adverse Childhood Experiences and Parenting Stress." *Journal of Youth and Adolescence* 49(10): 2160–2173.

Wang, M.-T., and S. Sheikh-Khalil (2014). "Does Parental Involvement Matter for Student Achievement and Mental Health in High School?" *Child Development* 85(2): 610–625.

Wasserman, M. (2020). "The Disparate Effects of Family Structure." In *How Cultural Factors Shape Economic Outcomes*, 55–81. Princeton, NJ and Washington, DC: Woodrow Wilson School of Public and International Affairs and The Brookings Institution.

Waters, M. C., P. J. Carr, M. J. Kefalas, and J. Holdaway (2011). *Coming of Age in America: The Transition to Adulthood in the Twenty-First Century.* Berkeley: University of California Press.

Williams, B. (2022). "Many Determined College Students Are Also Dedicated Parents: A Preview of the Student Parent Affordability Report." Washington, DC: The Education Trust.

Women in Academia Report (2022, November 9). "The Significant Gender Gap in College Graduation Rates." *WIA Report.* https://www.wiareport.com/2022/11/the-significant-gender-gap-in-college-graduation-rates/#:~:text=Some%2066.4%20percent%20of%20all,for%2Dprofit%20colleges%20and%20universities.

Zaloom, C. (2019). *Indebted: How Families Make College Work at Any Cost.* Princeton, NJ: Princeton University Press.

Zimmer-Gembreck, M., W. Ducat, W., Boislard-Pepin, M.A., et al. (2011). "Autonomy, Development of." In *Encyclopedia of Adolescence*, ed. B. Brown and M. Prinstein, 66–67. New York: Academic Press.

Index

middle adolescence, 45
middle-class mothers
  college (post–high school), 176–83
  dealing with trouble, 129–30
  designation of, 228
  emerging adulthood and, 203–5
  interviewing, 14
  limitations on mothers' ability to help teens,
    124–28
  preparing for post-graduation, 148–51
  resources for promoting school success,
    136–37
  supporting teens who are stressed, 117
motherhood, reflecting on
  children becoming nice people, 210
  giving back, 211–12
  having hand in growth of teens, 209
  satisfaction in changed roles, 210–11
  warm relationships, 212–13
  when children are doing well, 208–9
mothers
  accounts of, ix–x
  book overview and, 18–23
  gender and, 15–17
  impact of pulling away on, 28–32
  interviewing, 12–15
  keeping teens safe, 58–109
  race and, 17–18
  work of, 9–12
motivation and schoolwork, promoting
  addressing failure, 121
  addressing schoolwork, 120–21
  changing work situation, 122–23
  difficulties, 124
  personal days and employment, 121–22
  research, 119–20
mutual identification, loss of, 28

neighborhoods, keeping teens safe, 89–91
new freedoms, granting, 73
  developing trust, 73–76
  negotiating agreements, 76–79
  role of institutions, 79–83
  teens gaining control, 83–86
no college (post–high school), young adults
    and, 192
  falling behind, 194–98
  steps toward independence, 192–94
  teen pregnancies, 198–99
Northeastern City, 12

parenthood, young adulthood
    and, 198–99

parenting, vii–xii
  communication and, 32–39
  contributing to further research, 224
  exercising control, 47–55
  expanding understanding of, 218
  keeping teens safe, 58–109
  key elements of, 223
  negotiated nature of, 10–12
  negotiations with teens, 39–47
  new challenges in, 32–55
  popular narratives about, viii
  promoting school success, 110–60
  stakes of, x–xi
  top-down models, 1–2
  understanding process of, vii–viii
  young adults, 161–217
parent-teen negotiations, 39
  avoiding conflict, 44–45
  conflict frequency, 45–46
  conflict occurrence, 41–44
  contentiousness, 46
  defying conventional norms, 43–44
  finances, 42–43
  rebellion and, 39–41
  walking away, 46–47
permissiveness-restrictiveness balance, 49–51
personal days and employment, 121–22
physical growth, adolescents, 25–27
planning, strategic interactions, 37
post-graduation, preparing for, 140–42
  middle-class mothers, 148–51
  upper-middle-class mothers, 142–48
  working-class mothers, 151–58
privacy
  cell phones and, 69–73
  considering, 66–67
  disregarding issues considering, 67–68
  monitoring teens' activities, 68–69
  situations as always changing, 68
procrastination, dealing with, 124–26
public narratives, 9–10
pulling away, 56–57
  coming together, 56
  impact on mothers, 28–32
  new challenges in parenting, 32–55
  overview, 24–28

race, 17–18
racial background, 229, 230t
rebellion, 39–41
  adolescence as time of, 24–25
regrets, dealing with, 213–16
relationships, changes in, 29–32